Access 2007 Workbook For Dummies®

D1411277

Keyboard Shortcuts

Keystroke	Function
Ctrl+n	Creates a new blank database
Ctrl+o	Opens an existing database
F11	Shows/hides Navigation Pane
Alt+f	Opens the Microsoft Office Button menu
Alt+h	Displays Home tab on the Ribbon
Alt+c	Displays the Create tab on the Ribbon
Alt+x	Displays the External Data tab on the Ribbon
Alt+a	Displays the Database Tools tab on the Ribbon
Ctrl+c	Copies selection to the clipboard
Ctrl+v	Pastes selection to the clipboard
Ctrl+z	Undoes last operation
Ctrl+;	Inserts the current date
Ctrl+:	Inserts the current time
Ctrl+'	Copies same field data from previous record
F2	Selects all data in the field or places cursor in edit mode
F9	Recalculates fields on a form or refreshes a lookup combo or list box list
Ctrl+Enter	Inserts a line break in datasheet and form view
Ctrl+Shift++	Inserts a new record
Ctrl+Shift+-	Deletes current record
Ctrl+Enter	Opens selected object from Navigation Pane in design view
F4	Toggles property sheet in design or layout view
Ctrl+Right Arrow	Moves selected control to the right in design or layout view
Ctrl+Left Arrow	Moves selected control to the left in design or layout view
Ctrl+Down Arrow	Moves selected control down in design or layout view
Ctrl+Up Arrow	Moves selected control up in design or layout view
Shift+Right Arrow	Increases selected control width in design or layout view
Shift+Left Arrow	Decreases selected control width in design or layout view
Shift+Down Arrow	Increases selected control height in design or layout view
Shift+Up Arrow	Decreases selected control height in design or layout view
F4	Toggles property sheet in design view
Shift+F2	Zooms in on current field in datasheet and form view

For Dummies: Bestselling Book Series for Beginners

Access 2007 Workbook For Dummies®

Cheat Sheet

Navigating the Ribbon with Key Tips

1. **Press the Alt key.**

   Key Tips appear on the Ribbon, the Microsoft Office Button, and the Quick Access Toolbar.

2. **Press a Key Tip to set the focus to that item (like C in this case for the Create tab).**

   Key Tips appear for the item.

3. **Press a Key Tip (like T to create a new table).**

   The command assigned to the Key Tip runs.

Access Functions

Function	Description
Abs	Absolute value of a number
Avg	Arithmetic mean
Count	Number of records
Int	Integer value of a number
LCase	Converts a string to lowercase
Left	Returns a specified number of characters from the left side of a string
Len	Length of a string
LTrim	Removes extra spaces from the beginning of a string
Max	Maximum value
Min	Minimum value
Now	Current date and time
Replace	Replaces a string with a different string
Right	Returns a specified number of characters from the right side of a string
Rnd	Random number
Round	Rounds a number
RTrim	Removes extra spaces from the end of a string
Sum	The sum of values
Time	Current system time
Trim	Removes extra spaces from both ends of a string
UCase	Converts a string to uppercase

For Dummies: Bestselling Book Series for Beginners

Access® 2007 Workbook

FOR

DUMMIES®

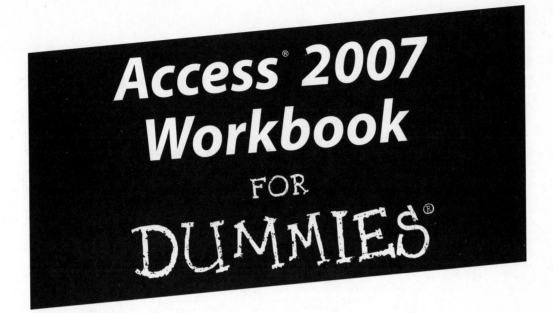

Access® 2007 Workbook FOR DUMMIES®

by Joseph C. Stockman

BICENTENNIAL
1807
WILEY
2007
BICENTENNIAL

Wiley Publishing, Inc.

Access® 2007 Workbook For Dummies®

Published by
Wiley Publishing, Inc.
111 River Street
Hoboken, NJ 07030-5774

www.wiley.com

About the Author

Joe Stockman is an independent consultant, software designer, and author who has been using Microsoft Access since its initial release. He's also developed courseware and taught classes in Access and VBA. Joe developed his first application in Access, and then migrated into Visual Basic and VB.NET, where he specializes in creating applications for the Windows Mobile platform. He's worked for several software companies before forming his consulting business in 2002, where he deals with all types of clients including healthcare, financial, government, manufacturing, and small business. His ability to turn his customers' wishes into working applications keeps them satisfied. Joe is the co-author of the *Access 2007 Bible* and *Access 2007 VBA Programming For Dummies* and also writes for the *Advisor Guide to Microsoft Access* magazine.

Dedication

To my mom, as always. And again to all my friends and family for their support, understanding, and encouragement throughout this project.

Author's Acknowledgments

Even though a single name appears on the cover of this book, this book was a team effort. I'd like to thank the many people who have contributed to this book. To Carole McClendon and everyone at Waterside Productions, thanks for finding this project and making it happen. Also, many thanks to Kyle Looper at Wiley for seeing the potential for a workbook on Access and letting me work with this format. To Pat O'Brien and the rest of the editorial and manufacturing team, thanks for working with me on all the little things that come up during the process, and keeping me on track. And finally, to Microsoft, for continuing to enhance Access and keeping it a wonderful development environment.

Publisher's Acknowledgments

We're proud of this book; please send us your comments through our online registration form located at www.dummies.com/register/.

Some of the people who helped bring this book to market include the following:

Acquisitions, Editorial, and Media Development

Project Editor: Pat O'Brien

Acquisitions Editor: Kyle Looper

Copy Editors: Heidi Unger, Laura K. Miller

Technical Editor: Eric Legault

Editorial Manager: Kevin Kirschner

Media Development Manager: Laura VanWinkle

Editorial Assistant: Amanda Foxworth

Sr. Editorial Assistant: Cherie Case

Cartoons: Rich Tennant (www.the5thwave.com)

Composition Services

Project Coordinator: Kristie Rees

Layout and Graphics: Stacie Brooks, Carl Byers, Erin Zeltner

Proofreaders: Laura Albert, David Faust, John Greenough, Shannon Ramsey

Indexer: Potomac Indexing, LLC

Anniversary Logo Design: Richard Pacifico

Publishing and Editorial for Technology Dummies

    Richard Swadley, Vice President and Executive Group Publisher

    Andy Cummings, Vice President and Publisher

    Mary Bednarek, Executive Acquisitions Director

    Mary C. Corder, Editorial Director

Publishing for Consumer Dummies

    Diane Graves Steele, Vice President and Publisher

    Joyce Pepple, Acquisitions Director

Composition Services

    Gerry Fahey, Vice President of Production Services

    Debbie Stailey, Director of Composition Services

Contents at a Glance

Table of Contents

Table of Exercises

Introduction

· ·

Microsoft Office Access 2007 is one of the most popular database packages in the world, and perhaps, the universe. Since Access was introduced with version 1.0 a long time ago, it's grown and evolved just like everything in the computer industry. For millions of users all over the globe, Access lets them create databases for storing all types of information from highly sensitive data to grandma's recipes.

As part of the 2007 Microsoft Office System, Access stands at the top of confusing information. Many users routinely use Word to create letters and documents, Excel to build spreadsheets, and Outlook to schedule and get their precious e-mail. And although they might fumble through using these applications for the first time, they figure out how to use them rather quickly. With Access, it's not so simple, which is probably why you're reading this right now.

About This Book

As the title suggests, *Access 2007 Workbook For Dummies* is designed to give you a hands-on experience to start using Access to create databases. This book is primarily composed of step-by-step exercises that give you the opportunity to learn about the features of Access while you're performing those exercises.

By doing the exercises in this book, you'll learn the basic skill for building and maintaining databases with Microsoft Access 2007. You'll master some skills necessary to use Access on a daily basis and be introduced to other skills that lightly touch a particular area of the program. This book won't teach you everything you need to know about Access, but it will get you on your way to becoming an Access guru.

Conventions Used in This Book

By convention, all the text entries that you type yourself appear in bold. In addition, all file-names appear in italicized type even though they are not italicized when you see their names in Windows Explorer or the Access interface.

When it comes to instructions in the exercises throughout this workbook, you'll notice a few conventions:

✔ Ribbon commands are introduced by naming the tab on the Ribbon, the group, followed by the command, as in "On the Home tab, in the Clipboard group, click the Copy command".

✔ Mouse commands are introduced with the word click or select, as in "Click OK" or "Select the Yes option button".

✔ Keyboard commands are introduced with the word press, as in "Press Tab" or "Press Enter".

For some commands, you can use either the keyboard or the mouse to make a selection on the screen. The method you use is completely up to you and your comfort level with the mouse or keyboard. For example, pressing the Enter key is equivalent to clicking the default OK button in most dialog boxes. You can also press the Alt key to show the keyboard shortcuts for the Ribbon.

One other convention that you'll notice used throughout the text is the display of names for Ribbon commands, dialog box and wizard options, and other screen elements in the title case, wherein all major words are capitalized, even though they don't appear that way on the screen. Microsoft doesn't always follow this convention, often preferring to capitalize the first letter of the option name.

Foolish Assumptions

Even though the word "Dummies" appears quite big on the front of this book, I don't presume that you've just crawled out of a cave and discovered fire. I do assume that you're a new Access user that has never seen Access before or you've used previous versions of Access and want to learn how to use Access 2007. Further, I assume you want to take a hands-on approach to learning Access.

To complete most of the exercises in this workbook, you only need to have Microsoft Access installed on a computer running Windows XP or Windows Vista. For exercises on printing reports, you'll benefit from having a printer installed on our system, although it's not required. For the importing and exporting exercises in Part VIII, you'll benefit from having Microsoft Excel installed as well.

This workbook is designed to be used with Access 2007 and Access 2007 only. Previous versions of Access have a completely different interface and you won't be able to follow along with versions prior to 2007. If you bought this book and you don't have Access 2007, I strongly recommend that you get Access 2007 and don't return this book. In fact, you should buy an extra copy just in case you spill coffee or it spontaneously combusts.

How This Book Is Organized

The workbook is organized into nine parts, each of which contains a few related chapters. Each of the chapters follows a similar pattern of introductory text followed by exercises. Although the exercises within any given chapter build upon one another, you're certainly not expected to complete them in strict chapter order. Feel free to work on the exercises in any order that feels comfortable and fits your learning needs.

Part I: Learning Database Fundamentals

This part introduces you to databases and Access. The two chapters in this section get you up and running with Access, all the way from starting the program to creating a new database.

Part II: Creating and Using Tables

Tables are where the information in your database lives and breathes. This part gives you practice with building and using tables, the core of any database. Because of the importance of tables in Access, the four chapters in this part concentrate solely on tables — no chairs allowed.

Part III: Viewing Data with Select Queries

This part teaches you to use select queries in Access to view data. Queries let you ask a question about your data and the three chapters in this part teach you how to build queries to ask these questions.

Part IV: Manipulating Data with Action Queries

This part demonstrates how to use action queries to manipulate data in your database. Action queries let you change, copy, and remove data from your tables and the four chapters in this part show you how to use the four types of action queries.

Part V: Building Forms

Forms let you present and edit data in a structured format. This part shows you how to create and use forms to view and edit your information. The five chapters in this part (the most in any part) cover the basics of building and designing forms.

Part VI: Advanced Form Design

This part shows you more about designing forms, one area of Access where you're likely to spend a lot of time. This book could easily be filled with information about all of the designing forms, and the four chapters in this part cover some additional topics on form design.

Part VII: Building Reports

Reports are designed to print information from your database. The three chapters in this part show you how to create reports to get data from your database onto the stack of paper. So order extra ink or toner now so when you get to this part, you don't run out.

Part VIII: Automating Access

This part shows you how to automate certain tasks within Access. The four chapters in this part show you the basics of adding buttons and creating macros which let you perform operations repeatedly.

- ✔ Chapter 26 shows you how to add buttons to forms.
- ✔ Chapter 27 teaches you the basics of creating macros.
- ✔ Chapter 28 demonstrates how to create a switchboard.
- ✔ Chapter 29 explains how to import and export data from other sources.

Part IX: The Part of Tens

This part gives you tips for using Access on your own after you complete the exercises in this book. The tips in these three chapters will save you time and make your Access life more productive.

The CD-ROM that comes with this workbook is an integral part of the workbook experience. It contains the practice material that you need to complete most of the exercises as well as videos that demonstrate select exercises. Appendix A contains the instructions.

Icons Used in This Book

Icons are sprinkled throughout the text of this workbook in high hopes that they draw your attention to particular features. Some of the icons are of the heads-up type, while others are more informational in nature:

This icon indicates that the file referred to in an exercise or some part of it is supplied to you on the CD-ROM that comes with this workbook.

This icon points out a tidbit of information that can make your work somewhat easier when using Access.

This icon indicates the information is technical in nature and gets into the nuts and bolts in Access. It's not required that you know this information to use Access.

This icon indicates the information is essential to the topic being discussed and is, therefore, worth remembering for later use.

This icon indicates a bit of trickery in the topic that, if ignored, can lead to some real trouble in your database.

Where to Go from Here

This workbook is organized to allow you the freedom of moving from part to part or chapter to chapter in any order that you want. However, each of the chapters builds upon the concepts and databases from the previous chapters; so if you're new to Access, I recommend that you start at the front of the book and work towards the back. If you're already familiar with Access, you might want to skim the first couple of chapters and dive right in to Chapter 3.

This book was written with the assumption that you know very little about Access 2007. Although I cover many different topics and walk you through many exercises on using Access, I don't go into too much detail into every available option and what its benefits and consequences are. If you'd like more detail into some topic in this book, I recommend *Access 2007 All-In-One Desk Reference For Dummies.*

Rome wasn't built in a day, and your skills in using Access won't be either, but completing the exercises in this book and applying the techniques to your own databases can help you reach the next level in database design. No matter where your new found database skills take you, be sure to have fun and remember we all learn from our mistakes.

Part I
Learning Database Fundamentals

The 5th Wave   By Rich Tennant

"Once I told Mona that Access was an 'argument' based program, she seemed to warm up to it."

In this part . . .

The chapters and exercises in Part I teach the basics of using Microsoft Office Access 2007. In Chapter 1, you'll learn what a database is, how to start Access and navigate around the interface, and how to create and open databases. In Chapter 2 you'll backup your database, set Access options, and learn about the Trust Center — which deals with security, not a forgotten trust fund.

Chapter 1

Getting Started with Access

• •

• •

Microsoft Office Access 2007 — which I refer to as *Access* throughout this book — is the database component of the 2007 Microsoft Office System. If you're familiar with other programs in the 2007 Microsoft Office System — such as Word, Excel, PowerPoint, and Outlook — you might already be familiar with the interface in Access. However, Access contains many components not found anywhere else within the Microsoft Office System.

In this chapter, you learn the very basics of databases, how to start and navigate Access, and how to find help both online and offline.

Understanding What a Database Is

A *database* is just a collection of related information. The library's card catalog, your grandmother's recipe cards, and the phone book are all examples of databases. Even if they aren't on the computer, they contain information you can retrieve relatively easily.

Putting these manual databases on the computer speeds up the retrieval of information. You may have begun keeping lists in *Excel* (Microsoft's spreadsheet application). Or perhaps you maintain your contacts in *Outlook* (Microsoft's e-mail application). And you've no doubt used an *Internet search engine* to look up information online. These are all computerized databases that harness the power of the microprocessor to organize and retrieve the information you need.

Defining two types of databases

A *database management system* (DBMS) is a computer software package designed for managing databases. A DBMS controls the organization, storage, and retrieval of data from a database. A DBMS contains data structures optimized to deal with large amounts of data — some DBMS's handle this data better than others.

A *relational database management system* (RDBMS) is a type of database management system that stores data in related *tables*.

For example, a table containing contact information (name, address, phone number) may be related to a table containing items each contact purchases (product, quantity, price). The RDBMS lets you retrieve answers to questions such as "What is the cost of the products each contact ordered?" from the related tables.

Exploring the basic parts of Access databases

Access is an RDBMS that stores data in a relational database. Each Access database is an automated version of the filing system where you define what type of information is being stored. An Access database is the container for this information which is stored in *tables*, plus other components such as *queries, forms, reports, macros,* and *modules.* You learn more about these components (also known as *database objects*) throughout this book.

Here's a brief overview of each of these database components.

Tables

A *table* serves as the primary container for the data in a database and has the following characteristics (shown in Figure 1-1):

Figure 1-1:
Viewing
the table
structure.

	Field a	Field b	Field c
Record 1	Value 1a	Value 1b	Value 1c
Record 2	Value 2a	Value 2b	Value 2c
Record 3	Value 3a	Value 3b	Value 3c

✔ Each table contains *records* (rows) that represent a set of information.

   For example, a record in a database of contact information for your clients contains the client's name, address, e-mail address, cell phone number, work phone number, and so on depending on what fields the database contains.

✔ Each record contains *fields* (columns) that represent attributes of the record.

   For example, a table of contact information contains such fields as Name, Address, and City.

✔ Each field contains a *value*.

   The *value* is the actual information you're storing.

Queries

A *query* retrieves or manipulates information in a database.

To retrieve information, you ask the database a question such as "What are all the CDs that I purchased in 2007?" using a specialized language called *Structured Query Language* (SQL).

Forms

A *form* presents data from a table or query in a structured view instead of the row and column format that a table shows. You create forms to

- ✔ Make data entry easier and more intuitive.
- ✔ Limit fields the user sees and changes.

Reports

A *report* presents information from your database in a printed format. You can format reports to display lists sorted by one or more columns. They can display totals and subtotals and pull data from one or more tables. You can apply a common theme to your reports to ensure that the printed output from your database has a consistent look and feel.

Macros

A *macro* is an action or set of actions that performs database operations. Macros let you automate your database by automatically performing tasks or performing tasks at the touch of a button. Macros perform such database functions as opening forms, printing reports, and manipulating data.

Modules

A *module* is a set of functions and procedures written in the Visual Basic for Application (VBA) programming language. Like macros, modules are also used for performing operations on your database, but go far beyond the limitations of macros.

 VBA isn't covered in this book. If (after you're done with this workbook) you're interested in learning how to use VBA to perform operations in your databases, pick up a copy of *Access 2007 VBA Programming For Dummies,* coauthored by yours truly and Alan Simpson (Wiley).

Launching Access

In order to be proficient in its use, you need to be familiar with all the various ways of launching Access.

Exercise 1-1: Launching Access

You can use any of the following techniques to start Access:

- ✔ Click Start on the Windows taskbar and then choose All Programs⇨Microsoft Office⇨Microsoft Office Access 2007.
- ✔ Double-click an Access database file in any folder on any drive to which your computer has access.
- ✔ Double-click the Microsoft Access program icon on your computer's desktop.
- ✔ Click the Microsoft Access icon on the taskbar's Start menu.
- ✔ Click the Access icon on the Quick Launch toolbar.

Exercise 1-2: Creating Additional Icons to Launch Access

The icons for launching Access are available only if you've added the Access program to the desktop, the Start menu, and the Quick Launch toolbar, respectively. In this exercise, add the Access program icon to your computer.

- ✔ Add a Microsoft Office Access shortcut to the Windows desktop by right-clicking the Microsoft Office Access item as it appears on the Start⇨All Programs⇨Microsoft Office submenu and then clicking Send To⇨Desktop from the pop-up menu.

- ✔ Add Access to the Start menu by right-clicking the Microsoft Office Access desktop shortcut and then clicking Pin to Start Menu on its shortcut menu.

- ✔ Add Access to the Quick Launch toolbar on the Windows taskbar by holding down Ctrl as you drag and drop the Microsoft Office Access desktop shortcut on to the toolbar.

Creating and Opening Databases

When you launch Access by clicking the Start button or a desktop shortcut (but not when you double-click an Access database file), the Getting Started with Microsoft Office Access page appears. (See Figure 1-2.) This page is the starting point for working with Access.

Microsoft Office Button

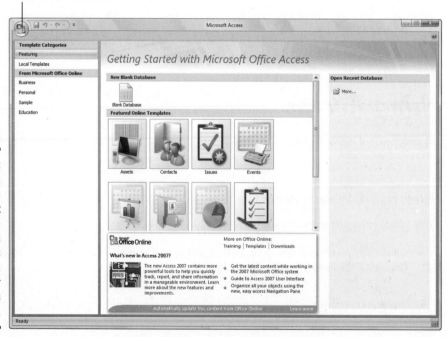

Figure 1-2:
The Getting Started with Microsoft Office Access page is where you begin your Access journey.

The Getting Started with Microsoft Office Access page contains various sections and panes that allow you to create blank databases, open existing databases, and create databases from *templates* (formatted examples), either online or local.

Creating a new database

Creating a new database is a simple task. The major decision you need to make is whether you want to

- ✔ Create a new *blank* database (as shown in Exercise 1-3 and Exercise 1-4).
- ✔ Create a new database that already contains a *structure* you'd like to use (as shown in Exercise 1-5).

Blank databases

You typically use a new blank database when you want to start from scratch in creating an Access application.

Exercise 1-3: Creating a New Blank Database from Access

In this exercise, you create a *new blank database,* which is a blank container that doesn't contain tables, queries, forms, reports, macros, or modules.

To create a new blank database, follow these steps:

1. Launch Microsoft Office Access by clicking the Start button or a desktop shortcut.

   The Getting Started with Microsoft Office Access page appears.

2. Under the New Blank Database section near the top of the Access window centered on the page, click the Blank Database icon.

   The right pane in the Access window switches to the Blank Database pane.

3. Type **Exercise1-3.accdb** in the File Name text box.

   If you don't want to change the database's location, skip to Step 5.

4. (Optional) If you need to change the location of the database, follow these steps:

   a. Click the Folder icon to the right of the File Name text box.

      The File New Database dialog box opens.

   b. Navigate to a folder on your computer or network where you'd like to save the new blank database.

   c. Click OK.

      The File New Database dialog box closes, and you return to the Getting Started with Microsoft Office Access page.

5. Click the Create button underneath the File Name text box in the Blank Database pane.

   Access creates the `Exercise1-3.accdb` database in the specified folder and opens the database showing Table1.

6. Click the Microsoft Office Button and click Close Database to close the new blank database and return to the Getting Started with Microsoft Office Access page.

> To show the Blank Database pane on the right side of the Getting Started with Microsoft Office Access page, you can click the Microsoft Office Button and click New.

Exercise 1-4: Creating a New Blank Database from Explorer

In this exercise, you create a new blank database without using Access. Windows lets you create databases right from Explorer. Follow these steps:

1. Close Microsoft Office Access and open Windows Explorer.

2. Navigate to a folder on your computer or network where you'd like to save the new blank database.

3. Right-click a blank area in the right pane of Windows Explorer and select New⇨Microsoft Office Access 2007 Database from the pop-up menu.

    A new database named `New Microsoft Office Access 2007 Database.accdb` appears in Windows Explorer with the database name highlighted.

4. Rename the database `Exercise1-4.accdb`.

Templates

A *database template* provides the structure of the database (tables, queries, forms, reports, and macros) necessary to perform common tasks. Access automatically installs a number of templates on your computer, and you can use templates from Microsoft Office Online.

Exercise 1-5: Creating a Database from a Local Template

In this exercise, you create a new database based on a *local template*, which is a template that's installed when you install Access. Follow these steps:

1. Launch Microsoft Office Access by clicking the Start button or a desktop shortcut.

    The Getting Started with Microsoft Office Access page appears.

2. Under the Template Categories section near the top left of the Access window, click Local Templates.

    The center section of the Access window switches to the Local Templates pane and displays a list of available templates (such as Assets, Contacts, and Events) installed on your computer.

3. Click Tasks in the Local Templates pane.

    The right section of the Access window switches to a description of the Tasks template database.

> For this example, I chose the Tasks template which is used to track work items that need to be completed, but you can choose any of the other templates (such as Assets, Contacts, or Projects) and create a database that's useful to you.

4. Type **Exercise1-5.accdb** in the File Name text box.

   If you don't want to change the database's location, skip to Step 6.

5. (Optional) Click the Folder icon to the right of the File Name text box to change the location of the database.

   The File New Database dialog box opens. Navigate to the desired folder and click OK to change the location of the database.

6. Make sure the Create and Link Your Database to a Windows SharePoint Services Site check box isn't selected.

   Windows SharePoint Services lets you share your database across an intranet, which isn't covered in this book.

7. Click the Create button underneath the File Name text box.

   Access creates the `Exercise1-5.accdb` database in the specified folder and opens the database, showing the Task List form.

8. Click the Microsoft Office Button and click Close Database to close the new template database and return to the Getting Started with Microsoft Office Access page.

Exercise 1-6: Creating a Database from an Online Template

In this exercise, you create a new database based on a template from Microsoft Office Online. (You need an active Internet connection.) Follow these steps:

1. Launch Microsoft Office Access by clicking the Start button or a desktop shortcut.

   The Getting Started with Microsoft Office Access page appears.

2. Under the From Microsoft Office Online section in the left pane of the Access window, click Personal.

   The center section of the Access window switches to the Personal pane and displays a list of available templates (such as Contacts, Home Inventory, Lending Library, and so forth) from Microsoft Office Online. It may take a few moments for the list of templates to appear.

3. Click Nutrition in the Personal pane.

   The right section of the Access window switches to a description of the Personal template database, showing you an approximate download time and a user rating.

4. Type **Exercise1-6.accdb** in the File Name text box.

   If you don't want to change the database's location, skip to Step 6.

5. (Optional) Click the Folder icon to the right of the File Name text box to change the location of the database.

   The File New Database dialog box opens. Navigate to the desired folder and click OK to change the location of the database.

6. Make sure the Create and Link Your Database to a Windows SharePoint Services Site check box isn't selected.

   Windows SharePoint Services lets you share your database across an intranet, which isn't covered in this book.

7. Click the Download button underneath the File Name text box.

Access displays a message to verify you're running a genuine copy of Microsoft Office.

8. Click Continue to validate your version of Microsoft Office.

Access validates your version of Office; if it's valid, Access downloads the template from Microsoft Office Online and creates the `Exercise1-6.accdb` database in the specified folder and opens the database showing the Nutrition Tracker Startup Screen form.

9. Click the Microsoft Office Button and click Close Database to close the new template database and return to the Getting Started with Microsoft Office Access page.

Check the From Microsoft Office Online section out regularly, as Microsoft routinely updates this with new and revised templates.

Opening an existing database

After you create a new database — blank or from a template — and close it, you must open it again to use it. You also need to open an existing database if someone else creates it and sends it to you.

The My Practice Databases folder on the CD-ROM (which you copied to your My Documents folder on your hard disk) contains the database files used throughout this book. If you haven't copied the files to your computer yet, see Appendix A.

Exercise 1-7: Opening an Existing Database

In this exercise, you open an existing database (`Exercise1-7.accdb`) that you copied from the CD-ROM.

1. Launch Microsoft Office Access by clicking the Start button or a desktop shortcut.

The Getting Started with Microsoft Office Access page appears.

2. Click the Microsoft Office Button and click Open.

The Open dialog box appears.

3. Navigate to the Documents\My Practice Databases\Chapter01 folder (or the folder where you saved the practice files from the CD-ROM).

4. Click `Exercise1-7.accdb`.

5. Click Open.

Access opens the `Exercise1-7.accdb` database, which displays contact information.

TIP

In addition to clicking Open under the Microsoft Office button, you should be familiar with the following methods of opening an existing Access database:

✓ Click a name in the Open Recent Database list on the right side of the Getting Started with Microsoft Office Access page.

✓ Click the More link in the Open Recent Database list on the right side of the Getting Started with Microsoft Office Access page to show the Open dialog box.

✓ Double-click an Access database file in any folder on any drive to which your computer has access.

Exploring the Access Interface

Microsoft Access 2007 has a newly designed user interface (UI), which is the result of extensive research and usability testing. This user interface consists of different elements, shown in Figure 1-3.

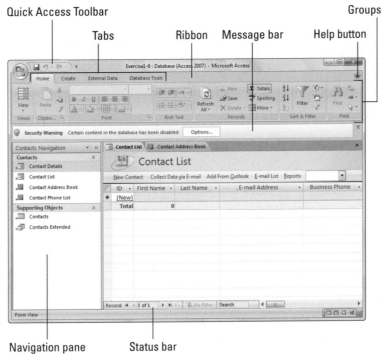

Figure 1-3:
The Access 2007 user interface.

The Ribbon contains commands necessary to perform operations in Access. The Ribbon is broken down into tabs that contain different groups of commands:

- The Ribbon contains four standard tabs: Home, Create, External Data, and Database Tools.

- Each tab contains groups, which categorize related commands.

- The Ribbon can also contain one or more *contextual tabs,* which appear when additional commands become available.

The Microsoft Office Button appears in the top left side of the Access window. Use the Microsoft Office Button to create, open, close, and manage databases.

The Quick Access Toolbar appears to the right of the Microsoft Office Button by default. You can change the location of this toolbar and customize the commands that appear.

The Navigation pane is where you access the database objects in your database. From here, you have access to all the tables, queries, forms, reports, macros, and modules in your application.

The Message bar appears underneath the Ribbon when special attention is needed, such as enabling security.

The Status bar appears at the bottom of the window and displays relevant information about the active screen element.

Using the Ribbon

The Ribbon is where you find the commands to perform most of the database operations while working with Access. In order to successfully use the Ribbon, you need to be aware of the different tabs and what types of commands appear on each tab.

Exercise 1-8: Using the Ribbon

In this exercise, you view the different tabs and commands on the Access Ribbon. Open the `Exercise1-8.accdb` file in the Chapter01 folder and do the following:

- Click the Home tab to use commands that change the view of the current object, access the clipboard, change fonts, navigate and create records, sort and filter data, and find specific information.

- Click the Create tab to use commands that create new tables, forms, reports, queries, macros, and modules.

- Click the External Data tab to use commands that import and export data to and from a variety of formats (Excel, Access, XML), collect data using Outlook 2007, and move data to and from SharePoint Lists.

- Click the Database Tools tab to run macros, create relationships, analyze the database, move data to SQL Server or another Access database, and other database functions.

Using the Navigation pane

The Navigation pane is where you access the objects in your database. You can collapse the Navigation pane so you have more room to work with the database objects. You can also change how the objects are listed in the Navigation pane. Figure 1-4 shows a few different views in the Navigation pane.

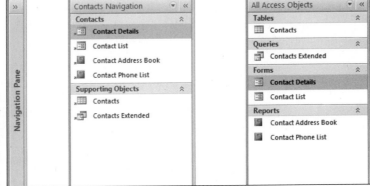

Figure 1-4: Different views of the Navigation pane.

Exercise 1-9: Manipulating the Navigation Pane

In this exercise, you change the look of the Navigation pane. Open the `Exercise1-9.accdb` file in the Chapter01 folder and do the following:

✔ Click the Shutter Bar Open/Close button to alternate between collapsed and open views.

✔ Press F11 to alternate between collapsed and open views.

✔ With the Navigation pane open, click the drop-down list icon to the left of the Shutter Bar Open/Close button and click Object Type to list the objects by type (tables, queries, forms, reports, macros, modules). In this view, you can expand/collapse each section using the arrows.

✔ Click the drop-down list icon and select Tables and Related Views to see the objects listed by what table each object is based on.

✔ Click the drop-down list icon and select Created Date to see the objects listed by when they were created.

✔ Click the drop-down list icon and select Modified Date to see the objects listed by when they were last modified.

✔ In each open view, click the drop-down list icon and select a different option under Filter by Group to narrow the list of objects. This is particularly useful when your database contains many objects.

Experiment with the different views and use whichever one works best for you. What works in one database may not work in another.

Finding help on Access topics

Access provides help in a number of ways. You can always access the help files on your local machine. If you have an active Internet connection, you have access to the resources of Microsoft Office Online. The Help window (Figure 1-5) is where you browse and search for help on different topics.

Search box   Links

Figure 1-5:
Using the
Help
window.

Online/Offline button

Exercise 1-10: Getting Help

In this exercise, you explore the different methods of getting help in Access. Open the `Exercise1-10.accdb` file in the Chapter01 folder and do the following:

- ✔ Click the Help button in the top right corner of the Access window (refer to Figure 1-3) to launch the Help window.

- ✔ Press F1 to launch the Help window.

- ✔ In the bottom-right of the Help window, click the Online/Offline button to switch between using local help files and online help files.

- ✔ Use the Search box to find help on a specific keyword. For example, to find help on tables, type **tables** in the Search box and click Search.

- ✔ Browse the help by clicking the links in the main area of the Help window.

Chapter 2

Managing Databases

· ·

In This Chapter

▶ Making a backup copy of your database

▶ Dealing with a bloated or broken database

▶ Saving a database that was created in an earlier version of Access

▶ Customizing what you see in Access

▶ Keeping your database and computer safe

· ·

*W*hen working with Access, it's inevitable that you must "take care" of databases. In this chapter, you learn the recommended maintenance procedures for Access databases, as well as how to set options for both Access and an individual database. You also use the Trust Center to see how different security settings affect how your database operates.

Backing up Databases

Before you begin making major changes to a database, it's always a good idea to make a backup copy of the database. This way, if you really mess something up and need to undo all of your changes, you can simply open the backup copy. You can use Access (Exercise 2-1) or Windows Explorer (Exercise 2-2) to make a backup copy of your database.

Exercise 2-1: Backing up a Database from Access

Access lets you create a backup of your database. Open the `Exercise2-1.accdb` file and follow these steps:

1. Click the Microsoft Office Button⇨Manage⇨Back Up Database.

   The Save As dialog box appears with the name of the current database followed by today's date (such as `Exercise2-1_2007-09-15.accdb`) in the File Name text box.

2. (Optional) To give the database a different name or change the folder, change the name in the File Name text box and/or navigate to a different destination folder.

   If you make multiple backups during a day, you might

   • Add the time or a letter to the end of the file name.

   • Save the backup copy to a different folder.

3. Click Save.

The Save As dialog box closes, and Access saves a copy of the database. You return to Access, where you can continue working on the original database.

Exercise 2-2: Backing up a Database from Windows Explorer

Windows lets you create a backup of your database without using Access. Follow these steps:

1. Close Access and use Windows Explorer to navigate to the folder containing the Exercise2-2.accdb file.

2. Right-click Exercise2-2.accdb and choose Copy from the pop-up menu.

3. Right-click a blank area of the Windows Explorer window and choose Paste from the pop-up menu.

Windows creates a copy of the database (for instance, Exercise2-2-Copy.accdb).

4. (Optional) To give the database a new name, right-click the new file, choose Rename from the pop-up menu, and type a new name.

Regardless of how you back up your database, you should also copy the backup copy of the database to your network or removable media (CD-ROM, USB drive, tape backup). If your computer dies, you won't lose months of hard work.

Compacting and Repairing Databases

In the day-to-day use of an Access database, the database file can become bloated, for these reasons:

✔ Access increases the file size when performing database tasks.

✔ When you delete information from the database, the file size doesn't decrease and recoup that empty space.

Also, *corruption* can occur, where Access loses track of the objects (tables, queries, forms, reports) in the database. Your database can become corrupt for a number of reasons, such as not closing Access properly, using faulty hardware, experiencing a power failure, or simply because it's a nice day and Access wants to toy with you.

Watch for these signs of corruption:

✔ When opening a database, you get a message saying the file isn't an Access database, is an unrecognized database format, or the database needs to be repaired.

✔ You're prompted for a database password when you open the database, and you know that the database doesn't have a password.

✔ You get random error messages when working with the database.

✔ Access routinely crashes when working with the database.

Compacting and repairing a database reclaims the empty space created from deleting information and fixes (or attempts to fix as some databases can't be fixed) the corruption in your database.

Exercise 2-3: Compacting and Repairing an Open Database

For general maintenance of an Access database, you can compact and repair the database when it's already open. Open the `Exercise2-3.accdb` file and follow this step:

✔ Choose Microsoft Office Button⇨Manage⇨Compact and Repair Database.

Access compacts and repairs the database and then reopens it. Depending on the size of the database, this might happen instantaneously or take a few moments.

Exercise 2-4: Compacting and Repairing Any Database

If for some reason (such as database corruption) you can't open a database, you must compact and repair the database without opening it. Follow these steps:

1. Launch Microsoft Office Access.

The Getting Started with Microsoft Office Access page appears.

2. Click the Microsoft Office Button⇨Manage⇨Compact and Repair Database.

The Database to Compact From dialog box appears.

3. Navigate to the Documents\My Practice Databases\Chapter02 folder (or the folder where you saved the practice files from the CD-ROM).

4. Click `Exercise2-4.accdb`.

5. Click Compact.

The Compact Database Into dialog box opens.

6. (Optional) Navigate to the desired folder to change the location of the database.

7. Type **Exercise2-4_Repaired.accdb** in the File Name text box.

8. Click Save.

Access compacts and repairs the database and saves it with a new file name (`Exercise2-4_Repaired.accdb`). The original database (`Exercise2-4.accdb`) remains unchanged.

Before making a backup copy of your database, compact and repair the database so it takes up less space. You can even right-click the database file in Windows Explorer, select Send To ⇨ Compressed (Zipped) Folder to compress the file so it takes up even less space.

Saving a Database in a Different Format

Access 2007 databases (which have `.accdb` extensions) are compatible only with Access 2007. So here's what to do if everyone involved with the database you're using isn't using the latest and greatest version of Access:

✔ If other users work in Access 2000, 2002, or 2003, you must convert your Access 2007 database to an earlier database format (which has a .mdb extension).

✔ If other users work in versions of Access *before Access 2000,* you can't share information with them.

Exercise 2-5: Saving an Access Database to an Earlier Version

To convert an Access 2007 database (.accdb) to an earlier version (.mdb), open the Exercise2-5.accdb file and follow these steps:

1. Click the Microsoft Office Button⇨Save As⇨Access 2002-2003 Database.

Or you can click Access 2000 Database if you want to save it in an Access 2000 format.

A dialog box appears, asking if you want Microsoft Office Access to close all open objects.

2. Click Yes to close all the database objects.

One of the following occurs:

• The Save As dialog box appears.

You can proceed to Step 3.

• The following message appears: You cannot save this database in an earlier version format, because it uses features that require the current file format.

If you see this message, you can't convert the database to an earlier format. The current database contains features that are available only in Access 2007 databases.

3. (Optional) Navigate to the desired folder to change the location of the database.

4. Type **Exercise2-5.mdb** in the File Name text box.

5. Click Save.

Access converts the Access 2007 database (.accdb) to the earlier Access 2002-2003 format (.mdb), or the Access 2000 format if that's what you've chosen, and opens the older database in Access 2007. Now you can open this database in Access 2007 and other users can open the same database in Access 2002 or Access 2003 (or Access 2000).

Setting Access Options

The more you use Access, the more you want to personalize your experience. Access provides a variety of options so you can use it the way you want, not the way those engineers at Microsoft tell you. Sure, you can't do whatever you want, but you can customize whether you want to default to Access 2007 or earlier formats, change the color schemes of the windows and datasheets, customize the title bar of your database, change certain defaults when creating new objects, and set different security settings to ensure the safety of your computer and possibly everyone else's computer on your network.

ON THE CD

Exercise 2-6: Exploring Access Options

In this exercise, you view the different options available in Access. Setting individual options is covered throughout this book, so don't worry about learning each and every option. Open the Exercise2-6.accdb file and practice these actions:

✔ Click the Microsoft Office Button and click Access Options in the lower right section of the menu.

The Access Options window appears (shown in Figure 2-1).

✔ In the left pane of the Access Options window, click Popular to display the most popular options in Access.

Popular options include customizing screen tips and changing the color scheme, the default folder, and file type for new databases, and your name and initials.

✔ Click Current Database to display options that pertain to the currently open database (Exercise2-6.accdb) only.

Current Database options include changing the title bar and icon, deciding whether to compact the database when you close it, showing the navigation pane, and customizing the Ribbon.

✔ Click Datasheet to display options that customize the way datasheets (such as tables) appear in Access.

Datasheet options include choosing the following: the color schemes, how gridlines appear between rows and columns, and the default font for the data.

✔ Click Object Designers to display options that customize the creation and modification of database objects in Access.

Object Designer options include customizing how you create and modify tables, queries, forms, and reports.

✔ Click Proofing to display options that change how Access automatically corrects and formats the contents of your databases and how it indicates the errors that it finds.

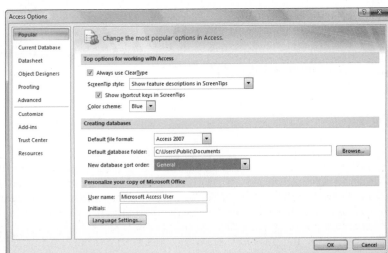

Figure 2-1:
The Access
Options
window.

✔ Click Advanced to display Advanced customization options for Access.

Advanced options include changing how the keyboard operates when moving around datasheets and forms, choosing whether to confirm record changes and object deletions, and deciding whether to show or hide the status bar, default print margins, and date formatting.

✔ Click Customize to change the commands that appear on the Quick Access Toolbar.

✔ Click Add-ins to view and manage Microsoft Office add-ins.

Add-ins provide additional functionality that isn't native to Microsoft Office Access.

✔ Click Trust Center to learn how to keep your documents safe and your computer secure and healthy, as well as set up trusted publishers and locations, which is covered in the section "Using the Trust Center," later in this chapter.

✔ Click Resources to contact Microsoft, find online resources, and maintain the health and reliability of your Microsoft Office programs.

Using the Tabbed Documents interface

When you install Access, the default setting for opening database objects in the document window is the Tabbed Documents interface. The Tabbed Documents interface opens each object with a tab at the top of the document window. (The tabs allow you to easily switch between open database objects.) The *document window* is the area of the Access window where you view database objects such as tables, queries, forms, and reports.

Exercise 2-7: Using the Tabbed Documents Interface

To open Access objects using the Tabbed Documents interface, open the `Exercise2-7.accdb` file and follow these steps:

1. In the Navigation pane, double-click Contacts under the Tables group.

The table Contacts opens with a tab to the right of the Contact List form's tab, which opens when `Exercise2-7.accdb` opens.

2. In the Navigation pane, double-click Contact Address Book under the Reports group.

The Contact Address Book report opens, with a tab to the right of the Contacts table's tab, shown in Figure 2-2.

3. Right-click the Contacts tab in the document window and choose Close from the pop-up menu.

The table Contacts closes and the Contact Address Book tab moves left to take the space where the Contacts tab appeared.

4. (Optional) To close all the open objects, right-click any tab in the document window, and then click Close All from the pop-up menu.

The Contact List form and the Contact Address Book report close, leaving an empty document window.

Document tabs

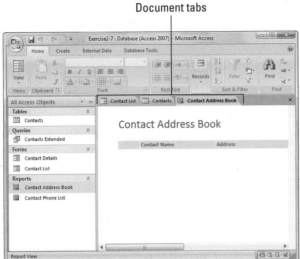

Using the Overlapping Windows interface

The *Overlapping Windows* interface is sometimes referred to as the *classic interface*. It's the interface used by all previous versions of Access.

When opening objects using the Overlapping Windows interface, each object opens in its own window, which can overlap with one on top of the other. Each object can be a different size and you can view more than one window at a time.

Exercise 2-8: Using the Overlapping Windows Interface

To open Access objects using the Overlapping Windows interface, open the `Exercise2-8.accdb` file and follow these steps:

1. Click the Microsoft Office Button and click Access Options in the lower right section of the menu.

The Access Options window appears.

2. Click Current Database to display options that only pertain to the currently open database (`Exercise2-8.accdb`).

3. Under Document Window Options in the Application Options section, click the Overlapping Windows option button (shown in Figure 2-3).

4. Click OK.

The Access Options window closes and Access displays a message box to close and reopen the current database for the specified option to take effect.

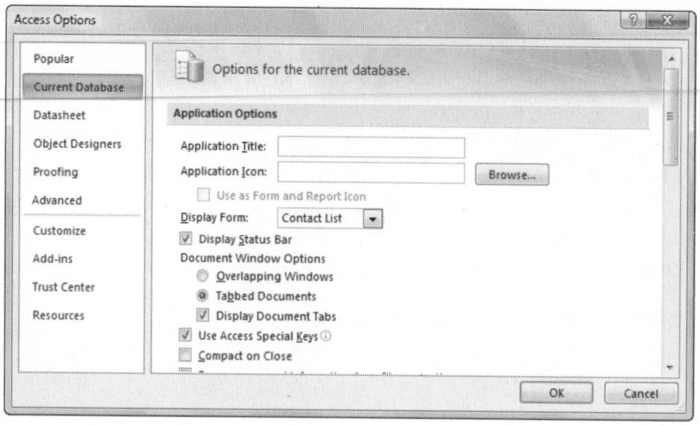

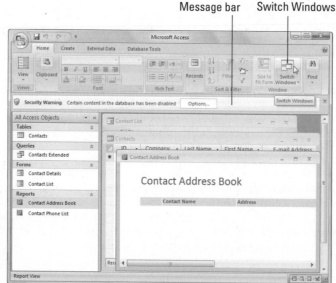

Figure 2-3:
Switching
from the
Tabbed
Documents
and
Overlapping
Windows
interface.

5. Click the Microsoft Office Button and click Close Database.

   `Exercise2-8.accdb` closes, and the Getting Started with Microsoft Office Access page appears.

6. In the Open Recent Database pane on the right side of the Getting Started with Microsoft Office Access page, click `Exercise2-8.accdb`.

   `Exercise2-8.accdb` opens and the Contact List form opens in the document window.

7. In the Navigation pane, double-click Contacts under the Tables group.

   The table, Contacts, opens in a new window on top of the Contact List form.

8. In the Navigation pane, double-click Contact Address Book under the Reports group.

   The Contact Address Book report opens in a new window on top of the Contacts table (shown in Figure 2-4).

Message bar   Switch Windows

Figure 2-4:
Viewing the
Overlapping
Windows
interface.

9. (Optional) To switch to a window that is completely behind another window, click the Switch Windows command on the Home tab and select the desired window from the drop-down menu.

10. Use one of these options to close a window:

    • Right-click the title bar of the window and then click Close from the pop-up menu.

    • Click the Close button in the top right corner of the window.

    • Double-click the icon in the top left corner of the window.

11. (Optional) To close all the open windows, right-click any title bar in the document window, and then click Close All from the pop-up menu.

    All open windows close, leaving an empty document window.

Understanding Access Security

Like most computer programs, Access databases are vulnerable to attack from hackers who get a kick out of writing malicious software that messes up as many computers as possible. You're probably aware of the dangers of opening e-mail attachments, and these dangers apply to Access databases as well. Unless you're sure the database is safe, you should make sure the dangerous contents of the database are disabled.

Exercise 2-9: Enabling Database Content

To enable all of the content in a database, open the `Exercise2-9.accdb` file and follow these steps:

1. In the Message Bar, which appears under the Ribbon (see Figure 2-4), click the Options button.

   The Microsoft Office Security Options dialog box appears.

2. If you trust the contents of this database (read the message), click the Enable this Content option button.

3. Click OK.

   The Microsoft Office Security Options dialog box closes, and the database closes and reopens without the Message Bar; all contents are enabled.

Using the Trust Center

If you routinely receive databases from a particular person or company, or you want to specify a location on your computer or network for databases you know are safe, use the Trust Center. In the Trust Center, you can set up trusted publishers and locations, define settings for add-ins and macros, choose to display the Message Bar, and set privacy options for sharing your information with Microsoft.

Exercise 2-10: Setting a Trusted Location

A *trusted location* is a folder on your computer where you place databases you know are safe. To set up a trusted location on your computer, open the `Exercise2-10.accdb` file and follow these steps:

1. Click the Microsoft Office Button and click Access Options in the lower right section of the menu.

   The Access Options window appears.

2. In the left pane of the Access Options window, click Trust Center.

3. In the right pane of the Access Options window under the Microsoft Office Access Trust Center section, click Trust Center Settings.

   The Trust Center window appears.

4. In the right pane of the Trust Center window, click Add New Location near the bottom of the window.

   The Microsoft Office Trusted Location dialog box appears.

5. Click Browse.

   The Browse dialog box appears.

6. Navigate to the Documents\My Practice Databases folder (or the folder where you saved the practice files from the CD-ROM).

7. Click OK.

   The Browse dialog box closes, showing the Microsoft Office Trusted Location dialog box, displaying the full path of the My Practice Databases folder in the Path text box.

8. Select the Subfolders of this Location are Also Trusted check box.

   Selecting this check box makes all of the subfolders in this folder (Chapter01, Chapter02, and so forth) trusted.

9. (Optional) To give this trusted location a description, type **Access 2007 Workbook Practice Files** in the Description text box.

10. Click OK.

   The Microsoft Office Trusted Location dialog box closes, displaying the Trust Center window, with the new location listed in the User Locations section. Now when you open any database from this folder or any of its subfolders, you won't see the security warning in the Message Bar because it's considered a trusted database.

11. Click OK to close the Trust Center window.

12. Click OK to close the Access Options window.

Encrypting a database

When you want to make sure prying eyes don't see the important data you keep in your databases, you should *encrypt* the database using a database password. Encrypting a database basically makes it readable to only the person who knows the password. Access jumbles up all of the information in the database, so it isn't easy for hackers to break into.

No database is 100 percent secure, even with encryptions, so you should still lock your office door at night.

Exercise 2-11: Encrypting a Database

To encrypt a database with a password, follow these steps:

1. Launch Microsoft Office Access.

   The Getting Started with Microsoft Office Access page appears.

2. Click the Microsoft Office Button and click Open.

   The Open dialog box appears.

3. Navigate to the Documents\My Practice Databases\Chapter02 folder (or the folder where you saved the practice files from the CD-ROM).

4. Click Exercise2-11.accdb.

5. Click the drop-down list on the Open button and click Open Exclusive.

   Access opens the Exercise2-11.accdb database exclusively, which ensures no other users can open the database. You must open a database exclusively in order to encrypt the database with a password.

6. On the Database Tools tab, click Encrypt with Password.

   The Set Database Password dialog box appears.

7. Type **test** in the Password text box.

8. Type **test** in the Verify text box.

9. Click OK.

   Access encrypts the database, and the Encrypt with Password command on the Database Tools tab changes to Decrypt Database.

10. Click the Microsoft Office Button and click Close Database.

    Exercise2-11.accdb closes, and the Getting Started with Microsoft Office Access page appears.

11. In the Open Recent Database pane on the right side of the Getting Started with Microsoft Office Access page, click Exercise2-11.accdb.

    The Password Required dialog box appears.

12. Type **test** in the Enter Database Password text box.

13. Click OK.

    Exercise2-11.accdb opens.

To decrypt a database, click the Decrypt Database command on the Database Tools tab on an encrypted database. You need the password to decrypt a database.

Part II

Creating and Using Tables

The 5th Wave   By Rich Tennant

"Your database is beyond repair, but before I tell you our backup recommendation, let me ask you a question. How many index cards do you think will fit on the walls of your computer room?"

In this part . . .

Tables are to a database what legs are to chairs; without tables, you don't really have a database. The chapters and exercises in Part II teach all about tables in Access. You start out by building tables (put away your hammer and saw), then move to entering and viewing data. Finally, you tie tables together using relationships.

Chapter 3

Creating and Modifying Tables

· ·

In This Chapter

▶ Adding tables to your database

▶ Working with tables in Datasheet view and Design view

▶ Understanding data types

▶ Making changes to field properties

· ·

*T*ables are the backbone of any Access database. Tables are where your information lives, and in order to create a functional database, you must carefully plan what type of information you want to store in your tables and create the table structure accordingly.

In this chapter, you can begin creating the table structures for the MyMediaStore database. You can learn different ways to create tables, add and change fields to a table, and set field properties.

Creating Tables

When you create a new blank database, it doesn't have any database objects in it. For most database applications, you start by creating tables. You can create tables in Datasheet view and Design view.

Using Datasheet view

Datasheet view is similar to a spreadsheet in which you see rows *(records)* and columns *(fields)*. In Datasheet view, you can add new fields and rename existing fields in your tables if you decide to change the field name later. You also can add and edit data in Datasheet view.

Exercise 3-1: Creating a Table in Datasheet View

You start building your Access application from the ground up — meaning you start with nothing. To create a new table to track artists in a blank database, launch Access and follow these steps:

1. Click the Microsoft Office Button and click New.

The right pane in the Access window switches to the Blank Database pane.

2. Type **Exercise3-1.accdb** in the File Name text box.

If you don't want to change the database's location, skip to Step 4.

3. (Optional) If you need or want to change the location of the database, click the folder icon to the right of the File Name text box and navigate to the desired folder.

4. Click the Create button underneath the File Name text box in the Blank Database pane.

Access creates the `Exercise3-1.accdb` database in the specified folder and opens the database showing Table1 in Datasheet view (shown in Figure 3-1). This table contains two fields: ID and Add New Field.

ID Field Add New Field heading

Design View command   (Table Tools) Datasheet tab

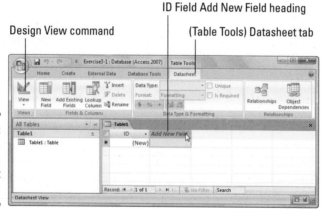

Figure 3-1: Creating a table in Datasheet view.

5. To add a new field, double-click the Add New Field column heading.

The words Add New Field disappear, and a blinking cursor appears.

6. Type **ArtistName** in the column heading.

7. Press Tab.

The column heading to the right of the ArtistName column switches to a blinking cursor.

8. Type **Genre** in the column heading.

9. Press Tab.

The column heading to the right of the Genre column switches to a blinking cursor.

10. Use one of these options to stop creating new columns:

- Press Tab without entering text in the column heading.
- Press Enter without entering text in the column heading.
- Click any other column heading or field in the table.

Exercise 3-2: Saving a Table

After you create a new table or make structural changes to an existing table, you must save your changes. Follow these steps to save the new table created in Exercise 3-1:

1. Use one of the following methods to save your table structure:

- Click the Save button on the Quick Access Toolbar.
- Click the Microsoft Office Button and choose Save in the menu that appears.
- Right-click the Table1 tab and choose Save from the pop-up menu that appears.
- Press Ctrl+S.

The Save As dialog box appears.

2. Type **tblArtists** in the Save As dialog box.

3. Click OK.

Access saves the table structure and changes Table1 on the document tab and in the Navigation pane to tblArtists.

By placing a prefix (tbl) before the table name, you know this object is a table. When you create different database objects, adding a prefix lets you know whether an object is a query (qry), form (frm), report (rpt), or macros (mcr).

Exercise 3-3: Renaming a Field in Datasheet View

If you want to rename a field name (maybe because you're a bad typist), you can change it in Datasheet view. Continue working with the database from Exercise 3-2 or open the `Exercise3-3.accdb` file in the Chapter03 folder, then follow these steps:

1. Double-click tblArtists in the Navigation pane.

The table opens in Datasheet view showing three fields: ID, ArtistName, and Genre.

2. Use one of the following methods to place the ID column heading in edit mode:

- Double-click the ID column heading.
- Right-click the ID column heading and choose Rename Column from the pop-up menu that appears.

3. Type **ArtistID** in the column heading.

4. Press Enter.

Access changes the column heading to ArtistID.

Using Design view

Design view lets you add and rename fields, just like Datasheet view does, but Design view gives you the ability to change other field properties. In Design view, you don't see the rows and columns; instead, you see a list of field names, data types, and descriptions (as shown in Figure 3-2).

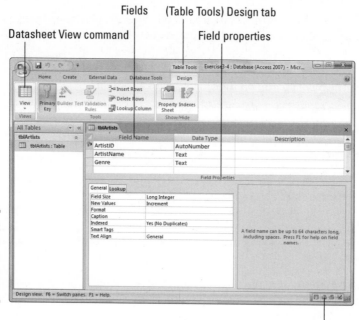

Figure 3-2:
Viewing a table in Design view.

Fields   (Table Tools) Design tab
Datasheet View command   Field properties

View shortcuts

Exercise 3-4: Switching Between Datasheet View and Design View

When designing a table, you routinely switch between Datasheet view and Design view. Continue working with the database from Exercise 3-3 or open the `Exercise3-4.accdb` file in the Chapter03 folder, then follow these steps:

1. Open tblArtists in Datasheet view if it isn't already open.

2. Use one of the following methods to switch to Design view:

- Click the Design View command on the left side of the Home tab (the command looks like a triangle, ruler, and pencil, as shown in Figure 3-1).

- Right-click the table's document tab and choose Design View from the pop-up menu that appears.

- Right-click the table name (tblArtists) in the Navigation pane and choose Design View from the pop-up menu that appears.

- Click the Design View button in the view shortcuts at the bottom-right of the Access window.

3. Use one of the following methods to switch to Datasheet view:

   • Click the Datasheet View command on the left side of the Home tab (the command looks like a spreadsheet, as shown in Figure 3-2).

   • Right-click the table's document tab and choose Datasheet View from the pop-up menu that appears.

   • Right-click the table name (tblArtists) in the Navigation pane and choose Open from the pop-up menu that appears.

   • Double-click the table name (tblArtists) in the Navigation pane.

   • Click the Datasheet View button in the view shortcuts at the bottom-right of the Access window.

4. Use one of the methods from Step 2 to switch back to Design view.

The Design view window consists of two halves:

✔ **Fields:** In the top half of the window, this section contains three columns:

   • **Field Name:** A unique name for each column in the table.

   • **Data Type:** This column specifies what kind of data (such as text, numbers, or dates), which you select from a drop-down list of available values. Table 3-1 lists the data types and describes when to choose each.

   • **Description:** This optional column supplies each field with additional information to assist the user in entering data. The text you enter here appears in the Status bar in Datasheet view.

✔ **Field Properties:** In the lower half of the Design view window, you can set properties for the field that you select in the top half. These properties vary based on the field's data type.

Table 3-1	Data Types	
Data Type	*What It Holds*	*When to Use It*
Text	Numbers, letters, punctuation, spaces, and special characters (up to 255 characters)	For all text fields, except really long ones. Also good for phone numbers and zip codes. You can't do mathematical calculations with a text field.
Memo	Text, and a lot of it — up to 63,999 characters	When you have a lot of text, such as in a comments or notes field.
Number	Numbers	For numbers you might want to add, multiply, or do other calculations with.
Date/Time	Dates and times	To store a date or time value, or both.
Currency	Numbers with a currency sign in front of them	To store currency data, such as prices.

(continued)

Table 3-1 *(continued)*

Data Type	What It Holds	When to Use It
AutoNumber	A unique number generated by Access for each record	To give each record in a table a unique value that you don't have to type in.
Yes/No	Binary data, such as Yes/No, True/False, and On/Off	When you want a field that has only two possible entries. Fields with this data type appear as a check box in Datasheet view.
OLE Object	An object, such as a sound, picture, or an OLE compatible file	To store something in Access or link to something created with another application, such as Paint or Microsoft Excel.
Hyperlink	URLs, e-mail addresses, and other links	To link to a Web page, e-mail address, or file on your computer or network.
Attachment	One or more attachments	To store compatible files, such as spreadsheets, documents, charts, and other types of files.
Lookup Wizard	Not really a data type, but it starts the Lookup Wizard that creates a drop-down list in your table	To look up a value in another table or choose from a predefined list of values.

Exercise 3-5: Adding a Field to a Table from Design View

You can add a field to a table from Design view. In this exercise, you add a field for each Artist's Web site. Continue working with the database from Exercise 3-4 or open the `Exercise3-5.accdb` file in the Chapter03 folder, then follow these steps:

1. Open tblArtists in Design view if it isn't already open.

2. Click in the Field Name column in the blank cell underneath the Genre field.

3. Type **ArtistWebSite** in the Field Name column.

4. Press Tab.

   The cursor moves to the Data Type column, which switches from blank to Text (the default selection).

5. Click the arrow on the right side of the Data Type column and select **Hyperlink** from the drop-down list that appears.

To delete a field in Design view, click in the row of the field name that you want to delete, then click the Delete Rows command on the (Table Tools) Design tab.

Exercise 3-6: Creating a New Table in Design View

You can create new tables by using Design view. In this exercise, you create a new table to track the Artists' albums. Continue working with the database from Exercise 3-5 or open the `Exercise3-6.accdb` file in the Chapter03 folder, then follow these steps:

1. Click Table Design on the Create tab.

    A new table opens in Design view with the cursor in the Field Name column.

2. Type **AlbumID** in the Field Name column.

3. Click the arrow on the right side of the Data Type column and select **AutoNumber** from the drop-down list that appears.

4. Press Tab.

    The cursor moves to the Description column.

5. Type **Unique Identifier for Each Album** in the Description column.

6. Press Tab.

    The cursor moves to the Field Name column in the next row.

7. Add the remaining fields by using the following list:

Field Name	Data Type	Description
ArtistID	Number	ArtistID from tblArtists
AlbumTitle	Text	Title of Album
YearOfRelease	Number	Year Album Released
Quantity	Number	Quantity On Hand
PurchaseDate	Date/Time	Date of Purchase
PurchasePrice	Currency	Amount Paid
SaleDate	Date/Time	Date of Sale
SalePrice	Currency	Amount Sold For

8. Click AlbumID in the first row of the field list.

9. On the (Table Tools) Design tab, click the Primary Key command.

    The AlbumID field becomes the primary key, and Access places a key icon to the left of the AlbumID field.

    A *primary key* is a field or group of fields that uniquely identifies each record in a table. Although primary keys aren't required, each table should have one. For this example, you set the AlbumID (an AutoNumber field) as the primary key.

10. Save the table as **tblAlbums**.

    Access saves the table structure, changes Table1 on the document tab to tblAlbums, and adds tblAlbums to the Navigation pane. The table's design is shown in Figure 3-3.

Primary Key command

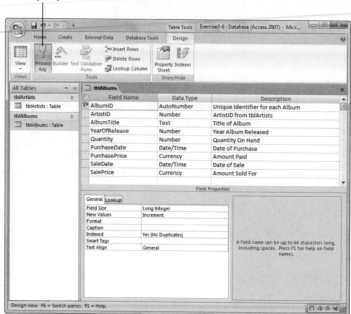

Figure 3-3:
Creating
tblAlbums
in Design
view.

Exercise 3-7: Inserting a Lookup Column in Design View

In order to make data entry easier, you can add a lookup column to the table. In this exercise, you insert a new field to select the media type (such as CDs or Cassettes) from a drop-down list. Continue working with the database from Exercise 3-6 or open the Exercise3-7.accdb file in the Chapter03 folder, then follow these steps:

1. Open tblAlbums in Design view if it isn't already open.

2. Click the YearOfRelease field name.

3. On the (Table Tools) Design tab, click the Insert Rows command.

Access inserts a new row above the YearOfRelease field. When in a table's Design view, Access always inserts rows above the selected field.

4. Type **MediaType** in the Field Name column.

5. Click the arrow on the right side of the Data Type column and select **Lookup Wizard** from the drop-down list.

The Lookup Wizard dialog box appears.

6. Select the I Will Type in the Values that I Want option button.

7. Click Next.

The next page of the wizard appears. On this page, you specify the number of columns (the default is one) and type the values you want in your lookup column.

8. Type the following values in each row of the grid, pressing Tab after each entry to move to the following row:

CD

Cassette

DVD-Audio

SA-CD (Super Audio)

Vinyl Record

9. Click Next.

The next page of the wizard appears, in which you specify the label for the lookup column (the default is MediaType, which you typed in Step 4).

You can also choose to allow multiple values to be selected by selecting the Allow Multiple Values check box on this page. Allowing multiple values lets you pick more than one value from a drop-down list.

10. Click Finish.

The wizard closes and changes the data type of the MediaType field to Text.

11. Click in the Description column for the MediaType field.

12. Type **Select the Media Type** in the Description column.

13. Click Save on the Quick Access Toolbar to save the table.

Because the table already has a name (tblAlbums), you aren't prompted for a table name.

14. Switch to Datasheet view.

15. Click in the MediaType column.

A drop-down arrow appears, indicating you can select a value from a drop-down list.

16. Click the drop-down arrow in the MediaType column.

The drop-down list of values you typed in Step 8 appears.

Setting Field Properties

In addition to the field name, data type, and description, each field has additional properties that appear at the bottom of the table's Design view. You can set properties for only one field at a time. To see the field properties for a particular field, click in any column for that field in the top half of the Design view window.

Setting the Field Size property

The Field Size property sets how much data a particular field can hold. For text fields, you can set the Field Size to any value from 1 to 255. For number fields, setting the Field Size is a bit more complicated. Table 3-2 shows the choices for the Field Size of a number field.

Table 3-2	Field Sizes for Number Fields	
Setting	*What It Holds*	*When to Use It*
Bytes	Integers from 0–255.	When values are integers less than 256.
Integer	Integers from –32,768 to 32, 767.	For most fields needing integers, unless you need to store values greater than 32,768 or less than -32,767.
Long Integer	Integers from –2,147,483,648 to 2,147,483,647.	When the range of values for the Integer setting is too small or when you're using a field to link to an AutoNumber field in another table.
Single	Numbers from about –3.4E38 to –1.4E–45 for negative numbers and from about 1.4E–45 to 3.4E38 for positive values. Decimal precision to seven places.	For numbers with decimal values. Holds big numbers and a lot of decimal places.
Double	Numbers from about –1.8E308 to –4.9E–324 for negative numbers and from about 4.9E–324 to 1.8E308 for positive values. Decimal precision to 15 places.	For numbers that the Single setting can't hold. Generally speaking, Single is sufficient, but you can change to Double if you need to store numbers within a larger range of values.
Decimal	Numbers from $-10^{28}-1$ through $10^{28}-1$ with decimal precision up to 28 places.	For numbers with a ton of decimal places.
ReplicationID	Globally unique identifier (GUID) used for replication (which is supported in only older `.mdb` files).	For an AutoNumber field that's the primary key when you replicate a database. (Not a common choice!)

Exercise 3-8: Setting the Field Size Property

Access has default settings for the Field Size property when creating fields. After you create fields, verify or set the Field Size property for each field to ensure each field is storing the right amount of information. Continue working with the database from Exercise 3-7 or open the `Exercise3-8.accdb` file in the Chapter03 folder, then follow these steps:

1. Open tblAlbums in Design view if it isn't already open.

2. Click the AlbumTitle field name in the top pane.

   The field properties in the bottom pane of the table's Design view change to show the properties of the AlbumTitle field.

3. Type **50** in the Field Size property in the bottom pane (the default value for a text field is 255).

   Changing the Field Size property to a smaller value limits how many characters you can enter for a value in this field.

4. Click the MediaType field name in the top pane.

5. Type **20** in the Field Size property in the bottom pane.

6. Click the YearOfRelease field name in the top pane.

7. Select Integer from the Field Size property drop-down list in the bottom pane.

   The default value for a number field is Long Integer.

8. Click the Quantity field name in the top pane.

9. Select Integer in the Field Size property drop-down list in the bottom pane.

10. Click Save on the Quick Access Toolbar to save tblAlbums.

11. Open tblArtists in Design view if it isn't already open.

12. Change the Field Size properties for the following fields:

Field Name	*Field Size*
ArtistName	50
Genre	20

13. Click Save on the Quick Access Toolbar to save tblArtists.

To change the default values when you add new fields to a table, follow these steps:

1. Open the Access Options window.

2. Click Object Designers in the left pane.

3. Change the values in the Table Design section.

For more information on changing Access Options, see Chapter 2.

Setting other field properties

In addition to the Field Size property, fields have additional properties that you can set. Not all properties are available for all data types.

You probably won't set or change all of these common field properties, but you should know what these properties do:

✔ **Format:** Changes how the data is displayed.

You select from predefined formats for Number, Currency, Date/Time, and Yes/No fields, or you set custom formats for these fields, as well as Text and Memo fields (which don't have any predefined formats).

✔ **Input Mask:** Sets a pattern for all data entered in this field.

The Input Mask Wizard (which you can access by clicking the ellipsis button on the right side of the Input Mask property setting) guides you through setting up an Input Mask.

✔ **Caption:** Changes the column heading in Datasheet view.

Changing the caption also changes the label that appears to the left of or above a field when you create a form or report.

✔ **Default Value:** Sets a value that's automatically entered in the field for a new record.

✔ **Validation Rule:** An expression that limits the values that can be entered in the field.

✔ **Validation Text:** The message that appears when you enter a value that violates the expression in the Validation Rule property.

If you don't enter a value here, a generic message appears.

✔ **Required:** Determines whether data must be entered in this field.

✔ **Indexed:** Sets an index on this field. An *index* speeds up searches and sorting on the field, but it may slow updates. An index can also prohibit duplicate data.

A primary key field automatically has this property set to Yes (No Duplicates).

✔ **Decimal Places:** For numeric fields, sets the number of decimal places displayed.

✔ **Show Date Picker:** For Date/Time fields, determines if a pop-up calendar is available (which makes entering date values easier).

Exercise 3-9: Setting Other Field Properties

To set additional field properties, continue working with the database from Exercise 3-8 or open the `Exercise3-9.accdb` file in the Chapter03 folder, then follow these steps:

1. Open tblAlbums in Design view if it isn't already open.

2. Click the Quantity field name in the top pane.

The field properties in the bottom pane of the table's Design view change to show the properties of the Quantity field.

3. In the bottom pane, set the following field properties for the Quantity field:

Field Property	Setting
Default Value	1
Validation Rule	>=0
Validation Text	Enter a value of 0 or higher
Required	Yes

Setting these properties makes the Quantity field a required field, defaults the value to 1 for new records, and requires you to enter a value of 0 or higher. The settings are shown in Figure 3-4.

Field properties of Quantity field   Description of selected property

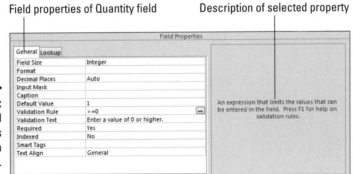

Figure 3-4:
Setting field
properties
in Design
view.

4. Click the PurchaseDate field name in the top pane.

   The field properties in the bottom pane of the table's Design view change to show the properties of the PurchaseDate field.

5. In the bottom pane, set the following field properties for the PurchaseDate field:

Field Property	*Setting*
Format	Short Date
Default Value	=Date()
Show Date Picker	For dates

   Setting these properties makes the PurchaseDate display in the Short Date format (10/1/2007), defaults the value to today's date for new records, and lets you use a calendar to select a different date.

6. Click Save on the Quick Access Toolbar to save the tblAlbums.

7. Switch to Datasheet view.

   The empty row under the column headings contains a default value of 1 in the Quantity field and today's date in the PurchaseDate field.

Chapter 4

Entering Data in Tables

· ·

In This Chapter

▶ Adding and editing records

▶ Deleting a record

▶ Moving around in your records with the navigation buttons

▶ Using Access tools to find and replace data

▶ Checking your spelling in a datasheet

· ·

*A*ll of the data in your database is stored in tables. The data doesn't just magically appear; somebody has to enter it. You can enter and manipulate data directly in a table's Datasheet view, which you might prefer if you're familiar with the row-and-column format used in a spreadsheet.

In this chapter, I explain how to fill in the table structures for the MyMediaStore database. You can learn different ways to add and change values in a table, how to navigate around the datasheet, and how to use the spell checker.

Adding Data to a Table

When you create a new table, it doesn't contain any data. After you define the structure (covered in Chapter 3), you're ready to begin entering data. Now, you can really hone your typing skills.

Exercise 4-1: Adding Records to a Table

A table without data isn't very useful. To add records to tblArtists, continue working with the database from Exercise 3-9 or open the `Exercise4-1.accdb` file in the Chapter04 folder, then follow these steps:

1. Double-click tblArtists in the Navigation pane.

The table opens in Datasheet view with the cursor in the ArtistID field (an AutoNumber field), which contains the text (New). The asterisk (*) in the *Record Selector* (the column to the left of the ArtistID field) also indicates a new row.

2. Press Tab.

The cursor moves to the ArtistName field (a Text field).

3. Type **John E. Blue** in the ArtistName field.

4. Press Tab.

The cursor moves to the Genre field (a Text field), and the ArtistID field changes to 1.

5. Type **Pop/Rock** in the Genre field.

6. Press Tab.

The cursor moves to the ArtistWebSite field (a Hyperlink field).

7. Type **www.dummies.com** in the ArtistWebSite field.

The text you type appears blue and underlined.

8. Press Tab.

The cursor moves to the ArtistID field in the row beneath the data you entered in Steps 3 through 7, which is now the New row (shown in Figure 4-1). When you leave a row, the record you entered in that row is automatically saved.

9. Press Tab and enter the following information in the table:

ArtistName	*Genre*	*ArtistWebSite*
Christy Aguadilla	Pop/Rock	www.aguadilla.com
Gnu Farm	Alternative	<leave blank>
Left Sisters	Country	<leave blank>
The Weedwackers	Country	<leave blank>
MC Smoothie	R&B	<leave blank>

The ArtistID field fills in sequentially as you enter the Artist information.

To save a record without leaving the row, click Save in the Records group on the Home tab.

Record Selector New record indicator Records group

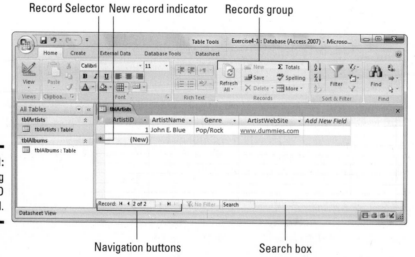

Figure 4-1: Accessing the ArtistID field.

Navigation buttons Search box

Editing Data in a Table

After you enter data in a table, there's a pretty good chance that, at some point, you'll need to change it. Whether you had a bad day and entered the wrong information or the data is outdated and you need to update it, you must edit the information. If you end up changing something you didn't intend to change, you can also undo those changes.

Exercise 4-2: Editing Records in a Table

If you make a mistake during data entry, or you simply need to update information, you need to edit a record. To edit records in tblArtists, continue working with the database from Exercise 4-1 or open the `Exercise4-2.accdb` file in the Chapter04 folder, then follow these steps:

1. Open tblArtists in Datasheet view if it isn't already open.

2. Highlight the word Country in the Genre field for the Left Sisters by clicking to the right of the word and dragging the mouse to the left.

3. Type **Alternative** in the Genre field.

   When you begin typing, a pencil appears in the Record Selector for the row you're editing (shown in Figure 4-2).

Editing record indicator (pencil)

Figure 4-2: Editing data in a table's Datasheet view.

tblArtists				
ArtistID ▾	ArtistName ▾	Genre ▾	ArtistWebSite ▾	Add New Field
1	John E. Blue	Pop/Rock	www.dummies.com	
2	Christy Aguadilla	Pop/Rock	www.aguadilla.com	
3	Gnu Farm	Alternative		
4	Left Sisters	Alternative		
5	The Weedwackers	Country		
6	MC Smoothie	R&B		
*	(New)			

4. Press the Down Arrow (↓).

   Access saves the record, the cursor moves to the Genre field in the row beneath the row you just edited, and the pencil disappears from the Record Selector.

Exercise 4-3: Undoing Changes while Editing

If you make a mistake and realize it before you save the record, you can undo your changes without saving. To undo changes to a record in tblArtists, continue working with the database from Exercise 4-2 or open the `Exercise4-3.accdb` file in the Chapter04 folder, then follow these steps:

1. Open tblArtists in Datasheet view if it isn't already open.

2. Highlight the word Alternative in the Genre field for the Left Sisters by clicking to the right of the word and dragging the mouse to the left.

3. Type **Country** in the Genre field.

   When you begin typing, a pencil appears in the Record Selector for the row you're editing (shown in Figure 4-2).

4. Press Tab.

   The cursor moves to the ArtistWebSite field (a Hyperlink field).

5. Type **www.country.com** in the ArtistWebSite field.

6. Press Esc.

   The text www.country.com disappears from the ArtistWebSite field. The first time you press Esc undoes the change to the current field.

7. Press Esc again.

   The word Country in the Genre field changes back to Alternative, its value at the beginning of this exercise. The second time you press Esc undoes all the changes to the current record.

TIP

If after editing data in a record, you move the cursor to a different row (which saves the record), then realize you made a mistake and want to undo the changes to that record, click Undo on the Quick Access Toolbar. You must click this command before you begin editing another record, otherwise, you can't undo your changes to the record you were working on previously. If you can't use the Undo command, you have to use a backup copy of your database (or hope your memory's good).

Removing Data from a Table

If you want to remove a record from your database, you must delete the entire row. It isn't enough to simply clear out all of the fields in a particular row. After you delete a record, you can't get the data back unless you use a backup copy of your database.

ON THE CD

Exercise 4-4: Deleting One Record from a Table

To delete a record in tblArtists, open the `Exercise4-4.accdb` file (do not use the database from Exercise 4-3) in the Chapter04 folder and follow these steps:

1. Open tblArtists in Datasheet view if it isn't already open.

2. Click the Record Selector on the left side of the Datasheet for the row containing Left Sisters (the row you want to delete).

   The row's background color gets darker, and a box outlines the entire row, indicating that the row's selected.

3. Use one of these steps to delete the Left Sisters record:

   • Click Delete in the Records group on the Home tab.

   • Right-click anywhere on the highlighted row and choose Delete Record from the pop-up menu.

   • Press Delete.

   The record disappears, and a message box appears confirming you're about to delete one record and you won't be able to undo the delete.

4. Click Yes.

Access deletes the Left Sisters row from the table.

Exercise 4-5: Deleting Multiple Records from a Table

Sometimes, you want to delete more than one record at a time from a table, which can take a while if you delete them one by one. To delete multiple records in tblArtists, continue working with the database from Exercise 4-4 or open the `Exercise4-5.accdb` file in the Chapter04 folder, then follow these steps:

1. Open tblArtists in Datasheet view if it isn't already open.

2. Click and hold the Record Selector on the left side of the datasheet for the row containing John E. Blue (the first record).

The row's background color gets darker, and a box outlines the entire row, indicating that the row's selected.

3. Drag the mouse down to the third row in the table and release the mouse button.

Each selected row's background color gets darker, and a box outlines the three rows, indicating multiple rows are selected.

4. Press Delete.

The records disappear, and a message box appears confirming that you're about to delete three records and you won't be able to undo the delete.

5. Click No.

The records reappear. Clicking No is your last chance to keep the data before it's gone.

6. To delete all data from a table, use one of the following methods to select all records:

• Press Ctrl+A.

• Choose Select All from the Select drop-down list in the Find group on the Home tab.

• Select the box in the top-left of the datasheet, above the Record Selectors and to the left of the first column (shown in Figure 4-3).

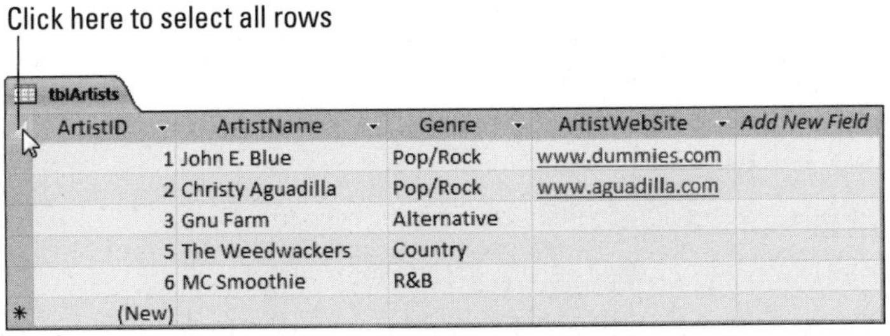

Click here to select all rows

Figure 4-3:
Deleting all rows from a table.

tblArtists				
ArtistID	ArtistName	Genre	ArtistWebSite	Add New Field
1	John E. Blue	Pop/Rock	www.dummies.com	
2	Christy Aguadilla	Pop/Rock	www.aguadilla.com	
3	Gnu Farm	Alternative		
5	The Weedwackers	Country		
6	MC Smoothie	R&B		
*	(New)			

7. Press Delete.

The records disappear, and a message box appears confirming that you're about to delete five records and you won't be able to undo the delete.

8. Click Yes.

Access deletes all the rows from the table.

To select more than one row, click the Record Selector on the first row you want to delete, scroll to the last row you want to delete, and hold Shift while clicking the Record Selector on the last row. Access selects the two rows you click, plus all the rows in between. You can select only sequential rows in a Datasheet (you can't delete only rows 1, 3, and 5 in one operation).

Using the Navigation Buttons

In addition to scrolling to find data in the table's Datasheet view, Access provides *navigation buttons,* which appear at the bottom of the datasheet (refer to Figure 4-1). The navigation buttons allow you to navigate to the first, previous, next, or last record, or to add a new record (shown in Figure 4-4).

Figure 4-4:
Using the
navigation
buttons.

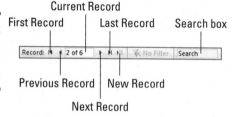

Exercise 4-6: Using the Navigation Buttons

To practice navigating records by using the navigation buttons, open tblArtists in the `Exercise4-6.accdb` file in the Chapter04 folder to practices these actions:

✔ Click the Last Record button.

The Current Record switches to 6 of 6.

✔ Click the Previous Record button.

The Current Record switches to 5 of 6.

✔ Click the First Record button.

The Current Record switches to 1 of 6.

✔ Click the Next Record button.

The Current Record switches to 2 of 6.

✔ Click in the Current Record box, type **4**, and press Enter.

The Current Record switches to 4 of 6.

✔ Click the New (Blank) Record button.

The Current Record switches to 7 of 7, and the new row (with the asterisk in the Record Selector) is selected.

Finding and Replacing Data

If you know you typed something in a datasheet but can't remember where exactly it is, or you want to replace one value with another, you can use the tools that Access provides to locate data and make changes. You can

✔ Search for the first instance the data appears

✔ Search for each subsequent instance of the data

✔ Change every instance of one value to another value

Exercise 4-7: Finding Data by Using the Search Box

When you type a value into the *Search box* (refer to Figure 4-4), it locates the first instance of that value. To find data in tblArtists by using the Search box, either continue working with the database from Exercise 4-6 or open the `Exercise4-7.accdb` file in the Chapter04 folder, then follow these steps:

1. Open tblArtists in Datasheet view if it isn't already open.

2. Click in the Search box and type **g**.

The g in Christy Aguadilla (row 2) is highlighted.

3. Type an **n** after the g in the Search box.

The Gn in Gnu Farm (row 3) is highlighted.

4. Clear the Search box and type **cou**.

As you enter the **c** and then the **o**, the c and the o in www.dummies.com (row 1) are highlighted. Then, when you add the **u**, the Cou in Country (row 5) is highlighted.

Exercise 4-8: Finding Data by Using the Find and Replace Dialog Box

The Find and Replace dialog box lets you find the first instance of a value in your table, as well as any subsequent instance of that value. To find data in tblArtists by using the Find and Replace dialog box, continue working with the database from Exercise 4-7 or open the `Exercise4-8.accdb` file in the Chapter04 folder, then follow these steps:

1. Open tblArtists in Datasheet view if it isn't already open.

2. Use one of the following methods to display the Find and Replace dialog box:

    • Click Find in the Find group on the Home tab.

    • Press Ctrl+F.

The Find and Replace dialog box appears (shown in Figure 4-5).

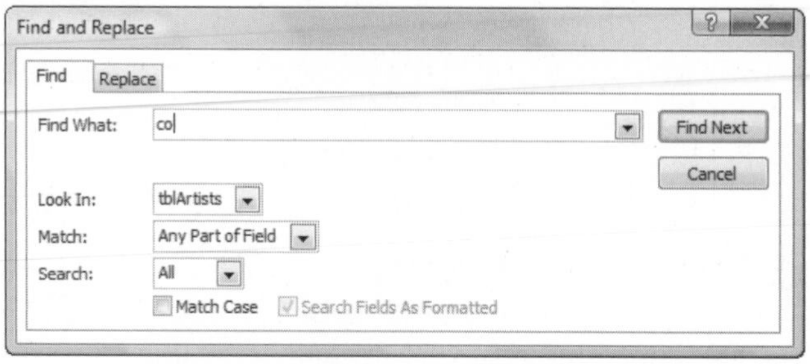

Figure 4-5:
Using the
Find and
Replace
dialog box.

> Find and Replace
>
> Find | Replace
>
> Find What: | co
>
> Look In: | tblArtists
> Match: | Any Part of Field
> Search: | All
>
> ☐ Match Case | ☑ Search Fields As Formatted
>
> Find Next
> Cancel

   3. Type **co** in the Find What text box.

   4. Click Find Next.

   The co in www.dummies.com (row 1) is highlighted. You might have to move the
   Find and Replace dialog box to see the values highlighted in the datasheet.

   5. Click Find Next in the Find and Replace dialog box.

   The co in www.aguadilla.com (row 2) is highlighted.

   6. Click Find Next in the Find and Replace dialog box.

   The Co in Country (row 5) is highlighted.

   7. Click Find Next in the Find and Replace dialog box.

   A message box appears stating that Access searched the records and didn't find
   the search item. All instances of co in tblArtists were found.

   8. Click OK.

   The message box closes.

   9. Click Cancel in the Find and Replace dialog box.

   The Find and Replace dialog box closes.

Exercise 4-9: Replacing Data by Using the Find and Replace Dialog Box

The Find and Replace dialog box lets you replace data in your database. To replace data
in tblArtists by using the Find and Replace dialog box, continue working with the database from Exercise 4-8 or open the `Exercise4-9.accdb` file in the Chapter04 folder,
then follow these steps:

   1. Open tblArtists in Datasheet view if it isn't already open.

   2. Click in the Genre field.

   Clicking a field before opening the Find and Replace dialog box lets you find and
   replace data in only a particular column.

   3. Use one of the following methods to display the Replace tab in the Find and
   Replace dialog box:

   • Click Replace in the Find group on the Home tab.

   • Press Ctrl+H.

The Find and Replace dialog box appears with the Replace tab selected. You can also just click the Replace tab when the Find and Replace dialog box is open to the Find tab.

4. Type **Alternative** in the Find What text box.

5. Type **Punk** in the Replace With text box.

6. Make sure **Genre** is selected from the Look In drop-down list.

If you select the table name (tblArtists) from this list, the Replace operation occurs for the entire table, not just a single field.

7. Click Find Next.

Alternative in row 3 is highlighted.

8. Click Replace.

The Genre for row 3 changes to Punk. Alternative in row 4 is highlighted.

9. Click Replace.

The Genre for row 4 changes to Punk.

10. Click Cancel in the Find and Replace dialog box.

The Find and Replace dialog box closes.

To replace all instances of a word or phrase with another word or phrase, click Replace All in the Find and Replace dialog box. After you perform this operation, you can't undo the changes.

Checking Spelling

Even if you're the best speller in the world, it's almost inevitable that you make a spelling or typing error when entering data. If you want to make sure your data doesn't contain any misspelled words, you should check the table for spelling.

Exercise 4-10: Checking Spelling in a Datasheet

The spelling check utility lets you check spelling in your database. To check the spelling in tblArtists, continue working with the database from Exercise 4-9 or open the `Exercise4-10.accdb` file in the Chapter04 folder, then follow these steps:

1. Open tblArtists in Datasheet view if it's not already opened.

2. Change Gnu Farm to **Gnu Farmm**.

3. Click Spelling in the Records group on the Home tab.

The Spelling dialog box appears with the misspelled word Farmm in the Not In Dictionary text box.

4. Select Farm (the correct spelling) in the Suggestions list.

5. Click Change.

Access changes Farmm to Farm, and the Spelling dialog box shows the next unrecognized word: Weedwackers.

6. Click Ignore.

A message box appears saying the spelling check utility is complete.

7. Click OK.

The message box closes, and you're returned to tblArtists.

Chapter 5

Viewing Data in Tables

· ·

In This Chapter

▶ Changing the order of data in a table

▶ Displaying only certain data in a table by using filters

▶ Adjusting the appearance of your datasheet

· ·

*A*fter you put the data in your tables, you may want to look at that data in different ways. You might want to view data in alphabetical order or from the largest number to the smallest number. You might want to see data in only a particular category or two. You can also change the fonts and background of the datasheet.

In this chapter, you sort the data in the table by one or more columns, narrow down the number of records you're viewing by using filters, and change the appearance of the datasheet.

Sorting Data in a Table

When you enter data in a table, you see the data in the order in which you entered it. As you add more and more information to your table, you might want to view the data in a different order. You can sort the data by one or more fields.

Exercise 5-1: Sorting Data by One Column

To sort records in tblArtists, continue working with the database from Exercise 4-10 or open the `Exercise5-1.accdb` file in the Chapter05 folder, then follow these steps:

1. Double-click tblArtists in the Navigation pane.

   The table opens in Datasheet view with the records sorted by ArtistID from 1 to 6 (the order in which you entered the data).

2. Click in the ArtistID field.

3. Use one of the following methods to reverse the sort order of the records:

   • Click the Descending command in the Sort & Filter group on the Home tab (shown in Figure 5-1).

Ascending (start with A)

Descending (start with Z)

Figure 5-1:
Using the
Sort & Filter
group.

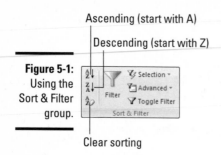

Clear sorting

- Click the arrow on the right side of the ArtistID column heading and select Sort Largest to Smallest from the drop-down list that appears.

- Right-click in any one of the ArtistID fields and choose Sort Largest to Smallest from the pop-up menu that appears.

The order of the records changes, with the records now sorted by ArtistID from 6 to 1. The arrow in the ArtistID column heading changes to include a down arrow to the right of the list arrow — indicating the column is sorted in descending order (shown in Figure 5-2).

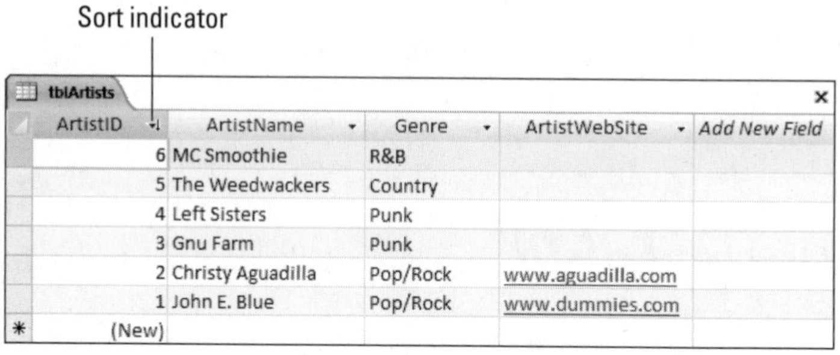

Sort indicator

Figure 5-2:
Determining
whether
data is
sorted.

tblArtists				✕
ArtistID ↓	ArtistName ▾	Genre ▾	ArtistWebSite ▾	Add New Field
6	MC Smoothie	R&B		
5	The Weedwackers	Country		
4	Left Sisters	Punk		
3	Gnu Farm	Punk		
2	Christy Aguadilla	Pop/Rock	www.aguadilla.com	
1	John E. Blue	Pop/Rock	www.dummies.com	
*	(New)			

When you close a table that's been sorted, you're prompted to save the changes to the table. Because you didn't make any table design changes (such as field names or data types), you may be wondering what you changed. Changing the sort on a table is a change of the table's design. If you save the changes, the next time you open the table, the records are sorted in the order you had them in when you last saved.

Exercise 5-2: Clearing the Sort

To clear the sort on the records in tblArtists, continue working with the database from Exercise 5-1 or open the `Exercise5-2.accdb` file in the Chapter05 folder, then follow these steps:

1. Double-click tblArtists in the Navigation pane.

The table opens in Datasheet view with the records sorted by ArtistID from 6 to 1 (the last sort saved in the table).

2. Click the Clear All Sorts command in the Sort & Filter group on the Home tab (refer to Figure 5-1).

   The order of the records changes back to the original state when you first entered them, with the records now sorted by ArtistID from 1 to 6, and the sort indicator in the ArtistID column heading disappears.

Depending on the type of data you're sorting, the commands that appear in the drop-down list when you click the arrow in the column heading change. The following list shows you the choices for each data type:

✔ Number, Currency, and AutoNumber data types:

  • Sort Smallest to Largest

  • Sort Largest to Smallest

✔ Text, Memo, and Hyperlink data types:

  • Sort A to Z

  • Sort Z to A

✔ Yes/No data type:

  • Sort Selected to Cleared

  • Sort Cleared to Selected

✔ Date/Time data type:

  • Sort Oldest to Newest

  • Sort Newest to Oldest

Exercise 5-3: Sorting Data by Multiple Columns

To sort records in tblArtists by Genre and, within each Genre, sort by ArtistName, continue working with the database from Exercise 5-2 or open the `Exercise5-3.accdb` file in the Chapter05 folder, then follow these steps:

1. Double-click tblArtists in the Navigation pane.

   The table opens in Datasheet view with the records sorted by ArtistID from 1 to 6 (the order you entered the data).

2. Identify the fields that will act as the innermost and outermost sort fields:

   • Genre is the outermost sort field (the field to sort on first).

   • ArtistName is the innermost sort field (the field to sort on last, after sorting on Genre).

3. Click the arrow on the right side of the ArtistName column heading (the innermost sort field) and select Sort A to Z from the drop-down list that appears.

   The order of the records changes, with the records now sorted by ArtistName from Christy Aguadilla to The Weedwackers. The arrow in the ArtistName column heading changes to include an up arrow to the right of the list arrow — indicating the column is sorted in ascending order.

4. Click the arrow on the right side of the Genre column heading (the outermost sort field), and select Sort A to Z from the drop-down list that appears.

The order of the records changes, with the records now sorted by Genre from Country to R&B. The arrow in the Genre column heading changes to include an up arrow to the right of the list arrow — indicating the column is sorted in ascending order. Within each Genre that includes multiple artists (Pop/Rock and Punk), the ArtistName is sorted in alphabetical order.

When sorting on multiple columns, always start with the innermost sort field and work your way out, ending with the sort on the outermost sort field. After you apply all the sorts in Datasheet view, you can't see the order in which you applied the sorts.

Filtering Data in a Table

A *filter* changes the data that a table displays without altering the structure of that table. By using filters, you can limit the records you're viewing so that you see only certain subsets of data. Like sorting, you can filter the data on one or more fields.

Exercise 5-4: Filtering Data by Selection (One Value)

To filter records in tblArtists by one Genre, continue working with the database from Exercise 5-3 or open the `Exercise5-4.accdb` file in the Chapter05 folder, then follow these steps:

1. Double-click tblArtists in the Navigation pane.

   The table opens in Datasheet view with the records sorted by Genre and ArtistName.

2. Click in the Genre field on a record that contains Pop/Rock.

3. Use one of the following methods to filter the records to show only the Pop/Rock genre:

   • Right-click the field containing Pop/Rock and choose Equals "Pop/Rock" from the pop-up menu that appears.

   • Click the Selection command in the Sort & Filter group on the Home tab, then select Equals "Pop/Rock" from the drop-down list that appears (shown in Figure 5-3).

Figure 5-3:
Filtering using the Selection command.

All records that contain Pop/Rock in the Genre column remain in Datasheet view, and the other records disappear. Various screen changes occur, letting you know the data is filtered (shown in Figure 5-4).

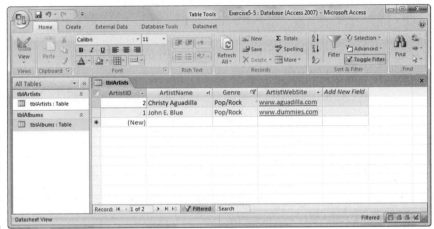

Figure 5-4:
Determining whether data is filtered.

Depending on the type of data you're filtering, the choices that appear in the drop-down list when you filter by selection change. The following list shows you the choices for each data type:

✔ Number, Currency, and AutoNumber data types:

- Equals <selected value>
- Does Not Equal <selected value>
- Less Than or Equal To <selected value>
- Greater Than or Equal To <selected value>

✔ Text, Memo, and Hyperlink data types:

- Equals "<selected value>"
- Does Not Equal "<selected value>"
- Contains "<selected value>"
- Does Not Contain "<selected value>"

✔ Yes/No data type:

- Is Selected
- Is Not Selected

✔ Date/Time data type:

- Equals <selected value>
- Does Not Equal <selected value>
- On or Before <selected value>
- On or After <selected value>

Exercise 5-5: Turning the Filter On and Off

To turn the filter on and off in tblArtists, continue working with the database from Exercise 5-4 or open the `Exercise5-5.accdb` file in the Chapter05 folder, then use one of the following methods to adjust the filter setting:

- ✔ Click the Toggle Filter command in the Sort & Filter group on the Home tab.

  Clicking this command changes its setting from highlighted to not highlighted (or vice versa).

- ✔ At the bottom of the screen, to the right of the navigation buttons, click the Filtered indicator.

  Clicking this indicator changes its setting from Filtered to Unfiltered (or Unfiltered to Filtered).

When you close a table that you've filtered, you're prompted to save the changes to the filtered table, similar to what happens when you sort data in a table. Changing the filter on a table changes the table's design. If you save the changes, the next time you open the table, the records won't be filtered, but you can turn the last saved filter on by using the methods described in Exercise 5-5.

Exercise 5-6: Removing the Filter

To completely remove the filter from tblArtists, continue working with the database from Exercise 5-5 or open the `Exercise5-6.accdb` file in the Chapter05 folder, then use one of the following methods to remove the filter:

- ✔ Click the Advanced command in the Sort & Filter group on the Home tab, then choose Clear All Filters from the drop-down list that appears.

- ✔ Click the Filtered indicator on the right side of the Genre column and choose Clear Filter from Genre from the drop-down list that appears.

  These methods remove the filter and don't let you toggle the filter back on because Access deletes that filter from the design of the form. You must create a new filter to narrow down the results displayed in the datasheet.

Filters and sorts are saved in the table independent of each other. Clearing a filter doesn't affect the sort, and clearing the sort doesn't affect the filter.

Exercise 5-7: Filtering Data by Multiple Values

To filter records in tblArtists by more than one Genre, continue working with the database from Exercise 5-6 or open the `Exercise5-7.accdb` file in the Chapter05 folder, then follow these steps:

1. Double-click tblArtists in the Navigation pane.

   The table opens in Datasheet view with the records sorted by Genre and ArtistName.

2. Click the arrow on the right side of the Genre column heading.

   The drop-down list appears (shown in Figure 5-5), featuring check boxes to the left of data from the table in the lower portion of the window.

Figure 5-5:
Filtering by
multiple
values.

3. Clear the check box to the left of (Select All).

   All the other check boxes clear, as well. Because all the check boxes were checked, clearing (Select All) clears all the other check boxes.

4. Select the check box to the left of Pop/Rock.

5. Select the check box to the left of Country.

6. Click OK.

   The drop-down list disappears, and only the records with a Genre of Pop/Rock or Country remain in the datasheet.

7. Click the filter indicator on the right side of the Genre column heading.

   The drop-down list appears, featuring check boxes to the left of Pop/Rock and Country.

8. Clear the check box to the left of Country.

9. Select the check box to the left of Punk.

10. Click OK.

    The drop-down list disappears, and only the records with a Genre of Pop/Rock or Punk remain in the datasheet.

11. Click the Toggle Filter command in the Sort & Filter group on the Home tab.

    The filter turns off, and all the records are displayed.

Exercise 5-8: Filtering Data on Multiple Columns

To filter records in tblArtists by more than one column, continue working with the database from Exercise 5-7 or open the `Exercise5-8.accdb` file in the Chapter05 folder, then follow these steps:

1. Double-click tblArtists in the Navigation pane.

   The table opens in Datasheet view with the records sorted by Genre and ArtistName.

2. Click the arrow on the right side of the ArtistWebSite column heading.

   The drop-down list appears, featuring check boxes to the left of data from the table in the lower portion of the window.

3. Clear the check box to the left of (Select All).

   All the other check boxes clear, as well. Because all of the check boxes were checked, clearing (Select All) clears all the other check boxes.

4. Select the check box to the left of (Blanks).

5. Click OK.

   The drop-down list disappears, and only the records with a blank ArtistWebSite remain in the datasheet (four records). A filter indicator appears in the column heading of the ArtistWebSite field.

6. Click in the Genre field on a record that contains Country.

7. Click the Selection command in the Sort & Filter group on the Home tab, then choose Does Not Equal "Country" from the drop-down list that appears.

   The single record containing Country in the Genre field disappears, leaving three records. A filter indicator appears in the column heading of the Genre field.

8. Highlight the capital S in Left Sisters in the ArtistName field.

9. Right-click the field containing Left Sisters and choose Contains "S" from the pop-up menu that appears.

   The record containing Gnu Farm in the ArtistName field disappears because it doesn't contain the capital letter S, leaving two records. A filter indicator appears in the column heading of the ArtistName field.

10. Right-click in the ArtistID field that has a value of 4 and choose Less Than or Equal to 4 from the pop-up menu that appears.

    Only one record remains (Left Sisters) because that's the only record that satisfies all four criteria. A filter indicator appears in the column heading of the ArtistID field.

To see how a particular column is filtered, hover the mouse over the filter indicator in the column heading. A tool tip appears showing the filter for that column (such as Genre Does Not Equal "Country").

Exercise 5-9: Filtering Data by Form

To filter records in tblArtists by using a form, continue working with the database from Exercise 5-8 or open the `Exercise5-9.accdb` file in the Chapter05 folder, then follow these steps:

1. Double-click tblArtists in the Navigation pane.

   The table opens in Datasheet view with the records sorted by Genre and ArtistName.

2. Click the Advanced command in the Sort & Filter group on the Home tab, then choose Filter By Form from the drop-down list that appears.

The datasheet switches to Filter By Form mode, indicated by the caption on the table's document tab, as well as the Look For and Or tabs at the bottom of the window (shown in Figure 5-6). The criteria appears in the fields from the last applied filter (from Exercise 5-8).

ArtistID	ArtistName	Genre	ArtistWebSite
	<=4 Like "*S*"	<>"Country" Or Is Null	

Look for / Or

Figure 5-6:
Filtering
by form.

3. Click the Advanced command in the Sort & Filter group on the Home tab, then choose Clear Grid from the drop-down list that appears.

   The data in the grid disappears, leaving a blank slate to create a new filter.

4. In the Genre field, type **p***.

   The asterisk (*) is a wildcard character. A *wildcard* is a placeholder that represents any unknown character or characters in search criteria. The asterisk represents any number of characters, so typing **p*** in the Genre field indicates you want the Genre field to start with the letter p and don't care what characters appear after the p.

5. Click the Or tab at the bottom of the window.

   The data in the grid disappears, leaving a blank slate to create additional criteria on tblArtists. Another Or tab appears to the right of the Or tab you click in this step.

6. In the ArtistName field, type ***wackers**.

   Placing the asterisk (*) before a value indicates you want the ArtistName field to end with the phrase wackers and don't care what characters appear before the phrase.

7. Click Toggle Filter in the Sort & Filter group on the Home tab.

   The table switches back to Datasheet view and displays the records in which the Genre starts with p or the ArtistName ends with wackers.

When filtering by selection, each filter criteria you select narrows down the result set. These criteria are applied using the AND operator, which means each condition must be true in order to display the record. Using the Or tab in Filter By Form mode allows you to return additional records by applying the OR operator to the criteria. The OR operator displays a record if either condition is (or both conditions are) true.

Changing the Datasheet's Appearance

In addition to sorting and filtering the records on a datasheet, you can change the appearance of the datasheet. You can change the fonts, foreground and background colors, and the appearance of gridlines and alternating rows.

Exercise 5-10: Changing the Datasheet's Font

To change the fonts for the tblArtists datasheet, continue working with the database from Exercise 5-9 or open the `Exercise5-10.accdb` file in the Chapter05 folder, then follow these steps:

1. Double-click tblArtists in the Navigation pane.

   The table opens in Datasheet view.

2. In the Font group on the Home tab (shown in Figure 5-7), click the arrow on the right side of the Font drop-down (which contains Calibri) and select Courier New from the drop-down list that appears.

   The font for the entire datasheet changes to Courier New.

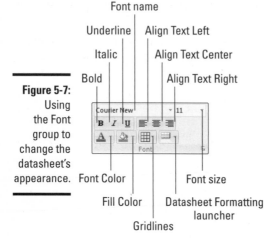

Figure 5-7: Using the Font group to change the datasheet's appearance.

3. In the Font group on the Home tab, click the arrow on the right side of the Font Size drop-down and select 14 from the drop-down list that appears.

   The font size for the entire datasheet changes to 14 point.

4. In the Font group on the Home tab, click the arrow on the right side of the Font Color drop down and select the color red from the drop-down gallery that appears.

   The font color for the entire datasheet (except the hyperlink field) changes to red.

5. Click the Bold, Italic, and Underline commands in the Font group on the Home tab.

   The font for the entire datasheet becomes bold, italicized, and underlined.

Exercise 5-11: Changing the Row Colors

To change the row colors in tblArtists, continue working with the database from Exercise 5-10 or open the Exercise5-11.accdb file in the Chapter05 folder, then follow these steps:

1. Double-click tblArtists in the Navigation pane.

The table opens in Datasheet view.

2. Select the color yellow from the Fill/Back Color drop-down gallery in the Font group on the Home tab (refer to Figure 5-7).

The background color for the odd-numbered rows changes to yellow.

3. Select the color light blue from the Alternate Fill/Back Color drop-down gallery in the Font group on the Home tab.

The background color for the even-numbered rows changes to light blue.

If you don't want the row colors to alternate, you don't have to match the colors in the Fill/Back Color and the Alternate Fill/Back Color drop-down galleries. If you select No Color from the Alternate Fill/Back Color drop-down gallery, the even-numbered rows match the odd numbered rows.

Exercise 5-12: Formatting Gridlines

To change the appearance of the gridlines in tblArtists, continue working with the database from Exercise 5-11 or open the Exercise5-12.accdb file in the Chapter05 folder, then follow these steps:

1. Double-click tblArtists in the Navigation pane.

The table opens in Datasheet view.

2. Set the Fill/Back Color and Alternate Fill/Back Color to Automatic in the Font group on the Home tab (refer to Figure 5-7).

3. Choose from the following settings in the Gridlines drop-down gallery (in the Font group on the Home tab):

- **Both:** Shows both horizontal and vertical gridlines
- **Horizontal:** Shows only horizontal gridlines between rows
- **Vertical:** Shows only vertical gridlines between columns
- **None:** Shows neither horizontal nor vertical gridlines

Exercise 5-13: Adding a 3-D Look to Your Datasheet

To give the tblArtists datasheet a three-dimensional look, continue working with the database from Exercise 5-12 or open the Exercise5-13.accdb file in the Chapter05 folder, then follow these steps:

1. Double-click tblArtists in the Navigation pane.

   The table opens in Datasheet view.

2. Click the Datasheet Formatting launcher (the diagonal-pointing arrow) in the lower-right corner of the Font group on the Home tab (refer to Figure 5-7).

   The Datasheet Formatting dialog box opens (shown in Figure 5-8).

Figure 5-8: Using the Datasheet Formatting dialog box.

3. Click the Sunken option button in the Cell Effect option group in the Datasheet Formatting dialog box.

4. Choose Automatic from the following color drop-down galleries:

   • Background Color

   • Alternate Background Color

   • Gridline Color

   The Sample section in the center of the Datasheet Formatting dialog box changes to show you what the datasheet will look like if you apply the settings you've selected. Changing the color settings to Automatic captures the true representation of a 3-D look (raised or sunken). If you choose different colors, the Sample might not appear 3-D (even if you put on those glasses).

5. Click OK.

   The Datasheet Formatting dialog box closes, and the datasheet switches to the sunken effect.

In the examples so far, any changes you make by using the Font group affect the entire datasheet. You can't apply any special colors or fonts to a particular row or column.

Exercise 5-14: Aligning Text in a Datasheet Column

To change the alignment of text in tblArtists, continue working with the database from Exercise 5-13 or open the `Exercise5-14.accdb` file in the Chapter05 folder, then follow these steps:

1. Double-click tblArtists in the Navigation pane.

   The table opens in Datasheet view.

2. Click in the ArtistID column.

3. Click the Align Text Left command in the Font group on the Home tab (refer to Figure 5-7).

   The numbers in the ArtistID column move from the right side of the column to the left side.

4. Click in the Genre column.

5. Click the Center command in the Font group on the Home tab.

   The text in the Genre column moves from the left side of the column to the center.

Aligning text in a column affects text only in the selected column, not the entire datasheet.

Chapter 6

Building Relationships

· ·

In This Chapter

▶ Finding out about database relationships

▶ Working in the Relationships window

▶ Creating and editing relationships

▶ Keeping your table relationships healthy with referential integrity

· ·

Access is a relational database management system (RDBMS). The relational part of RDBMS is what makes Access a powerful tool for managing data. Relationships link information in one table to information in another.

In this chapter, you can create and edit relationships between tables by using the Relationships window. You can also learn about referential integrity and how it affects how you update and delete data in your tables.

Defining Relationships

A *relationship* is an association between common fields in two tables. This association links information in one table to information in the related table. For example, you can establish a relationship based on a field in a table that contains artists' names to a field in a related table that contains each artist's albums.

Here are the three types of relationships:

✔ **One-to-many relationship:** In this type of relationship, records on the "one" side of the relationship can have many related records on the "many" side of the relationship.

This type of relationship is the most common and is what you create in this chapter.

✔ **One-to-one relationship:** In this type of relationship, records in one table can have only one related record in the other table. This type of relationship isn't very common because you can usually put all the fields in one table instead of breaking it up into two or more tables.

If you want to separate sensitive information (such as salary or medical information) from the main table that contains address information, use a one-to-one relationship.

✔ **Many-to-many relationship:** This isn't really a type of relationship at all; it's actually two one-to-many relationships tied together with a third table. For example, if you have a database that tracks orders, you can have many products on each order, and each product can be on many orders.

Using the Relationships Window

When you create relationships in your database, you use the Relationships window. The Relationships window lets you add tables and create relationships between tables.

Exercise 6-1: Adding Tables to the Relationships Window

To open the Relationships window for the first time and add tables to the layout, open the `Exercise6-1.accdb` file in the Chapter06 folder and follow these steps:

1. Click the Relationships command in the Show/Hide group on the Database Tools tab (shown in Figure 6-1).

Figure 6-1:
Opening the
Relationships
window.

The Relationships window opens, along with the Show Table dialog box. Because it's the first time you're opening the Relationships window and you don't have any tables in the layout, the Show Table dialog box appears automatically (shown in Figure 6-2).

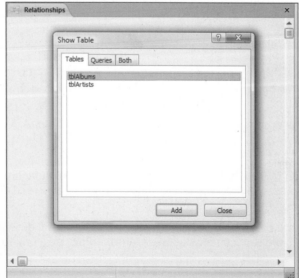

Figure 6-2:
Adding
tables to
the layout.

2. In the Show Table dialog box, click tblAlbums.

3. Click Add.

   Access adds tblAlbums to the Relationships window behind the Show Table dialog box. You might have to move the Show Table dialog box to see the table.

4. In the Show Table dialog box, double-click tblArtists.

   Access adds tblArtists to the right of tblAlbums to the Relationships window behind the Show Table dialog box. Double-clicking a table name is the same as selecting the table, then clicking Add.

5. In the Show Table dialog box, click Close.

   The Show Table dialog box disappears, revealing the Relationships window.

6. On the Quick Access Toolbar, click Save.

   This step saves the layout in the Relationships window. Any time you add or move tables in the Relationships window, saving the layout preserves any changes you make, so the next time you view the relationships, the window looks like it did when you saved it.

Exercise 6-2: Rearranging the Relationships Layout

To rearrange the tables in the layout of the Relationships window, continue working with the database from Exercise 6-1 or open the `Exercise6-2.accdb` file in the Chapter06 folder, then follow these steps:

1. Click the Relationships command in the Show/Hide group on the Database Tools tab (refer to Figure 6-1).

   The Relationships window opens, showing tblAlbums and tblArtists in the layout. Because the layout has tables displayed, the Show Table dialog box doesn't open automatically, as it did in Exercise 6-1.

2. Click the title of tblAlbums in the layout and drag it to the right of tblArtists.

3. Click the title of tblArtists in the layout and drag it to the left side of the Relationships window.

   tblArtists should now be to the left of tblAlbums. When you create relationships, put the "one" table on the left and the "many" table on the right. When creating the relationship, the tables appear "one" to "many" from left to right (as in a one-to-many relationship).

4. Click Close in the Relationships group on the (Relationship Tools) Design tab.

   A dialog box appears asking if you want to save changes to the layout of Relationships. Because you rearranged the layout of the Relationships window, you're prompted to save the changes.

5. Click Yes.

   Access saves the layout and closes the Relationships window.

Creating a Relationship

After you get the tables lined up how you want them in the Relationships window, you're ready to create the relationship. After you create a relationship, changing the layout doesn't have an effect on that relationship.

Exercise 6-3: Creating a Relationship

To create a one-to-many relationship between tblArtists and tblAlbums, continue working with the database from Exercise 6-2 or open the `Exercise6-3.accdb` file in the Chapter06 folder, then follow these steps:

1. Click the Relationships command in the Show/Hide group on the Database Tools tab (refer to Figure 6-1).

   The Relationships window opens, displaying tblArtists and tblAlbums as you left them in Exercise 6-2.

2. In tblArtists, click and hold ArtistID (the primary key field).

3. Drag the mouse over to tblAlbums.

4. Position the cursor over the ArtistID field in tblAlbums, then release the mouse button.

   The Edit Relationships dialog box opens (shown in Figure 6-3). ArtistID should appear in the first row of each column in the field grid. At the bottom of the dialog box, the Relationship Type is One-To-Many.

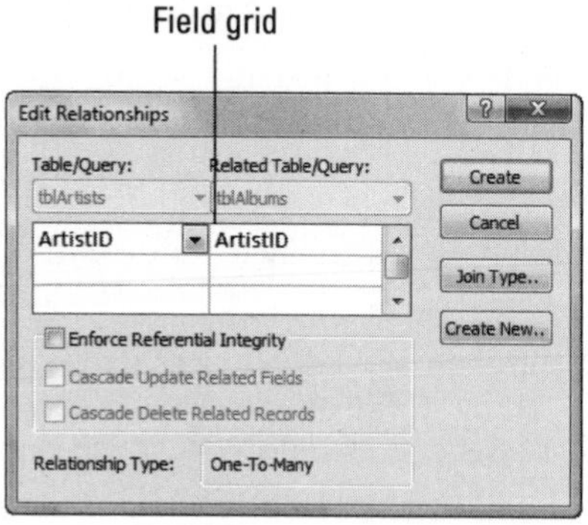

Figure 6-3: Creating a relationship by using the Edit Relationships dialog box.

5. (Optional) If you dragged from the wrong field in the tblArtists or released the mouse over the wrong field in the tblAlbums, follow these steps to correct your actions:

   a. Click the arrow on the left side of the field grid (under Table/Query: tblArtists) and select ArtistID from the drop-down list that appears.

   b. Click the arrow on the right side of the field grid (under the Related Table/Query: tblAlbums) and select ArtistID from the drop-down list that appears.

6. Click Create.

The Edit Relationships dialog box closes, and a line is drawn between the ArtistID fields in tblArtists and tblAlbums. This line represents the relationship between the two tables. The ArtistID field in tblAlbums is known as a *foreign key* because it's in the relationship used to link tblAlbums to tblArtists. A foreign key is a field in one table that refers to a field in another table to link the tables together.

7. Click Close in the Relationships group on the (Relationship Tools) Design tab.

The Relationships window closes and doesn't prompt you to save changes. Clicking Create in the Edit Relationships dialog box saves the actual relationships. Saving the layout of the Relationships window only preserves the size and location of the tables in the window.

Editing and Deleting a Relationship

After you create a relationship, you might decide later that you didn't set it up properly and want to change the properties of the relationship. You might even decide that you don't want the relationship to exist at all.

Exercise 6-4: Editing an Existing Relationship

To edit the relationship between tblArtists and tblAlbums, continue working with the database from Exercise 6-3 or open the `Exercise6-4.accdb` file in the Chapter06 folder, then follow these steps:

1. Click the Relationships command in the Show/Hide group on the Database Tools tab (refer to Figure 6-1).

   The Relationships window opens, displaying tblArtists and tblAlbums linked together with a relationship line.

2. Double-click the relationship line between tblArtists and tblAlbums (as shown in Figure 6-4).

Figure 6-4: Double-click the relation-ship line to edit the relationship.

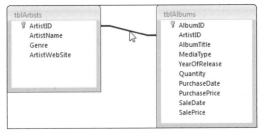

The Edit Relationships dialog box opens. You can make changes to the relationship in this dialog box.

3. Click Cancel to close the Edit Relationships dialog box.

Exercise 6-5: Deleting a Relationship

To delete the relationship between tblArtists and tblAlbums, continue working with the database from Exercise 6-4 or open the `Exercise6-5.accdb` file in the Chapter06 folder, then follow these steps:

1. Click the Relationships command in the Show/Hide group on the Database Tools tab (refer to Figure 6-1).

   The Relationships window opens, showing tblArtists and tblAlbums linked together with a relationship line.

2. Click the relationship line between tblArtists and tblAlbums.

3. Press Delete.

   A prompt appears asking if you're sure you want to permanently delete the selected relationship from your database.

4. Click Yes.

   The prompt disappears, and the relationship line between tblArtists and tblAlbums disappears.

5. Follow the steps in Exercise 6-3 to recreate the relationship between tblArtists and tblAlbums.

Enforcing Referential Integrity

Referential integrity ensures that all records in a related table (called a *child table*) have a record in the main table (referred to as the *parent table*). Any records in the child table that don't have records in the parent table are referred to as *orphan records*. Referential integrity makes sure you can't create orphan records in your database.

Exercise 6-6: Creating the Genre Table

One method to ensure that users enter a valid value in a field is to have a table related to that field. To create a new table (tblGenres), continue working with the database from Exercise 6-5 or open the `Exercise6-6.accdb` file in the Chapter06 folder, then follow these steps:

1. Click the Table Design command in the Tables group on the Create tab.

   A new table opens in Design view. For more detailed information on creating and entering data in a table, see Chapter 3 and Chapter 4.

2. Add a new field to the table with the following values:

   • Field Name: **Genre**

   • Date Type: **Text**

   • Description: **Musical Genre**

3. Set the Field Size property of the Genre field to **20**.

4. Click the Primary Key command in the Tools group on the (Table Tools) Design tab.

   This step makes the Genre field the primary key.

5. On the Quick Access Toolbar, click Save, then type **tblGenres** in the Save As dialog box.

6. Right-click the document tab for tblGenres and choose Datasheet View from the pop-up menu that appears.

7. Press Tab and enter the following information into tblGenres:

   Genre
   Pop/Rock
   Punk
   Country
   R&B

8. Right-click the document tab for tblGenres and choose Close from the pop-up menu that appears.

   tblGenres closes.

You must close the tables you're working with before creating and modifying relationships.

Exercise 6-7: Creating Relationships with Referential Integrity

To create relationships that enforce referential integrity between the tables, continue working with the database from Exercise 6-6 or open the `Exercise6-7.accdb` file in the Chapter06 folder, then follow these steps:

1. Click the Relationships command in the Show/Hide group on the Database Tools tab (refer to Figure 6-1).

   The Relationships window opens, displaying tblArtists and tblAlbums linked together with a relationship line.

2. Click the Show Table command in the Relationships group on the (Relationship Tools) Design tab.

   The Show Table dialog box opens.

3. In the Show Table dialog box, double-click tblGenres.

   Access adds tblGenres to the Relationships window behind the Show Table dialog box.

4. In the Show Table dialog box, click Close.

   The Show Table dialog box disappears, revealing the Relationships window.

5. In the Relationships window, click and drag the Genre field from tblGenres and drop it onto the Genre field in tblArtists.

   The Edit Relationships dialog box opens (refer to Figure 6-3). Genre appears in the first row of each column in the field grid.

6. Set the following options for enforcing referential integrity in this relationship:

   • **Enforce Referential Integrity:** Click the check box to the left of this option if you want to enforce referential integrity between tblGenres and tblArtists.

   • **Cascade Update Related Fields:** Click the check box to the left of this option if you want to ensure that if the primary key field changes in the parent table (tblGenres), the change *cascades* (meaning changes in the child tables) to all related records in the child table.

   • **Cascade Delete Related Records:** Leave the check box to the left of this option unchecked. Unchecking this option prevents you from deleting a Genre if it's being used in tblArtists. Checking the Cascade Delete Related Records check box can lead to some unwanted consequences; for example, with Cascade Delete Related Records turned on, deleting a Genre from tblGenres would also delete any record in tblArtists that contains that Genre. You might want to check this option if you want to delete related records (for example, if you delete a contact and have a separate table of phone numbers, you probably want to delete those phone numbers too).

7. Click Create.

   The Edit Relationships dialog box closes, and a line is drawn between the Genre fields in tblGenres and tblAlbums. Because referential integrity is enforced, a 1 appears next to the Genre field in tblGenres (representing the "one" side) and an infinity symbol (∞) appears next to the Genre field in tblArtists (representing the "many" side).

8. Double-click the relationship line between tblArtists and tblAlbums.

   The Edit Relationships dialog box opens for the tblArtists/tblAlbums relationship.

9. Check the Enforce Referential Integrity check box.

   Because the primary key in tblArtists is an AutoNumber field, this field can't change, so you don't need to check the Cascade Update Related Fields check box.

10. Click OK.

    The Edit Relationships dialog box closes, and the line between tblArtists and tblAlbums contains the 1 and ∞, indicating referential integrity is enforced.

11. Click Close in the Relationships group on the (Relationship Tools) Design tab.

    A dialog box appears asking if you want to save changes to the layout of the Relationships window. This dialog box appears because you added a table to the layout in the Relationships window, not because you added or edited a relationship.

12. Click Yes.

    Access saves the layout and closes the Relationships window.

In order to enforce referential integrity, the data in the tables must already conform to the rules of referential integrity. If you have potential orphan records in the child table, you can't create the relationship. Many developers create relationships before entering data in their tables so they don't run into this orphan problem.

Exercise 6-8: Testing Referential Integrity

To test relationships that have referential integrity enforced between the tables, continue working with the database from Exercise 6-7 or open the `Exercise6-8.accdb` file in the Chapter06 folder, then follow these steps:

1. Double-click tblArtists in the Navigation pane.

   The table opens in Datasheet view, displaying records from the Pop/Rock, Punk, Country, and R&B Genres.

2. Double-click tblGenres in the Navigation pane.

   The table opens in Datasheet view, displaying the same four Genres from Step 1.

3. In tblGenres, change Punk to **Alternative** and move the cursor to the record below (by pressing the down arrow or clicking on the next row) to save the changes.

4. Click the tblArtists document tab.

   The Datasheet view for tblArtists displays the artists; however, the records that previously contained Punk now contain Alternative. The changes you made in tblGenres in Step 3 cascaded into tblArtists because you have both referential integrity and cascade updates turned on for the relationship between these two tables (refer to Exercise 6-7).

5. In tblArtists, change the value of Genre in the first record (John E. Blue) from Pop/Rock to **Reggae** and move the cursor to the record below(by pressing the down arrow or clicking on the next row) to save the changes.

   A dialog box appears indicating you can't change the record because a related record is required in tblGenres. Because referential integrity is in place, the value Reggae must be in tblGenres before you can use it in tblArtists.

6. Click OK to close the dialog box.

7. Press Esc to undo the change, turning the Genre record from Reggae back to Pop/Rock.

8. Click the tblGenres document tab.

   The Datasheet view for tblGenres displays the list of Genres.

9. Right-click the Record Selector for the row containing Pop/Rock and choose Delete Record from the pop-up menu that appears.

   A dialog box appears indicating you can't delete the record because tblArtists includes related records. Because referential integrity is in place and cascade deletes are turned off, you can't delete Pop/Rock from tblGenres (because it's being used in tblArtists).

Part III

Viewing Data with Select Queries

The 5th Wave   By Rich Tennant

I told Russell he should data model before we go any further.

Miss Claudia Schiffer, please.

In this part . . .

Select queries let you ask your database simple or complex questions about the data. The chapters and exercises in Part III teach all about select queries in Access. You start out by creating single-table select queries and move to creating queries with more than one table. Finally, you build expressions and perform calculations in your queries.

Chapter 7

Creating Single-Table Queries

. . . .

In This Chapter

▶ Creating a select query

▶ Adjusting fields in a select query

▶ Rearranging the records in a select query

▶ Making your select query more specific by adding criteria

▶ Taking a peek at SQL view

. . . .

A *query* is a database object that locates information stored in one or more tables and allows you to view and manipulate the information it finds. A *select query* is a type of query that retrieves (or selects, hence the clever name) data that matches specified criteria from one or more tables. Access displays the results of a select query in a datasheet.

In this chapter, you can create single-table select queries by using the query design grid. You can learn how to add and remove fields, sort the data, and add criteria to the query to limit the results.

Creating a New Select Query

Just like when you create a new table, you start creating a new query with the Create tab. Creating a new query lets you start from scratch to begin viewing your data in different ways.

Using Design view

Design view lets you add tables and fields to your query. By using Design view, you can decide which fields you want to see and in what order you want to see them.

Exercise 7-1: Creating a New Select Query in Design View

To create a new select query that will show data from tblArtists, continue working with the database from Exercise 6-8 or open the `Exercise7-1.accdb` file in the Chapter07 folder, then follow these steps:

1. Click the Query Design command in the Other group on the Create tab (shown in Figure 7-1).

Create tab   Query Design command

The query Design view opens, along with the Show Table dialog box.

2. Use one of the following methods to add tblArtists to the query Design view:

   • Double-click tblArtists in the Show Table dialog box.

   • Click tblArtists in the Show Table dialog box, then click Add.

   The tblArtists table appears in the query Design view behind the Show Table dialog box.

3. In the Show Table dialog box, click Close.

   The Show Table dialog box closes, revealing the query Design view (shown in Figure 7-2). The top pane of the query Design view displays the query's data sources (tblArtists), and the Query By Example (QBE) grid in the bottom pane specifies the fields displayed in the query.

4. Use one of the following methods to add the ArtistID field to the QBE grid:

   • Double-click ArtistID in tblArtists in the top pane of the query Design view.

   • Click and drag ArtistID from tblArtists in the top pane of the query Design view to the first blank column of the QBE grid in the lower pane.

   • Click the arrow in the first column of the QBE grid in the lower pane and select ArtistID from the drop-down list that appears.

   ArtistID appears in the first column of the QBE grid.

5. Repeat Step 4 to add ArtistName, Genre, and ArtistWebSite to the second, third, and fourth columns of the QBE grid.

   The first four columns of the QBE grid contain the following fields: ArtistID, ArtistName, Genre, and ArtistWebSite.

Query Tools Design tab

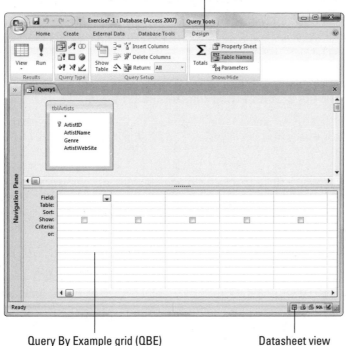

Figure 7-2:
Using the query Design view.

Query By Example grid (QBE)   Datasheet view

6. Use one of the following methods to save your select query:

   • Click the Save button on the Quick Access Toolbar.

   • Click the Microsoft Office Button and choose Save from the menu that appears.

   • Right-click the Query1 tab and choose Save from the pop-up menu that appears.

   The Save As dialog box appears.

7. Type **qryArtists** in the Save As dialog box.

8. Click OK.

   Access saves the query and changes Query1 on the document tab to qryArtists. The query also appears in the Navigation pane in the tblArtists group because it's based on tblArtists.

By placing a prefix (qry) before the query name, you know this object is a query. When you create different database objects, adding a prefix lets you know whether an object is a table (tbl), form (frm), report (rpt), or macros (mcr).

Using Datasheet view

A query's Datasheet view is similar to a table's Datasheet view in which you see rows *(records)* and columns *(fields)*. In Datasheet view, you can add, edit, and view data in the query's underlying table.

Exercise 7-2: Viewing a Select Query in Datasheet View

To view the data from qryArtists in Datasheet view, continue working with the database from Exercise 7-1 or open the `Exercise7-2.accdb` file in the Chapter07 folder, then follow these steps:

1. Right-click qryArtists in the Navigation pane and choose Design View from the pop-up menu that appears.

The query opens in Design view, displaying four fields in the QBE grid: ArtistID, ArtistName, Genre, and ArtistWebSite.

2. Use one of the following methods to switch from Design view to Datasheet view:

• Click the Datasheet View command in the Results group on the (Query Tools) Design tab (refer to Figure 7-2).

• Click the Run command in the Results group on the (Query Tools) Design tab (refer to Figure 7-2).

Running a select query displays the results in Datasheet view.

• Right-click the qryArtists document tab and choose Datasheet View from the pop-up menu that appears.

The query switches to Datasheet view, displaying data from the selected fields in tblArtists.

3. Use one of the following methods to switch from Datasheet view to Design view:

• Click the Design View command in the Views group on the Home tab. The Design View command icon contains a triangle, pencil, and ruler.

• Right-click the qryArtists document tab and choose Design View from the pop-up menu that appears.

The query switches to Design view.

Double-clicking a select query in the Navigation pane opens the query in Datasheet view.

Customizing Fields in a Select Query

A select query can do so much more than simply show the exact same fields from the underlying table. You can choose to show a subset of fields and change the order of the fields.

Exercise 7-3: Removing a Field from a Query

To remove a field from qryArtists, continue working with the database from Exercise 7-2 or open the `Exercise7-3.accdb` file in the Chapter07 folder, then follow these steps:

1. Right-click qryArtists in the Navigation pane and choose Design View from the pop-up menu that appears.

The query opens in Design view, displaying four fields in the QBE grid: ArtistID, ArtistName, Genre, and ArtistWebSite.

2. In the QBE grid (in the lower pane of the query Design view), move the cursor to the thin gray bar above the ArtistID field.

The cursor changes to a small black arrow pointing down.

3. When the cursor becomes a small black arrow pointing down, click to select the column.

The selected column turns black with light lettering (shown in Figure 7-3).

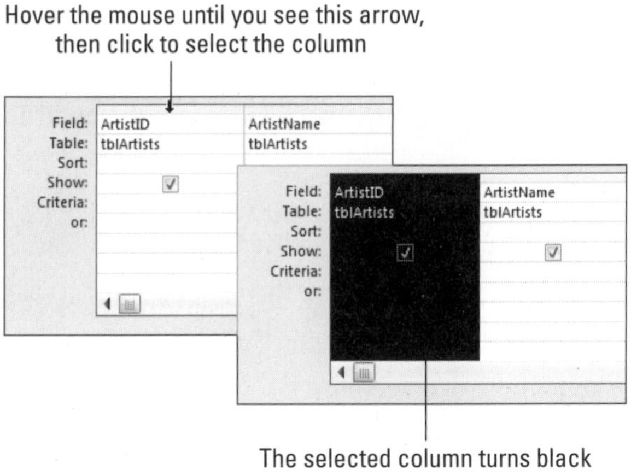

Hover the mouse until you see this arrow,
then click to select the column

Figure 7-3:
Selecting a
column in
query
Design
view.

The selected column turns black

4. Press Delete.

The selected column that contains ArtistID disappears.

5. Click the Run command in the Results group on the (Query Tools) Design tab.

The query switches to Datasheet view, displaying the data from tblArtists without the ArtistID column.

You can select multiple columns by clicking the thin gray bar above the field and dragging left or right.

Exercise 7-4: Rearranging Fields in a Query

To change the order of the fields in qryArtists, continue working with the database from Exercise 7-3 or open the `Exercise7-4.accdb` file in the Chapter07 folder, then follow these steps:

1. Right-click qryArtists in the Navigation pane and choose Design View from the pop-up menu that appears.

   The query opens in Design view, displaying three fields in the QBE grid: ArtistName, Genre, and ArtistWebSite.

2. In the QBE grid (in the lower pane of the query Design view), click the thin gray bar above the ArtistName field.

   The ArtistName column turns black with light lettering, indicating it's selected.

3. Click and hold the mouse near the top of the black area of the column (where the thin gray bar used to be).

   The cursor changes to an arrow with a box below it, indicating you've grabbed the selected object (the column).

4. Drag the mouse between the Genre and ArtistWebSite columns in the QBE grid.

   The line between Genre and ArtistWebSite turns to a thick black line, showing you where the ArtistName column will appear when you release the mouse.

5. Release the mouse.

   The ArtistName column appears between the Genre and ArtistWebSite columns, with the Genre column being the first column in the QBE grid.

6. Click the Run command in the Results group on the (Query Tools) Design tab.

   The query switches to Datasheet view, displaying the data from tblArtists with the Genre column first.

Sorting Data in a Select Query

Just like you have the ability to rearrange the columns in a select query, you can also rearrange the order of the records. Changing the order of the records is known as *sorting the data.*

Exercise 7-5: Sorting Data in a Query

To change the order of the records in qryArtists, continue working with the database from Exercise 7-4 or open the `Exercise7-5.accdb` file in the Chapter07 folder, then follow these steps:

1. Right-click qryArtists in the Navigation pane and choose Design View from the pop-up menu that appears.

   The query opens in Design view, displaying three fields in the QBE grid: Genre, ArtistName, and ArtistWebSite.

2. In the QBE grid (in the lower pane of the query Design view), click the arrow in the Sort row below Genre and select Ascending from the drop-down list that appears (shown in Figure 7-4).

Figure 7-4:
Sorting data
in a query.

Field:	Genre	ArtistName	ArtistWebSite
Table:	tblArtists	tblArtists	tblArtists
Sort:			
Show:	Ascending	✓	✓
Criteria:	Descending		
or:	(not sorted)		

3. Click the Run command in the Results group on the (Query Tools) Design tab.

   The query switches to Datasheet view, displaying the data from tblArtists sorted by Genre.

4. Right-click the qryArtists document tab and choose Design View from the pop-up menu that appears.

   The query switches to Design view.

5. In the QBE grid (in the lower pane of the query Design view), click the arrow in the Sort row below ArtistName and select Ascending from the drop-down list that appears.

6. Click the Run command in the Results group on the (Query Tools) Design tab.

   The query switches to Datasheet view, displaying the data from tblArtists sorted first by Genre, then by ArtistName.

When fields have their Sort rows set to either Ascending or Descending in the QBE grid, Access sorts those fields from left to right.

Adding Criteria to a Select Query

Adding criteria to a query is similar to filtering a table in Datasheet view. You decide which records you want to see in the query's results, then you set the criteria accordingly. You can add specific criteria, test for null values, and use wildcard characters.

Exercise 7-6: Adding Criteria to a Query

To add criteria to limit the results of qryArtists to one genre, continue working with the database from Exercise 7-5 or open the `Exercise7-6.accdb` file in the Chapter07 folder, then follow these steps:

1. Right-click qryArtists in the Navigation pane and choose Design View from the pop-up menu that appears.

   The query opens in Design view, displaying three fields in the QBE grid: Genre, ArtistName, and ArtistWebSite.

2. In the QBE grid (in the lower pane of the query Design view), click in the Criteria row below Genre and type **Alternative**.

3. Click in any other cell in the QBE grid.

   Access places quotation marks around Alternative (shown in Figure 7-5). Because Genre is a text field, criteria must be placed in quotation marks. If you don't include quotation marks when typing your criteria for a text field, Access adds them for you.

   Text fields require quotation marks (") around the criteria, Date/Time fields require pound signs (#) around the criteria, and numeric fields don't require any special characters around the criteria.

Criteria row

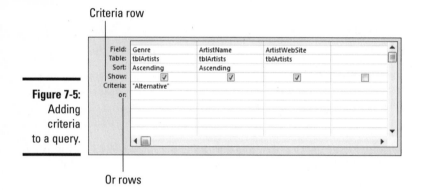

Figure 7-5:
Adding
criteria
to a query.

Or rows

4. Click the Run command in the Results group on the (Query Tools) Design tab.

   The query switches to Datasheet view, displaying the two records from tblArtists that feature Alternative as the Genre.

Exercise 7-7: Dealing with Null Values in a Query

To add criteria to check for null values (or non-null values) in qryArtists, continue working with the database from Exercise 7-6 or open the `Exercise7-7.accdb` file in the Chapter07 folder, then follow these steps:

1. Right-click qryArtists in the Navigation pane and choose Design View from the pop-up menu that appears.

   The query opens in Design view, displaying three fields in the QBE grid: Genre, ArtistName, and ArtistWebSite.

2. In the QBE grid (in the lower pane of the query Design view), clear "Alternative" from the Criteria row below Genre.

3. In the QBE grid (in the lower pane of the query Design view), type **Is Null** in the Criteria row below ArtistWebSite.

4. Click the Run command in the Results group on the (Query Tools) Design tab.

   The query switches to Datasheet view, displaying the four records from tblArtists in which the ArtistWebSite doesn't contain a value.

5. Right-click the qryArtists document tab and choose Design View from the pop-up menu that appears.

   The query switches to Design view.

6. In the QBE grid (in the lower pane of the query Design view), change Is Null to **Is Not Null** in the Criteria row below ArtistWebSite.

7. Click the Run command in the Results group on the (Query Tools) Design tab.

   The query switches to Datasheet view, displaying the two records from tblArtists in which the ArtistWebSite contains data.

Exercise 7-8: Using Wildcard Characters in a Query

To limit the results of qryArtists by using wildcard characters in the criteria, continue working with the database from Exercise 7-7 or open the `Exercise7-8.accdb` file in the Chapter07 folder, then follow these steps:

1. Right-click qryArtists in the Navigation pane and choose Design View from the pop-up menu that appears.

   The query opens in Design view, displaying three fields in the QBE grid: Genre, ArtistName, and ArtistWebSite.

2. In the QBE grid (in the lower pane of the query Design view), clear Is Not Null from the Criteria row below ArtistWebSite.

3. In the QBE grid (in the lower pane of the query Design view), type **T*** in the Criteria row below ArtistName.

4. Click in any other cell in the QBE grid.

   Access changes the criteria cell to Like "T*". Because ArtistName is a text field and you're using a wildcard character, you must use the Like operator with criteria placed in quotation marks.

   When using wildcard characters in the criteria for text fields, you must use the Like operator. If you don't include the Like operator when you type criteria that include a wildcard character, Access adds Like for you.

5. Click the Run command in the Results group on the (Query Tools) Design tab.

   The query switches to Datasheet view, displaying the single record from tblArtists in which the ArtistName starts with the letter T. Placing the asterisk (*) after the letter T tells the query that you want to see records that have the letter T as the first character in ArtistName and that you don't care what characters follow the letter T.

6. Right-click the qryArtists document tab and choose Design View from the pop-up menu that appears.

   The query switches to Design view.

7. In the QBE grid (in the lower pane of the query Design view), change the Criteria row below ArtistName to **Like "*S*"**.

8. Click the Run command in the Results group on the (Query Tools) Design tab.

The query switches to Datasheet view, displaying the four records from tblArtists in which the ArtistName contains the letter S. Placing the asterisk (*) before and after the letter S tells the query that you want to see records that have the letter S somewhere in the ArtistName field and that you don't care which characters appear before and after the letter S.

When adding criteria for text fields, the capitalization of the criteria doesn't matter. The criteria in Step 7 finds records where the ArtistName field contains an S or an s.

A *wildcard character,* such as the asterisk (*), is a placeholder that represents an unknown character or characters in search criteria. Table 7-1 shows a list of wildcard characters and how they work.

Table 7-1	Wildcard Characters	
Character	*Description*	*Example*
*	Matches any number of characters.	st* finds stairs, strong, and steam, but not cost or paste.
?	Matches any single alphabetic character.	c?t finds cat, cut, and cot, but not cast or crust.
[]	Matches any single character within the brackets.	c[au]t finds cat and cut, but not cot.
!	Matches any single character not in the brackets.	c[!au]t finds cot, but not cat or cut.
-	Matches any one range of characters. You must specify the range in ascending order (A–Z).	c[a-s]t finds cat, cot, and cst, but not cut.
#	Matches any single numeric character.	1#2 finds 102, 112, and 122, but not 1002.

Exercise 7-9: Prompting for Criteria in a Query

Prompting the user for criteria enables you to create one query that can show different results. To prompt the user for criteria by using qryArtists, continue working with the database from Exercise 7-8 or open the Exercise7-9.accdb file in the Chapter07 folder, then follow these steps:

1. Right-click qryArtists in the Navigation pane and choose Design View from the pop-up menu that appears.

The query opens in Design view, displaying three fields in the QBE grid: Genre, ArtistName, and ArtistWebSite.

2. In the QBE grid (in the lower pane of the query Design view), clear Like "*S*" from the Criteria row below ArtistName.

3. In the QBE grid (in the lower pane of the query Design view), click in the Criteria row below Genre and type **[Enter a Genre]**.

   Entering a word or phrase in brackets tricks Access into thinking it's an unrecognized field name. Whenever Access sees a field name it doesn't recognize, it prompts you for the data. By entering a clear instruction between the brackets, you can prompt users for values when they run a query.

   4. Click the Run command in the Results group on the (Query Tools) Design tab.

   The Enter Parameter Value dialog box opens, displaying the words Enter a Genre.

   5. In the Enter Parameter Value dialog box, type **Alternative** in the text box.

   6. Click OK.

   The query switches to Datasheet view, displaying the two records from tblArtists in which the Genre is Alternative.

   7. Right-click the qryArtists document tab and choose Design View from the pop-up menu that appears.

   The query switches to Design view.

   8. Click the Run command in the Results group on the (Query Tools) Design tab.

   The Enter Parameter Value dialog box opens, displaying the words Enter a Genre.

   9. In the Enter Parameter Value dialog box, type **Country** in the text box.

   10. Click OK.

   The query switches to Datasheet view, displaying the one record from tblArtists in which the Genre is Country.

Using SQL View

In addition to offering the QBE grid in Design view to help you build your query, Access gives you the ability to create your query in SQL view. *SQL* (Structured Query Language) is a computer language used to create, retrieve, update, and delete data from a relational database such as an Access database. Access provides the query Design view to simplify creating queries. Adding fields, sort orders, and criteria to the QBE grid simply changes the SQL behind the scenes.

Exercise 7-10: Using SQL View

To view the SQL that Access creates when you design qryArtists by using Design view, continue working with the database from Exercise 7-9 or open the `Exercise7-10.accdb` file in the Chapter07 folder, then follow these steps:

   1. Right-click qryArtists in the Navigation pane and choose Design View from the pop-up menu that appears.

   The query opens in Design view, displaying three fields in the QBE grid: Genre, ArtistName, and ArtistWebSite.

2. In the QBE grid (in the lower pane of the query Design view), click in the Criteria row below Genre and replace [Enter a Genre] with **Alternative**.

3. Click in any other cell in the QBE grid.

   Access places quotation marks around Alternative (refer to Figure 7-5).

4. Click the arrow below the View command in the Results group on the (Query Tools) Design tab, then choose SQL View from the drop-down gallery that appears.

   The query switches to SQL view, displaying the SQL statement used to retrieve the data from the database (shown in Figure 7-6).

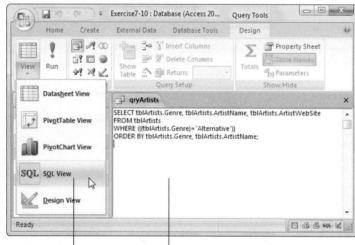

Figure 7-6:
Switching to
SQL view.

SQL view command   Selected view

 If you're familiar with SQL, you can edit the SQL statement in SQL view. Avoid editing SQL statements unless you know what you're doing. Teaching the nuances of SQL is outside the scope of this book, but here's what the SQL statement for the query in Exercise 7-10 looks like:

```
SELECT tblArtists.Genre, tblArtists.ArtistName, tblArtists.ArtistWebSite
FROM tblArtists
WHERE (((tblArtists.Genre)="Alternative"))
ORDER BY tblArtists.Genre, tblArtists.ArtistName;
```

Chapter 8

Creating Multi-Table Queries

- -

In This Chapter

▶ Using a select query to add data to a table

▶ Searching data from more than one table by using a multi-table query

▶ Changing your tables' join type

▶ Finding unmatched values by using a query

- -

*W*hen you use a relational database management system, you want to be able to store information in multiple related tables instead of using one single flat file system. Trying to view data in a child table and figuring out which record it belongs to in its parent table can be confusing, since you only see the primary key from the parent table. By creating multiple table select queries, you can see the information from two or more tables in one datasheet, allowing you to see the useful information from all of the included tables.

In this chapter, you can create multi-table select queries by using the query design grid. You can learn how to add tables to the query Design view and change the type of join between tables to get information.

Adding Data by Using a Select Query

If you want to view data from multiple tables in one datasheet, each table in the database should have data. In Chapter 4 and Chapter 6, you entered data in tblArtists and tblGenres, but you have yet to add any album information to tblAlbums. You can add this information by opening tblAlbums in Datasheet view and typing in data, or you can create a query that can enter this information. A query's Datasheet view works just like a table's; you can add, edit, and delete information.

Exercise 8-1: Adding Data by Using a Select Query

To create a new select query so you can enter data into tblAlbums, continue working with the database from Exercise 7-10 or open the Exercise8-1.accdb file in the Chapter08 folder, then follow these steps:

1. Click the Query Design command in the Other group on the Create tab.

The query Design view opens, along with the Show Table dialog box.

2. Double-click tblAlbums in the Show Table dialog box.

   The tblAlbums table appears in the query Design view behind the Show Table dialog box.

3. In the Show Table dialog box, click Close.

   The Show Table dialog box closes, revealing the query Design view.

4. In the top pane of the query Design view, double-click the title bar of tblAlbums.

   All the fields in tblAlbums become selected.

5. Click and drag the selected fields from tblAlbums to the QBE grid (in the lower pane of the query Design view), then release the mouse.

   All the fields in tblAlbums appear in the QBE grid.

6. Click the Run command in the Results group on the (Query Tools) Design tab.

   The query switches to Datasheet view, displaying the structure from tblAlbums with no data.

7. Use Table 8-1 to add album information via the query.

   The AlbumID field is an AutoNumber field and fills in automatically as you enter data. The ArtistID field is a foreign key to the ArtistID field in tblArtists. For now, leave the SaleDate and SalePrice fields blank.

Table 8-1		Entering Data in a Select Query				
ArtistID	*AlbumTitle*	*MediaType*	*YearOf Release*	*Quantity*	*Purchase Date*	*Purchase Price*
1	Gray Skies	CD	2007	1	9/1/2007	$8.99
2	Sucio	CD	2007	2	9/15/2007	$8.99
3	Gnu World Order	CD	2006	1	6/1/2006	$9.99
3	Start Spreading the Gnus	CD	2007	1	5/1/2007	$9.99

8. Click the Save button on the Quick Access Toolbar.

   The Save As dialog box appears.

9. Type **qryAlbums** in the Save As dialog box.

10. Click OK.

   Access saves the query and changes Query1 on the document tab to qryAlbums. This query also appears in the Navigation pane in the tblAlbums group because it's based on tblAlbums.

You can also drag the asterisk (*) from tblAlbums (which appears at the top of the list of fields) to the QBE grid (in the lower pane of the query Design view) to show all the fields in the query's results. Unlike the asterisk when you use it as a wildcard character (when it means "any characters"), the asterisk as a field name means "all fields."

Creating a Multi-Table Query

After you add data to the Albums table, you can display information from both tblArtists and tblAlbums in one datasheet.

Exercise 8-2: Creating a New Multi-Table Select Query

To create a new multi-table select query to show data from tblArtists and tblAlbums, continue working with the database from Exercise 8-1 or open the `Exercise8-2.accdb` file in the Chapter08 folder, then follow these steps:

1. Click the Query Design command in the Other group on the Create tab.

The query Design view opens, along with the Show Table dialog box.

2. Double-click tblArtists in the Show Table dialog box.

The tblArtists table appears in the query Design view behind the Show Table dialog box.

3. Double-click tblAlbums in the Show Table dialog box.

The tblAlbums table appears in the query Design view behind the Show Table dialog box to the right of tblArtists.

4. In the Show Table dialog box, click Close.

The Show Table dialog box closes, revealing the query Design view, which displays tblArtists and tblAlbums in the top pane with a join line between the two tables' ArtistID fields (shown in Figure 8-1).

Because you created a relationship between tblAlbums and tblArtists in Chapter 6, the join line appears with the 1 to the right of the tblArtists and the infinity symbol (∞) to the left of the tblAlbums, indicating referential integrity exists between these two tables.

If a relationship doesn't exist between two tables, Access might automatically guess which two fields should represent the join and draw a join line between those two fields. This guess is based on the field names and data types in each of the tables. This join line exists only in the query and doesn't affect the relationships defined in the Relationships window.

5. Double-click ArtistName in tblArtists in the top pane of the query Design view.

ArtistName appears in the first column of the QBE grid, and tblArtists appears below ArtistName in the Table row.

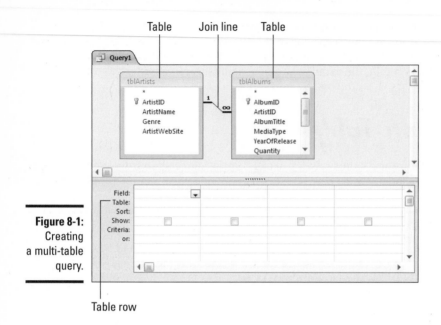

Table   Join line   Table

Figure 8-1:
Creating
a multi-table
query.

Table row

6. Double-click AlbumTitle in tblAlbums in the top pane of the query Design view.

   AlbumTitle appears in the second column of the QBE grid, and tblAlbums appears below AlbumTitle in the Table row.

7. Click the Run command in the Results group on the (Query Tools) Design tab.

   The query switches to Datasheet view, displaying the ArtistName values from tblArtists and AlbumTitle values from tblAlbums in which the ArtistID fields match (shown in Figure 8-2).

Figure 8-2:
Showing
data from
two differ-
ent tables.

ArtistName	AlbumTitle
John E. Blue	Gray Skies
Christy Aguadilla	Sucio
Gnu Farm	Gnu World Order
Gnu Farm	Start Spreading the Gnus

8. Click the Save button on the Quick Access Toolbar.

   The Save As dialog box appears.

9. Type **qryArtistsAndAlbums** in the Save As dialog box.

10. Click OK.

    Access saves the query and changes Query1 on the document tab to qryArtistsAndAlbums. The query also appears in the Navigation pane in both the tblAlbums group and the tblArtists group because it's based on both of those tables.

If your database doesn't have relationships defined, or if Access makes a bad guess (or no guess at all) about which fields to use to create a join, you can drag a field from one table onto a field in the other table to create a join (similar to creating a relationship, which you can read about in Chapter 6). This join exists only in the query and doesn't create a relationship between the tables.

Changing the Join Type

When you include multiple tables in a query, you use joins to help get the results you're looking for. A join helps a query find the records that you want to see from each table based on how those tables are related to each other. Depending on the join type, you can see records only when the joined fields match, or you can choose to see all the records from one table and only those records that match in the other table.

Exercise 8-3: Changing the Join Type

To change the join type between tblArtists and tblAlbums in qryArtistsAndAlbums, continue working with the database from Exercise 8-2 or open the `Exercise8-3.accdb` file in the Chapter08 folder, then follow these steps:

1. Right-click qryArtistsAndAlbums in the Navigation pane and choose Design View from the pop-up menu that appears.

The query opens in Design view, displaying tblArtists and tblAlbums in the top pane with a join line between them.

2. Double-click the join line between tblArtists and tblAlbums.

The Join Properties dialog box opens (shown in Figure 8-3).

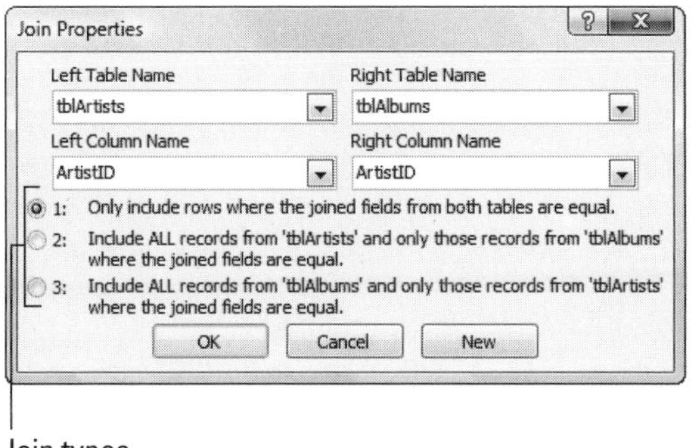

Figure 8-3:
Changing
the join type
in the Join
Properties
dialog box.

Join Properties

Left Table Name	Right Table Name
tblArtists	tblAlbums

Left Column Name	Right Column Name
ArtistID	ArtistID

- 1: Only include rows where the joined fields from both tables are equal.
- 2: Include ALL records from 'tblArtists' and only those records from 'tblAlbums' where the joined fields are equal.
- 3: Include ALL records from 'tblAlbums' and only those records from 'tblArtists' where the joined fields are equal.

OK   Cancel   New

Join types

You can choose from the following types of join in the Join Properties dialog box:

- 1: Only include rows where the joined fields from both fields are equal.

    This selection is the most common type of join and is known as an *inner join*.

• 2: Include ALL records from 'tblArtists' and only those records from 'tblAlbums' where the joined fields are equal.

This type of join is *a left outer join* because it displays all the records from the table on the left and only the records from the table on the right that match records from the table on the left.

• 3: Include ALL records from 'tblAlbums' and only those records from 'tblArtists' where the joined fields are equal.

This type of join is a *right outer join* because it displays all the records from the table on the right and only the records from the table on the left that match the table on the right.

3. Select the option button to the left of 2 to change the join type to a left outer join.

4. Click OK in the Join Properties dialog box.

The Join Properties dialog box closes, revealing the query Design view with an arrow pointing to tblAlbums on the right side of the join (shown in Figure 8-4).

Figure 8-4: Changing to a left outer join adds an arrow to the join line.

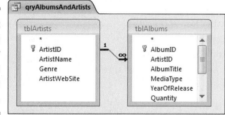

5. Click the Run command in the Results group on the (Query Tools) Design tab.

The query switches to Datasheet view, displaying all the ArtistName values from tblArtists and all the AlbumTitle values from tblAlbums in which the ArtistID fields match, leaving blanks where no matching records exist in tblAlbums (shown in Figure 8-5).

Matching records

Figure 8-5: Viewing the results of a left outer join.

No matching records

TIP

If you get confused trying to make the distinction between a left outer join and a right outer join, get in the habit of putting the table in which you want all the records on the left side of the join and the table which only includes related records on the right. Then you only have to worry about using a left outer join.

Creating a Find Unmatched Query

When you analyze the data in your database, you might come across a scenario in which you want to see the values in one table that *don't* have a matching value in another table. You can build this type of query by using an outer join between the tables.

ON THE CD

Exercise 8-4: Creating a Find Unmatched Query

To create a query that lists the values in tblArtists that don't have a matching record in tblAlbums, continue working with the database from Exercise 8-3 or open the `Exercise8-4.accdb` file in the Chapter08 folder, then follow these steps:

1. Right-click qryArtistsAndAlbums in the Navigation pane and choose Design View from the pop-up menu that appears.

The query opens in Design view, displaying tblArtists and tblAlbums in the top pane with a left outer join line between the two tables. The QBE grid shows ArtistName and AlbumTitle.

2. In the QBE grid (in the lower pane of the query Design view), click the arrow to the right of AlbumTitle and select ArtistID from the drop-down list that appears.

When you create a find unmatched query, include the foreign key field (in this case, ArtistID) from the table.

3. In the QBE grid (in the lower pane of the query Design view), type **Is Null** in the Criteria row below ArtistID.

By testing the ArtistID field for a null value, you're essentially asking for values that don't exist in tblAlbums.

4. In the QBE grid (in the lower pane of the query Design view), unselect the Show check box.

The X disappears from the check box. Because the values in the ArtistID field will be Null, you don't need to see this column in the query's results.

5. Click the Run command in the Results group on the (Query Tools) Design tab.

The query switches to Datasheet view, displaying the three ArtistName values from tblArtists that don't have a corresponding record in tblAlbums. These Artists are the same Artists that don't have matching records in Exercise 8-3 (refer to Figure 8-5).

6. Click the Microsoft Office Button and select Save As from the menu that appears.

The Save As dialog box appears.

7. Type **qryArtistsWithoutAlbums** in the Save As dialog box.

8. Click OK.

Access saves the query and changes qryArtistsAndAlbums on the document tab to qryArtistsWithoutAlbums. The query also appears in the Navigation pane in both the tblAlbums group and the tblArtists group because it's based on both of those tables.

When you create a new query, sometimes it's faster to change the design of an existing query and save it with a new query name instead of creating a new query from scratch.

Chapter 9

Performing Calculations in Queries

- -

In This Chapter

▶ Using calculated fields to show data not stored in the table

▶ Tallying information totals by using queries

- -

*W*hen you use queries to view data, you can perform calculations. Calculations can be anything from mathematical expressions that use data from one or more columns or rows to combining multiple text fields into one. Computers are good at computing, and you can use Access queries to let the computer do the work.

In this chapter, you can create calculated fields that show the product of two columns and summarize numerical data from multiple tables. You can also build a calculated text field, which shows data from two or more text fields as one column of data. Finally, you can use the grouping feature of a query to summarize data from multiple rows.

Creating Calculated Fields

In an Access query, you can create a *calculated field,* which is a field that doesn't exist in any of the underlying tables and displays the results of an expression. An expression can be anything from static text, to a mathematical expression between numbers and dates, to an alphanumeric expression that combines two text fields into one.

Creating numeric calculated fields

Crunching numbers is a task well suited for Access queries. By using calculated fields, you can create calculations between multiple columns and static values.

Exercise 9-1: Creating Numeric Calculated Fields

To create numeric calculated fields in a query, continue working with the database from Exercise 8-4 or open the `Exercise9-1.accdb` file in the Chapter09 folder, then follow these steps:

1. Click the Query Design command in the Other group on the Create tab.

The query Design view opens, along with the Show Table dialog box.

2. Double-click tblArtists in the Show Table dialog box.

The tblArtists table appears in the query Design view behind the Show Table dialog box.

3. Double-click tblAlbums in the Show Table dialog box.

The tblAlbums table appears in the query Design view behind the Show Table dialog box to the right of tblArtists.

4. In the Show Table dialog box, click Close.

The Show Table dialog box closes, revealing the query Design view with tblArtists and tblAlbums in the top pane.

5. Double-click ArtistName in tblArtists in the top pane of the query Design view.

ArtistName appears in the first column of the QBE grid (in the lower pane of the query Design view), and tblArtists appears below ArtistName in the Table row.

6. Double-click AlbumTitle, Quantity, and PurchasePrice in tblAlbums in the top pane of the query Design view.

AlbumTitle, Quantity, and PurchasePrice appear in the second, third, and fourth columns of the QBE grid (in the lower pane of the query Design view), and tblAlbums appears in the Table row below each field name.

7. In the QBE grid (in the lower pane of the query Design view), type **ExtPrice: [Quantity]*[PurchasePrice]** in the Field row of the first blank column to the right of the PurchasePrice field (shown in Figure 9-1).

Fields from tables

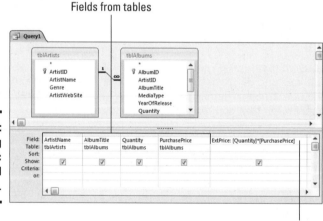

Figure 9-1:
Creating
a numeric
calculated
field.

Calculated field

This step creates a calculated field named ExtPrice (short for ExtendedPrice), which is equal to the value in the Quantity field multiplied by the value in the PurchasePrice field. In mathematical calculations, the asterisk (*) is used for multiplication.

The general syntax for creating a calculated field in a query is `Fieldname: Expression`.

8. Click the Run command in the Results group on the (Query Tools) Design tab.

   The query switches to Datasheet view, displaying the four fields from the underlying tables and the calculated field named ExtPrice (shown in Figure 9-2).

Fields from tables   Calculated fields

Figure 9-2:
Viewing the
results of a
calculated
field.

ArtistName	AlbumTitle	Quantity	PurchasePrice	ExtPrice
John E. Blue	Gray Skies	1	$8.99	$8.99
Christy Aguadilla	Sucio	2	$8.99	$17.98
Gnu Farm	Gnu World Order	1	$9.99	$9.99
Gnu Farm	Start Spreading the Gnu	1	$9.99	$9.99

The calculated field (ExtPrice) appears in Datasheet view just like a normal field. However, Access doesn't let you change the contents of the calculated field. The calculated field always shows the Quantity multiplied by the PurchasePrice.

9. Right-click the Query1 document tab and choose Design View from the pop-up menu that appears.

   The query switches to Design view.

10. In the QBE grid (in the lower pane of the query Design view), type **SalesTax: [ExtPrice]*0.06** in the Field row of the first blank column to the right of the ExtPrice field.

    This step creates a calculated field named SalesTax that multiplies the value in the calculated ExtPrice field by 0.06. Because ExtPrice is now a field in the query, you can use it in other calculated fields.

11. In the QBE grid (in the lower pane of the query Design view), type **TotalPrice: [ExtPrice]+[SalesTax]** in the Field row of the first blank column to the right of the SalesTax field.

    This step creates a calculated field named TotalPrice that adds the values from the ExtPrice and SalesTax fields.

12. Click the Run command in the Results group on the (Query Tools) Design tab.

    The query switches to Datasheet view, displaying the four fields from the underlying tables and the three calculated fields (ExtPrice, SalesTax, and TotalPrice).

13. Click the Save button on the Quick Access Toolbar.

    The Save As dialog box appears.

14. Type **qryAlbumPrices** in the Save As dialog box.

15. Click OK.

    Access saves the query and changes Query1 on the document tab to qryAlbumPrices. The query also appears in the Navigation pane in both the tblAlbums group and in the tblArtists group because it's based on both of those tables.

Creating concatenated text fields

Concatenation involves combining more than one field into a single field. By combining values from multiple fields, you can store values in separate fields (such as John in FirstName and Doe in LastName) and display them later in one field (Doe, John).

A concatenated field is a calculated field, even though it isn't performing any mathematical operations.

Exercise 9-2: Creating Concatenated Text Fields

To combine multiple columns into one column by using concatenation, continue working with the database from Exercise 9-1 or open the `Exercise9-2.accdb` file in the Chapter09 folder, then follow these steps:

1. Right-click qryAlbumPrices in the Navigation pane and choose Design View from the pop-up menu that appears.

   The query opens in Design view, displaying four fields from the underlying tables and three calculated fields.

2. In the QBE grid (in the lower pane of the query Design view), change the value of the second column (AlbumTitle) to **AlbumTitleYear: [AlbumTitle] & [YearOfRelease]**.

   The ampersand (&) operator concatenates two expressions together.

3. Click the Run command in the Results group on the (Query Tools) Design tab.

   The query switches to Datasheet view, displaying the data from AlbumTitle and YearOfRelease in one calculated field named AlbumTitleYear (shown in Figure 9-3).

Figure 9-3:
Viewing the results of a concatenated field.

qryAlbumPrices	
ArtistName ▾	AlbumTitleYear ▾
John E. Blue	Gray Skies2007
Christy Aguadilla	Sucio2007
Gnu Farm	Gnu World Order2006
Gnu Farm	Start Spreading the Gnus2007

The data from the two fields in the AlbumTitleYear column run together. You told the query to combine the two fields into one, and Access isn't smart enough to put a space between the fields.

4. Right-click the qryAlbumPrices document tab and choose Design View from the pop-up menu that appears.

   The query switches to Design view.

5. In the QBE grid (in the lower pane of the query Design view), change the value of the second column (AlbumTitleYear) to **AlbumTitleYear: [AlbumTitle] & " (" & [YearOfRelease] & ")"**.

   This value adds a space after the AlbumTitle and puts parentheses around the YearOfRelease.

6. Click the Run command in the Results group on the (Query Tools) Design tab.

The query switches to Datasheet view, displaying the data from AlbumTitle and YearOfRelease in one calculated field named AlbumTitleYear, this time with the data displayed more clearly with parentheses around the year (shown in Figure 9-4).

Figure 9-4:
Fixing up the results of a concatenated field.

ArtistName	AlbumTitleYear
John E. Blue	Gray Skies (2007)
Christy Aguadilla	Sucio (2007)
Gnu Farm	Gnu World Order (2006)
Gnu Farm	Start Spreading the Gnus (2007)

qryAlbumPrices

REMEMBER

When you concatenate fields, put the field names, brackets, and any other characters you're adding to the concatenation (including spaces) in quotation marks. Also, include an ampersand (&) between each field name and expression in quotation marks.

Calculating Totals

In addition to calculating values across columns, queries give you the ability to total information from multiple rows. Using totals, you can show the number of related records in the child table for each parent record. You can also calculate sums and show minimum and maximum values for the entire query, or grouped on a particular field.

ON THE CD

Exercise 9-3: Counting Records

To create a query that can count the number of albums (or records) that exist for each artist, continue working with the database from Exercise 9-2 or open the `Exercise9-3.accdb` file in the Chapter09 folder, then follow these steps:

1. Click the Query Design command in the Other group on the Create tab.

The query Design view opens, along with the Show Table dialog box.

2. Double-click tblArtists in the Show Table dialog box.

The tblArtists table appears in the query Design view behind the Show Table dialog box.

3. Double-click tblAlbums in the Show Table dialog box.

The tblAlbums table appears in the query Design view behind the Show Table dialog box to the right of tblArtists.

4. In the Show Table dialog box, click Close.

The Show Table dialog box closes, revealing the query Design view with tblArtists and tblAlbums in the top pane.

5. Double-click ArtistName in tblArtists in the top pane of the query Design view.

ArtistName appears in the first column of the QBE grid.

6. Double-click AlbumID in tblAlbums in the top pane of the query Design view.

AlbumID appears in the second column of the QBE grid.

7. Click the Totals column in the Show/Hide group on the (Query Tools) Design tab.

The Total row appears in the QBE grid, with Group By appearing under the ArtistName and AlbumID fields (shown in Figure 9-5).

Totals command

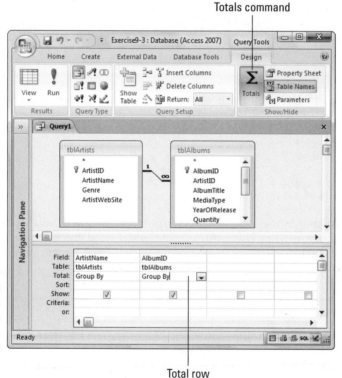

Figure 9-5:
Displaying
the Total
row.

Total row

8. In the QBE grid (in the lower pane of the query Design view), click the arrow in the Total row below ArtistID and select Count from the drop-down list that appears.

9. Click the Run command in the Results group on the (Query Tools) Design tab.

The query switches to Datasheet view, displaying three values in ArtistName and how many albums each artist has in a column which Access names CountOfArtistID. The query doesn't display the artists that have no albums.

10. Right-click the Query1 document tab and choose Design View from the pop-up menu that appears.

The query switches to Design view.

11. Double-click the join line between tblArtists and tblAlbums.

The Join Properties dialog box opens.

12. Select the option button to the left of 2 to change the join type from an inner join to a left outer join.

13. In the Join Properties dialog box, click OK.

    The Join Properties dialog box closes, and the join line in the top pane of the query Design view changes, displaying an arrow pointing to tblAlbums which indicates the join is a left outer join.

14. In the QBE grid (in the lower pane of the query Design view), click the arrow in the Sort row below ArtistID and select Descending from the drop-down list that appears.

15. Click the Run command in the Results group on the (Query Tools) Design tab.

    The query switches to Datasheet view, displaying all values in ArtistName and how many albums each artist has in a column which Access names CountOfArtistID, including artists with no albums. Because you sorted the CountOfArtistID in descending order in Step 14, the artist with the most albums appears first.

16. Click the Save button on the Quick Access Toolbar.

    The Save As dialog box appears.

17. Type **qryArtistAlbumCount** in the Save As dialog box.

18. Click OK.

    Access saves the query and changes Query1 on the document tab to qryArtistAlbumCount.

Exercise 9-4: Adding Values from Multiple Rows

To create a query that can add the purchase prices for the records in tblAlbums, continue working with the database from Exercise 9-3 or open the `Exercise9-4.accdb` file in the Chapter09 folder, then follow these steps:

1. Click the Query Design command in the Other group on the Create tab.

    The query Design view opens, along with the Show Table dialog box.

2. Double-click tblAlbums in the Show Table dialog box.

    The tblAlbums table appears in the query Design view behind the Show Table dialog box.

3. In the Show Table dialog box, click Close.

    The Show Table dialog box closes, revealing the query Design view with tblAlbums in the top pane.

4. Double-click PurchasePrice in tblAlbums in the top pane of the query Design view.

    PurchasePrice appears in the first column of the QBE grid.

5. Click the Totals command in the Show/Hide group on the (Query Tools) Design tab.

    The Total row appears in the QBE grid, with Group By appearing below the PurchasePrice field.

6. In the QBE grid (in the lower pane of the query Design view), click the arrow in the Total row below PurchasePrice and select Sum from the drop-down list that appears.

7. Click the Run command in the Results group on the (Query Tools) Design tab.

The query switches to Datasheet view, displaying one row containing the sum of all the PurchasePrice fields in tblAlbums.

8. Right-click the Query1 document tab and choose Design View from the pop-up menu that appears.

The query switches to Design view.

9. Click the Show Table command in the Query Setup group on the (Query Tools) Design tab.

The Show Table dialog box opens.

10. Double-click tblArtists in the Show Table dialog box.

The tblArtists table appears in the query Design view behind the Show Table dialog box to the right of tblAlbums.

11. In the Show Table dialog box, click Close.

The Show Table dialog box closes.

12. Double-click Genre in tblArtists in the top pane of the query Design view.

Genre appears in the second column of the QBE grid with Group By appearing in the Total row.

13. Click the Run command in the Results group on the (Query Tools) Design tab.

The query switches to Datasheet view, displaying two rows, each containing the sum of the PurchasePrice fields for the Genre of music. The results don't include all genres of music, because you only entered albums for artists in the Alternative and Pop/Rock genres.

14. Click the Save button on the Quick Access Toolbar.

The Save As dialog box appears.

15. Type **qryPriceByGenre** in the Save As dialog box.

16. Click OK.

Access saves the query and changes Query1 on the document tab to qryPriceByGenre.

Part IV
Manipulating Data with Action Queries

The 5th Wave   By Rich Tennant

"Our automated response policy to a large company-wide data crash is to notify management, back up existing data and sell 90% of my shares in the company."

In this part . . .

*A*ction queries let you manipulate data in your database, changing lots of data in one fell swoop. The chapters and exercises in Part IV teach all about action queries in Access. You start out by creating update queries to change existing data then move to creating append queries to add data to a table. Finally, you build delete queries to remove entire records from the database and make table queries to create a whole new table without using the table designer.

Chapter 10

Changing Data with Update Queries

● ●

In This Chapter

▶ Backing up your table before making changes

▶ Working with an update query

▶ Using criteria to update data

▶ Updating with calculated values

● ●

*A*ction queries are different than select queries because action queries manipulate data in your tables. You can use action queries to change existing data in your database, add data to a table, delete records from a table, and create new tables based on data in another table. An *update query* is a type of action query that modifies data in one or more fields across one or more rows of data. Use an update query when you want to change data that already resides in your database. This query is kind of like the Find and Replace dialog box on steroids.

In this chapter, you can create update queries by using the query design grid. You can learn how to update all the records in a table or just a select few records. You can update fields to a static value, a calculated value, and even a value from another table. And you can even update multiple fields at the same time.

Creating a Backup Table

It's always wise to make a backup copy of your database before changing information. If you make a mistake, you may find it difficult to get back the information you changed — so make that backup copy before you get started and save yourself hours of trying to figure out what you did wrong. In addition to creating a copy of the entire database, you can create a copy of just a table for practice.

Exercise 10-1: Making a Backup Copy of a Table

To make a backup copy of tblAlbums, continue working with the database from Exercise 9-4 or open the `Exercise10-1.accdb` file in the Chapter10 folder, then follow these steps:

1. Click the arrow in the top-right corner of the Navigation pane and select Object Type from the drop-down list that appears.

The Navigation pane displays the database objects grouped by Tables and Queries. After you add enough objects to a database, you might find it easier to locate them in this view, rather than using the Tables and Related Views setting (used up until this point).

2. In the Navigation pane, right-click tblAlbums and choose Copy from the pop-up menu that appears.

3. In the Navigation pane, right-click a blank area and choose Paste from the pop-up menu that appears.

The Paste Table As dialog box opens.

4. In the Paste Table As dialog box, type **tblAlbums_Backup** in the Table Name text box and make sure the Structure and Data option button is selected.

Selecting the Structure and Data option creates a copy of the table, including all the data from the original table.

5. In the Paste Table As dialog box, click OK.

tblAlbums_Backup appears in the Tables group in the Navigation pane.

Many Access users prefer to view their database objects (such as tables, queries, and forms) by Object Type. Chapter 1 outlines the different views in the Navigation pane and explains how to use the one that you like best.

Creating an Update Query

When you create an update query, start by creating a select query to view the data you want to update before updating it. This select query helps minimize the chance that you'll make a mistake when changing the data. After you know you're viewing the information you want to change, you can change the query to an update query and modify the data.

Exercise 10-2: Creating the Select Query

For this example, you fill in the SaleDate field with a known value. To create a select query to see the field you want to change in tblAlbums_Backup, continue working with the database from Exercise 10-1 or open the `Exercise10-2.accdb` file in the Chapter10 folder, then follow these steps:

1. Click the Query Design command in the Other group on the Create tab.

The query Design view opens, along with the Show Table dialog box.

2. Double-click tblAlbums_Backup in the Show Table dialog box.

   The tblAlbums_Backup table appears in the query Design view behind the Show Table dialog box.

3. In the Show Table dialog box, click Close.

   The Show Table dialog box closes, revealing the query Design view.

4. Double-click AlbumTitle and SaleDate in tblAlbums_Backup in the top pane of the query Design view.

   AlbumTitle and SaleDate appear in the first and second columns of the QBE grid. You can add more fields to the query than you want to change if seeing those extra fields can help you make sure you're going to update the correct records.

5. Click the Run command in the Results group on the (Query Tools) Design tab.

   The query switches to Datasheet view, displaying the album titles and blank SaleDate fields. Because you know you want to update those records, you're done with the select query.

6. Click the Save button on the Quick Access Toolbar.

   The Save As dialog box appears.

7. Type **qryUpdateSaleDate** in the Save As dialog box.

8. Click OK.

   Access saves the query and changes Query1 on the document tab to qryUpdateSaleDate. The query also appears in the Queries group in the Navigation pane.

If the select query doesn't show you the information you want to update, switch back to Design view and make changes to retrieve the correct data.

Exercise 10-3: Changing a Select Query to an Update Query

To change the query type from a select query to an update query, and to change the data in the query's underlying table, continue working with the database from Exercise 10-2 or open the `Exercise10-3.accdb` file in the Chapter10 folder, then follow these steps:

1. Right-click qryUpdateSaleDate in the Navigation pane and choose Design View from the pop-up menu that appears.

   The query opens in Design view.

2. Click the Update command in the Query Type group on the (Query Tools) Design tab.

   Access changes the query from a select query to an update query (indicated by the now-highlighted Update command) and adds the Update To row to the QBE grid in the lower pane of the query Design view (shown in Figure 10-1).

Query Type group

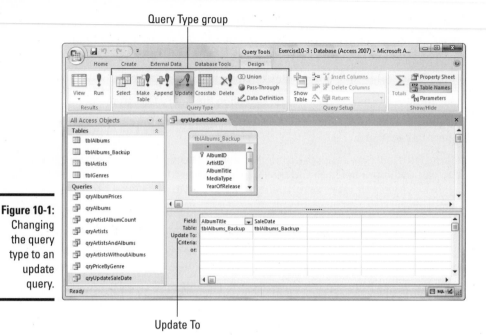

Figure 10-1:
Changing
the query
type to an
update
query.

Update To

3. In the QBE grid (in the lower pane of the query Design view), type **#11/2/2007#** in the Update To cell below SaleDate.

Because SaleDate is a Date/Time field, you must put pound signs (#) around the data you're entering. If you don't put pound signs around the date, Access puts them in for you.

Date/Time fields require pound signs (#) around the criteria, Text fields require quotation marks (") around the criteria, and numeric fields don't require any special characters around the criteria.

4. Click the Run command in the Results group on the (Query Tools) Design tab.

Access displays a confirmation dialog box (shown in Figure 10-2) telling you that you're about to update four rows and you won't be able to undo the changes.

Figure 10-2:
Confirming
you want
to update
the rows.

5. Click Yes in the dialog box.

The dialog box closes, and the update query runs, changing the data behind the scenes.

6. Click the Save button on the Quick Access Toolbar.

Access saves the query, and the icon to the right of qryUpdateSaleDate in the Navigation pane changes from the select query icon to the update query icon (a pencil with an exclamation point, shown in Figure 10-3).

Select queries

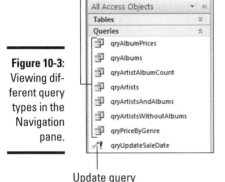

Figure 10-3: Viewing different query types in the Navigation pane.

Update query

7. Double-Click tblAlbums_Backup in the Navigation pane.

The table opens, and the SaleDate field for all four records appears as 11/2/2007.

Updating with Criteria

When you change data by using an update query, you don't have to update data in every row. Just like when you use criteria in select queries, you can add criteria to an update query to limit the number of rows you're updating.

Exercise 10-4: Updating with Criteria

To create an update query to clear the SaleDate field for the albums by Gnu Farm (which has the ArtistID of 3) in tblAlbums_Backup, continue working with the database from Exercise 10-3 or open the `Exercise10-4.accdb` file in the Chapter10 folder, then follow these steps:

1. Click the Query Design command in the Other group on the Create tab.

The query Design view opens, along with the Show Table dialog box.

2. Double-click tblAlbums_Backup in the Show Table dialog box.

The tblAlbums_Backup table appears in the query Design view behind the Show Table dialog box.

3. In the Show Table dialog box, click Close.

The Show Table dialog box closes, revealing the query Design view.

4. Double-click ArtistID, AlbumTitle, and SaleDate in tblAlbums_Backup in the top pane of the query Design view.

   ArtistID, AlbumTitle, and SaleDate appear in the QBE grid (in the lower pane of the query Design view).

5. In the QBE grid (in the lower pane of the query Design view), click in the Criteria row below ArtistID and type **3**.

6. Click the Run command in the Results group on the (Query Tools) Design tab.

   The query switches to Datasheet view, displaying the album titles (Gnu World Order and Start Spreading the Gnus) for which the ArtistID is 3.

7. Right-click the Query1 document tab and choose Design View from the pop-up menu that appears.

   The query switches to Design view.

8. Click the Update command in the Query Type group on the (Query Tools) Design tab.

   Access changes the query from a select query to an update query.

9. In the QBE grid (in the lower pane of the query Design view), type **Null** in the Update To row below SaleDate.

   The Null keyword in the Update To row tells Access to update the field to a null value (make it blank).

10. Click the Run command in the Results group on the (Query Tools) Design tab.

    Access displays a confirmation dialog box telling you that you're about to update two rows and you won't be able to undo the changes.

11. Click Yes in the dialog box.

    The dialog box closes, and the update query runs, changing the data behind the scenes.

12. Click the Save button on the Quick Access Toolbar.

    The Save As dialog box appears.

13. Type **qryUpdateSaleDateToNull** in the Save As dialog box.

14. Click OK.

    Access saves the query and changes Query1 on the document tab to qryUpdateSaleDateToNull.

15. Double-Click tblAlbums_Backup in the Navigation pane.

    The table opens, showing that the SaleDate field for two records has been cleared.

Updating to a Calculated Value

When you run an update query, you might not always know what value you're updating the field to. For instance, you might be updating one field to a value based on another field. You might even be updating a field to a value in another table. Whatever the case, update queries can be dynamic and aren't limited to updating to values you already know.

Exercise 10-5: Updating to a Calculated Value

This exercise shows you how to create a query that can update the SalePrice field to $4 more than the PurchasePrice field for all the albums in tblAlbums_Backup. Just continue working with the database from Exercise 10-4 or open the `Exercise10-5.accdb` file in the Chapter10 folder, then follow these steps:

1. Click the Query Design command in the Other group on the Create tab.

   The query Design view opens, along with the Show Table dialog box.

2. Double-click tblAlbums_Backup in the Show Table dialog box.

   The tblAlbums_Backup table appears in the query Design view behind the Show Table dialog box.

3. In the Show Table dialog box, click Close.

   The Show Table dialog box closes, revealing the query Design view.

4. Double-click PurchasePrice and SalePrice in tblAlbums_Backup in the top pane of the query Design view.

   PurchasePrice and SalePrice appear in the QBE grid (in the lower pane of the query Design view).

5. In the QBE grid (in the lower pane of the query Design view), type **SalePriceTest: [PurchasePrice] + 4** in the Field row of the first blank column to the right of the SalePrice field.

   This step creates a calculated field named SalePriceTest that acts as a test column that gives you a preview of what you're updating the SalePrice field to.

6. Click the Run command in the Results group on the (Query Tools) Design tab.

   The query switches to Datasheet view, displaying three columns — the PurchasePrice; SalePrice (which is blank); and SalePriceTest, which shows the data that you want to appear in the SalePrice field (shown in Figure 10-4).

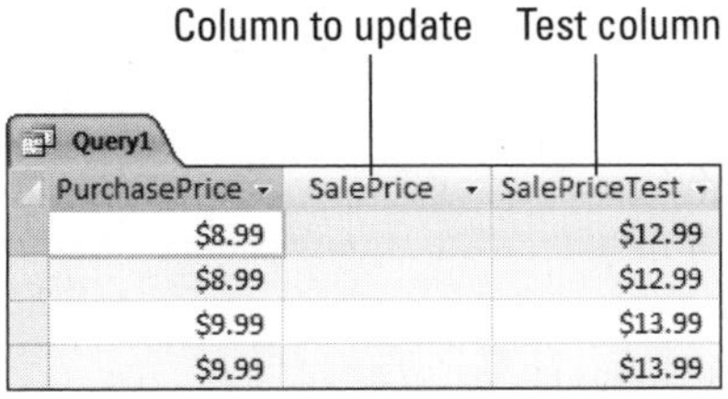

Column to update   Test column

Figure 10-4:
Previewing
calculated
data before
updating.

PurchasePrice	SalePrice	SalePriceTest
$8.99		$12.99
$8.99		$12.99
$9.99		$13.99
$9.99		$13.99

7. Right-click the Query1 document tab and choose Design View from the pop-up menu that appears.

   The query switches to Design view.

8. Click the Update command in the Query Type group on the (Query Tools) Design tab.

   Access changes the query from a select query to an update query.

9. In the QBE grid (in the lower pane of the query Design view), type **[PurchasePrice] + 4** in the Update To row below SalePrice.

When creating an update query, you can't use the calculated field name (SalePriceTest) in the Update To row. Instead, you must retype the expression (or copy and paste it) in the Update To row of the field you're updating.

10. Click the Run command in the Results group on the (Query Tools) Design tab.

Access displays a confirmation dialog box telling you that you're about to update four rows and you won't be able to undo the changes.

11. Click Yes in the dialog box.

The dialog box closes, and the update query runs, changing the data behind the scenes.

12. Click the Save button on the Quick Access Toolbar.

The Save As dialog box appears.

13. Type **qryUpdateSalePriceToPurchasePrice** in the Save As dialog box.

14. Click OK.

Access saves the query and changes Query1 on the document tab to qryUpdateSalePriceToPurchasePrice.

15. Double-click tblAlbums_Backup in the Navigation pane.

The table opens, and the SalePrice field for all the records displays a value $4 more than the PurchasePrice.

Exercise 10-6: Updating to Values from Another Table

To create a query that can update the SaleDate and SalePrice fields in tblAlbums to the values of SaleDate and SalePrice in tblAlbums_Backup, continue working with the database from Exercise 10-5 or open the Exercise10-6.accdb file in the Chapter10 folder, then follow these steps:

1. Click the Query Design command in the Other group on the Create tab.

The query Design view opens, along with the Show Table dialog box.

2. Double-click tblAlbums in the Show Table dialog box.

The tblAlbums table appears in the query Design view behind the Show Table dialog box.

3. Double-click tblAlbums_Backup in the Show Table dialog box.

The tblAlbums_Backup table appears in the query Design view behind the Show Table dialog box to the right of tblAlbums.

4. In the Show Table dialog box, click Close.

The Show Table dialog box closes, revealing the query Design view.

5. Drag the AlbumID field from tblAlbums and drop it onto the AlbumID field in tblAlbums_Backup.

A join line appears between the two tables in the top pane of the query Design view.

6. Double-click SaleDate and SalePrice in tblAlbums in the top pane of the query Design view.

SaleDate and SalePrice from tblAlbums appear in the QBE grid.

7. Double-click SaleDate and SalePrice in tblAlbums_Backup in the top pane of the query Design view.

SaleDate and SalePrice from tblAlbums_Backup appear in the QBE grid.

8. Click the Run command in the Results group on the (Query Tools) Design tab.

The query switches to Datasheet view, displaying four columns, two from tblAlbums and two from tblAlbums_Backup (shown in Figure 10-5).

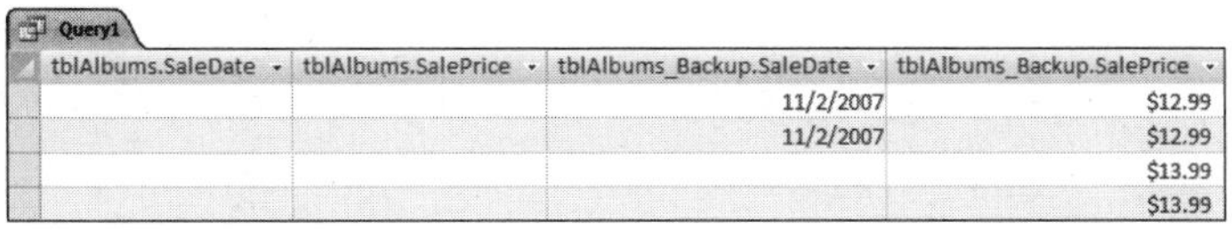

Figure 10-5:
Viewing fields from multiple tables that have the same name.

Query1			
tblAlbums.SaleDate ▾	tblAlbums.SalePrice ▾	tblAlbums_Backup.SaleDate ▾	tblAlbums_Backup.SalePrice ▾
		11/2/2007	$12.99
		11/2/2007	$12.99
			$13.99
			$13.99

When fields with the same name from two or more tables appear in a query, you must refer to those fields using the table name; otherwise, Access doesn't know which field you're talking about. To refer to a duplicate field name, use this syntax: `tablename.fieldname` OR `[tablename].[fieldname]`.

9. Right-click the Query1 document tab and choose Design View from the pop-up menu that appears.

The query switches to Design view.

10. Click the Update command in the Query Type group on the (Query Tools) Design tab.

Access changes the query from a select query to an update query.

11. In the QBE grid (in the lower pane of the query Design view), type **[tblAlbums_Backup].[SaleDate]** in the Update To row below SaleDate from tblAlbums.

12. In the QBE grid (in the lower pane of the query Design view), type **[tblAlbums_Backup].[SalePrice]** in the Update To row below SalePrice from tblAlbums.

13. Click the Run command in the Results group on the (Query Tools) Design tab.

Access displays a confirmation dialog box telling you that you're about to update four rows and you won't be able to undo the changes.

14. Click Yes in the dialog box.

The dialog box closes, and the update query runs, changing the data behind the scenes.

15. Click the Save button on the Quick Access Toolbar.

The Save As dialog box appears.

16. Type **qryUpdateSalesInfoFromAlbumBackup** in the Save As dialog box.

17. Click OK.

Access saves the query and changes Query1 on the document tab to qryUpdateSalesInfoFromAlbumBackup.

18. Double-click tblAlbums in the Navigation pane.

The table opens, and the SaleDate and SalePrice fields for all the records match the values from tblAlbums_Backup.

Chapter 11

Adding Data with Append Queries

In This Chapter

▶ Making a source table

▶ Appending records by using an append query

▶ Adding a single record to a table

A n *append query* is a type of action query that adds records to a table. Use append queries when you have data from some other source and you don't feel like retyping it into your database.

In this chapter, you can create append queries by using the query design grid. You can learn how to add records to a table based on records in another table or just add a single record to a table.

Creating a Source Table

Before you can use an append query to add data to your database, you need a source table from which you get the data you want to add. If the source table has the same structure as the destination table, creating an append query is a breeze. If the source table has a different structure than the destination table, you have to do a few more steps to build the append query.

Exercise 11-1: Creating a Source Table

To make a source table that contains new artists, continue working with the database from Exercise 10-6 or open the `Exercise11-1.accdb` file in the Chapter11 folder, then follow these steps:

1. In the Navigation pane, right-click tblAlbums and choose Copy from the pop-up menu that appears.

2. In the Navigation pane, right-click a blank area and choose Paste from the pop-up menu that appears.

   The Paste Table As dialog box opens.

3. In the Paste Table As dialog box, type **tblNewArtists** in the Table Name text box.

4. In the Paste As dialog box, select the Structure Only option button.

The Structure Only option makes a copy of the table's structure but doesn't copy any data from the original table.

5. In the Paste Table As dialog box, click OK.

tblNewArtists appears in the Tables group in the Navigation pane.

6. Double-click tblNewArtists in the Navigation pane.

The table opens in Datasheet view.

7. Enter the following information in the table:

ArtistName	*Genre*	*ArtistWebSite*
Precinct 40	Alternative	\<leave blank\>
Farm Gals	Country	\<leave blank\>
Breaker One Nine	R&B	\<leave blank\>

The ArtistID field fills in sequentially (1, 2, and 3) as you enter the Artist information.

8. Right-click the tblNewArtists document tab and choose Close from the pop-up menu that appears.

The query switches to Design view.

You might find it silly to create a table just to add it to an existing table. However, people might give you information in another Access database, an Excel spreadsheet, or some other format that you can import into your database (see Chapter 29) and add to a table by using an append query.

Creating an Append Query

After you have a source table from which you want to get the data, you're ready to build an append query that can copy the data from the source table into the destination table. When you build an append query, always start with the source table.

Always make a backup copy of your database before you run any type of action query against the data. For more information on making a backup copy of your database, see Chapter 2.

Exercise 11-2: Appending Records from a Source Table

To copy records from one table to another table, continue working with the database from Exercise 11-1 or open the `Exercise11-2.accdb` file in the Chapter11 folder, then follow these steps:

1. Click the Query Design command in the Other group on the Create tab.

The query Design view opens, along with the Show Table dialog box.

2. Double-click tblNewArtists in the Show Table dialog box.

   The tblNewArtists table appears in the query Design view behind the Show Table dialog box. When you build an append query, the query's underlying table is the source table.

3. In the Show Table dialog box, click Close.

   The Show Table dialog box closes, revealing the query Design view.

4. Double-click ArtistName, Genre, and ArtistWebSite in tblNewArtists in the top pane of the query Design view.

   ArtistName, Genre, and ArtistWebSite appear in the QBE grid. You didn't select ArtistID because you're appending the data to tblArtists, and ArtistID is an AutoNumber field in the destination table.

   When appending data to a table with an AutoNumber field, don't append data to that AutoNumber field since Access assigns a unique number automatically.

5. Click the Run command in the Results group on the (Query Tools) Design tab.

   The query switches to Datasheet view, displaying the artists from tblNewArtists.

   Start all your action queries as select queries to ensure that you're manipulating the correct data.

6. Right-click the Query1 document tab and choose Design View from the pop-up menu that appears.

   The query switches to Design view.

7. Click the Append command in the Query Type group on the (Query Tools) Design tab.

   The Append dialog box appears (shown in Figure 11-1).

Table Name drop-down list

Figure 11-1: Changing the query type to an append query.

8. In the Append dialog box, click the arrow to the right of Table Name and select tblArtists from the drop-down list that appears.

9. In the Append dialog box, click OK.

   The Append dialog box closes, and Access changes the query from a select query to an append query (indicated by the now-highlighted Append command) and adds the Append To row to the QBE grid (in the lower pane of the query Design view) with the field names from tblArtists filled in because they match the names in tblNewArtists (shown in Figure 11-2).

Append command   Query Type group

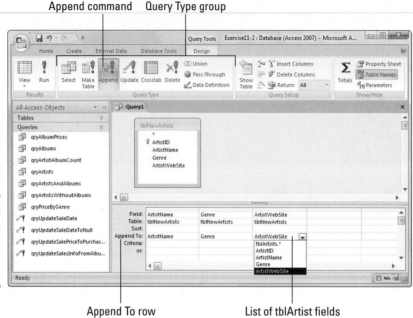

Figure 11-2:
Viewing the append query's design.

Append To row   List of tblArtist fields

The Append To row in the QBE grid contains drop-down lists that include the fields from tblArtists (the destination table you select in the Append dialog box in Step 8). These fields fill in automatically if the field names from the source table and the destination table are the same. If the field names in the Append To row are blank or incorrect, click the arrow in the Append To row and select the correct field name from the drop-down list that appears.

10. Click the Run command in the Results group on the (Query Tools) Design tab.

Access displays a confirmation dialog box telling you that you're about to append three rows and you won't be able to undo the changes.

11. Click Yes in the dialog box.

The dialog box closes, and the append query runs, adding the data behind the scenes.

12. Click the Save button on the Quick Access Toolbar.

The Save As dialog box appears.

13. Type **qryAppendNewArtists** in the Save As dialog box.

14. Click OK.

Access saves the query and changes Query1 on the document tab to qryAppendNewArtists, and the query appears in the Navigation pane with the append query icon (a plus sign with an exclamation) to the left of the name.

15. Double-click tblArtists in the Navigation pane.

The table opens, and the three new records from tblNewArtists appear in tblArtists (shown in Figure 11-3).

tblArtists			
ArtistID ▾	ArtistName ▾	Genre ▾	ArtistWebSite ▾
1	John E. Blue	Pop/Rock	www.dummies.com
2	Christy Aguadilla	Pop/Rock	www.aguadilla.com
3	Gnu Farm	Alternative	
4	Left Sisters	Alternative	
5	The Weedwackers	Country	
6	MC Smoothie	R&B	
7	Precinct 40	Alternative	
8	Farm Gals	Country	
9	Breaker One Nine	R&B	

Figure 11-3: Viewing the results of the append query.

Added records

Appending a Single Record

In addition to adding records from a source table, you can add a single record directly into a table without using a source table. You can even add a parameter to the expression in the field name to prompt for a value.

Exercise 11-3: Appending a Single Record

To add a single record to tblArtists, continue working with the database from Exercise 11-2 or open the `Exercise11-3.accdb` file in the Chapter11 folder, then follow these steps:

1. Click the Query Design command in the Other group on the Create tab.

The query Design view opens, along with the Show Table dialog box.

2. In the Show Table dialog box, click Close.

The Show Table dialog box closes, revealing the query Design view with no tables in the top pane.

3. Click the Append command in the Query Type group on the (Query Tools) Design tab.

The Append dialog box appears (refer to Figure 11-1).

4. In the Append dialog box, click the arrow to the right of Table Name and select tblArtists from the drop-down list that appears.

5. In the Append dialog box, click OK.

The Append dialog box closes, and Access changes the query from a select query to an append query.

6. In the QBE grid (in the lower pane of the query Design view), type **Artist: [Enter the Artist Name]** in the Field row of the first blank column.

This step creates a calculated field named Artist, which prompts you for an artist name when you run the query.

7. In the QBE grid (in the lower pane of the query Design view), click the arrow in the Append To row below the new Artist field and select ArtistName from the drop-down list that appears.

8. In the QBE grid (in the lower pane of the query Design view), type **Genre: "Pop/Rock"** in the Field row of the first blank column to the right of the Artist field.

   This step creates a field named Genre that contains the static value Pop/Rock. Because you're appending this column to a text field in tblArtists, you must surround the data with quotation marks so Access knows you're not appending from a field named Pop/Rock.

9. In the QBE grid (in the lower pane of the query Design view), click the arrow in the Append To row below the new Genre field and select Genre from the drop-down list that appears.

10. Click the Run command in the Results group on the (Query Tools) Design tab.

    The Enter Parameter Value dialog box opens, displaying the words Enter the Artist Name.

11. In the Enter Parameter Value dialog box, type **The Baddest** in the text box.

12. Click OK.

    Access displays a confirmation dialog box telling you that you're about to append one row and you won't be able to undo the changes.

13. Click Yes in the dialog box.

    The dialog box closes, and the append query runs, adding the data behind the scenes.

14. Click the Save button on the Quick Access Toolbar.

    The Save As dialog box appears.

15. Type **qryAppendSingleArtist** in the Save As dialog box.

16. Click OK.

    Access saves the query and changes Query1 on the document tab to qryAppendSingleArtist, and the query appears in the Navigation pane.

17. Double-click tblArtists in the Navigation pane.

    The table opens, and the single new record appears in tblArtists.

Chapter 12

Removing Data with Delete Queries

. . . .

In This Chapter

▶ Deleting all records from a table by using a delete query

▶ Adding criteria to a delete query

. . . .

A *delete query* is a type of action query that removes entire records from a table. Use delete queries when you want to remove one or more rows of data without having to delete them manually from Datasheet view.

Delete queries are a powerful feature, and you should handle them with as much care as you would dynamite; one wrong move, and all your data explodes into nothing.

In this chapter, you can create delete queries by using the query design grid. You can learn how to delete a single record from a table and how to delete all the records from a table.

Creating a Delete Query

When you create a delete query, start by creating a select query to see the data you want to delete. This approach minimizes the chance that you'll make a mistake and delete the wrong data. After you're sure that you're viewing the information you want to delete, you can change the query to a delete query to remove the data.

Always make a backup copy of your database before running any type of action query against the data. For more information on making a backup copy of your database, see Chapter 2.

Exercise 12-1: Creating the Select Query

To create a select query that displays all the records from tblAlbums_Backup (all of which you want to delete), continue working with the database from Exercise 11-3 or open the `Exercise12-1.accdb` file in the Chapter12 folder, then follow these steps:

1. Click the Query Design command in the Other group on the Create tab.

The query Design view opens, along with the Show Table dialog box.

2. Double-click tblAlbums_Backup in the Show Table dialog box.

   The tblAlbums_Backup table appears in the query Design view behind the Show Table dialog box.

3. In the Show Table dialog box, click Close.

   The Show Table dialog box closes, revealing the query Design view.

4. Double-click the asterisk (*) at the top of the field list in tblAlbums_Backup in the top pane of the query Design view.

   The asterisk (which represents all fields in the table) appears in the first column of the QBE grid.

5. Click the Run command in the Results group on the (Query Tools) Design tab.

   The query switches to Datasheet view, displaying all four rows from tblAlbums_Backup. Because you want to delete all the records from this table, you're finished with the select query.

6. Click the Save button on the Quick Access Toolbar.

   The Save As dialog box appears.

7. Type **qryDeleteAlbumsBackup** in the Save As dialog box.

8. Click OK.

   Access saves the query and changes Query1 on the document tab to qryDeleteAlbumsBackup. The query also appears in the Queries group in the Navigation pane.

Exercise 12-2: Changing the Select Query to a Delete Query

To change the query type from a select query to a delete query and remove all the data from tblAlbums_Backup, continue working with the database from Exercise 12-1 or open the Exercise12-2.accdb file in the Chapter12 folder, then follow these steps:

1. Right-click qryDeleteAlbumsBackup in the Navigation pane and choose Design View from the pop-up menu that appears.

   The query opens in Design view.

2. Click the Delete command in the Query Type group on the (Query Tools) Design tab.

   Access changes the query from a select query to a delete query (indicated by the now-highlighted Delete command) and adds the Delete row to the QBE grid in the lower pane of the query Design view (shown in Figure 12-1).

3. Click the Run command in the Results group on the (Query Tools) Design tab.

   Access displays a confirmation dialog box telling you that you're about to delete four rows and you won't be able to undo the changes.

4. Click Yes in the dialog box.

   The dialog box closes, and the delete query runs, deleting the data behind the scenes.

Query Type group   Delete command

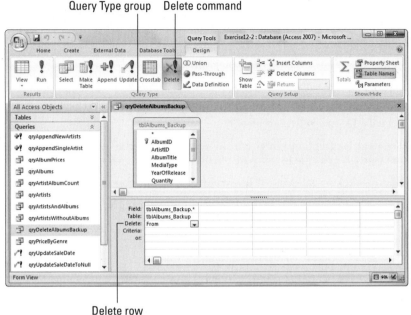

Figure 12-1:
Changing
the query
type to a
delete
query.

Delete row

5. Click the Save button on the Quick Access Toolbar.

   Access saves the query, and the icon to the left of qryDeleteAlbumsBackup in the Navigation pane changes to the delete query icon (a red X with an exclamation point).

6. Double-click tblAlbums_Backup in the Navigation pane.

   The table opens, and all the records are gone.

Deleting with Criteria

When you delete records by using a delete query, you can choose to delete only some of the records. Just like you can add criteria to a select query, you can add criteria to a delete query to delete a subset of data. You might want to delete a specific artist or all of your Country artists. Whatever the case, you can add criteria to limit the number of records you're deleting by using a delete query.

Exercise 12-3: Deleting with Criteria

To create a delete query that removes one record from tblNewArtists, continue working with the database from Exercise 12-2 or open the `Exercise12-3.accdb` file in the Chapter12 folder, then follow these steps:

1. Click the Query Design command in the Other group on the Create tab.

   The query Design view opens, along with the Show Table dialog box.

2. Double-click tblNewArtists in the Show Table dialog box.

   The tblNewArtists table appears in the query Design view behind the Show Table dialog box.

3. In the Show Table dialog box, click Close.

   The Show Table dialog box closes, revealing the query Design view.

4. Double-click the asterisk (*) at the top of the field list in tblNewArtists in the top pane of the query Design view.

   The asterisk (which represents all fields in the table) appears in the first column of the QBE grid (in the lower pane of the query Design view).

5. Double-click ArtistID in tblNewArtists in the top pane of the query Design view.

   ArtistID appears in the second column of the QBE grid (in the lower pane of the query Design view).

6. In the QBE grid (in the lower pane of the query Design view), click in the Criteria row below ArtistID and type **2**.

7. Click the Run command in the Results group on the (Query Tools) Design tab.

   The query switches to Datasheet view, displaying the one record to be deleted (Farm Gals with the ArtistID of 2).

8. Right-click the Query1 document tab and choose Design View from the pop-up menu that appears.

   The query switches to Design view.

9. Click the Delete command in the Query Type group on the (Query Tools) Design tab.

   Access changes the query from a select query to a delete query and adds the Delete row to the QBE grid (in the lower pane of the query Design view). From appears in the Delete row below the asterisk, and Where appears in the Delete row below the ArtistID field because ArtistID has criteria defined (shown in Figure 12-2). When defining criteria for a delete query, set the value in the Delete row to Where for the fields to which you're adding criteria.

Figure 12-2:
Adding
criteria to
a delete
query.

Field:	tblNewArtists.*	ArtistID
Table:	tblNewArtists	tblNewArtists
Delete:	From	Where
Criteria:		2
or:		

10. Click the Run command in the Results group on the (Query Tools) Design tab.

    Access displays a confirmation dialog box telling you that you're about to delete one row and you won't be able to undo the changes.

11. Click Yes in the dialog box.

The dialog box closes, and the delete query runs, deleting the data behind the scenes.

12. Click the Save button on the Quick Access Toolbar.

The Save As dialog box appears.

13. Type **qryDeleteOneNewArtist** in the Save As dialog box.

14. Click OK.

Access saves the query and changes Query1 on the document tab to qryDeleteOneNewArtist.

15. Double-click tblNewArtists in the Navigation pane.

The table opens, and one of the records (the Farm Gals record with the ArtistID of 2) has been deleted from the table.

When you want to delete data from one or more fields in a table, but you don't want to delete the records, you might be tempted to use a delete query. Because delete queries remove an entire record from a table, you should use an update query to clear the contents of the field(s). For more information on using update queries to set the value of a field to null, see Chapter 10.

Chapter 13

Creating Tables with Make Table Queries

● ●

In This Chapter

▶ Using a make table query

▶ Combining data from multiple tables

● ●

A *make table query* is a type of action query that creates a new table based on
selected rows and columns from one or more tables. Make Navigation pane, or
you can archive a subset of your table's data by using these queries.

In this chapter, you can create make table queries that back up your data at the table
level, as well as create entirely new structures based on data from two tables. But put
away your hammer and saw because the tables you're making are in Access.

Creating a Make Table Query

When you create a make table query, start by creating a select query to view the data
you want to put in a new table. After you're sure that you're viewing the information you
want to add to the new table, you can change the query to a make table query.

Always make a backup copy of your database before running any type of action query
against the data. For more information on making a backup copy of your database, see
Chapter 2.

Exercise 13-1: Creating the Select Query

To create a select query to view all the records from tblArtists that you want to put into
a new table, continue working with the database from Exercise 12-3 or open the
`Exercise13-1.accdb` file in the Chapter13 folder, then follow these steps:

1. Click the Query Design command in the Other group on the Create tab.

The query Design view opens, along with the Show Table dialog box.

2. Double-click tblArtists in the Show Table dialog box.

   The tblArtists table appears in the query Design view behind the Show Table dialog box.

3. In the Show Table dialog box, click Close.

   The Show Table dialog box closes, revealing the query Design view.

4. Double-click the asterisk (*) at the top of the field list in tblArtists in the top pane of the query Design view.

   The asterisk (which represents all fields in the table) appears in the first column of the QBE grid.

5. Click the Run command in the Results group on the (Query Tools) Design tab.

   The query switches to Datasheet view, displaying ten rows from tblArtists.

6. Click the Save button on the Quick Access Toolbar.

   The Save As dialog box appears.

7. Type **qryMakeArtistBackup** in the Save As dialog box.

8. Click OK.

   Access saves the query and changes Query1 on the document tab to qryMakeArtistBackup. The query also appears in the Navigation pane in the Queries group.

Exercise 13-2: Changing a Select Query to a Make Table Query

To change the query type from a select query to a make table query, and to copy the data to a new table, continue working with the database from Exercise 13-1 or open the `Exercise13-2.accdb` file in the Chapter13 folder, then follow these steps:

1. Right-click qryMakeArtistBackup in the Navigation pane and choose Design View from the pop-up menu that appears.

   The query opens in Design view.

2. Click the Make Table command in the Query Type group on the (Query Tools) Design tab.

   The Make Table dialog box appears (shown in Figure 13-1).

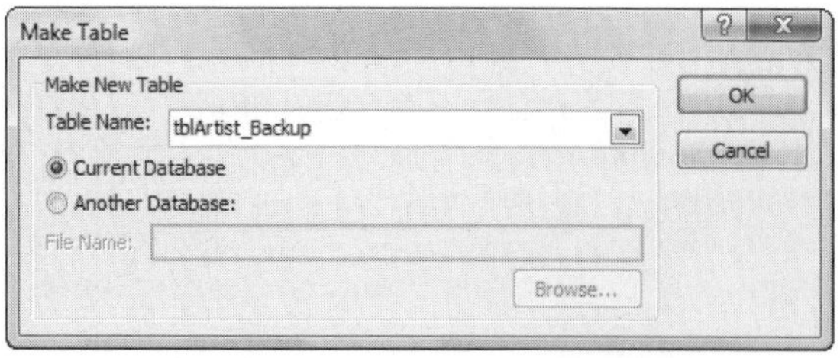

Figure 13-1:
Changing the query type to a make table query.

3. In the Make Table dialog box, type **tblArtist_Backup** in the Table Name combo box.

4. In the Make Table dialog box, click OK.

The Make Table dialog box closes, and Access changes the query from a select query to a make table query (indicated by the now-highlighted Make Table command) but doesn't add any rows to the QBE grid (shown in Figure 13-2).

Make Table command

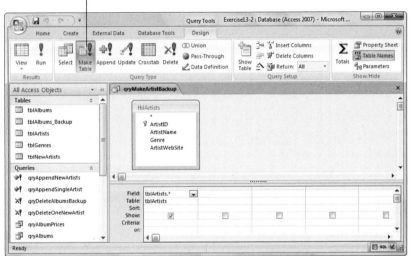

Figure 13-2:
Viewing the make table query's design.

5. Click the Run command in the Results group on the (Query Tools) Design tab.

Access displays a confirmation dialog box telling you that you're about to paste ten rows into a new table and you won't be able to undo the changes.

6. Click Yes in the dialog box.

The dialog box closes, and the make table query runs and creates the table. A new table named tblArtist_Backup appears in the Navigation pane.

7. Click the Save button on the Quick Access Toolbar.

Access saves the query, and the icon to the left of qryMakeArtistBackup in the Navigation pane changes to the make table query icon (a table with an asterisk and an exclamation point).

8. Double-click tblArtist_Backup in the Navigation pane.

The table opens, and all the records from tblArtists have been copied to the new table.

Combining Multiple Tables

In addition to simply creating a backup of an existing table, you can combine two or more tables into a single structure. You can choose the fields you want from each table and even limit the rows you add to the new table by using criteria.

Exercise 13-3: Combining Multiple Tables

To create a new table that combines fields from tblArtists and tblAlbums, continue working with the database from Exercise 13-2 or open the `Exercise13-3.accdb` file in the Chapter13 folder, then follow these steps:

1. Click the Query Design command in the Other group on the Create tab.

The query Design view opens, along with the Show Table dialog box.

2. Double-click tblArtists in the Show Table dialog box.

The tblArtists table appears in the query Design view behind the Show Table dialog box.

3. Double-click tblAlbums in the Show Table dialog box.

The tblAlbums table appears in the query Design view behind the Show Table dialog box to the right of tblArtists.

4. In the Show Table dialog box, click Close.

The Show Table dialog box closes, revealing the query Design view.

5. Double-click ArtistName in tblArtists in the top pane of the query Design view.

ArtistName appears in the first column of the QBE grid (in the lower pane of the query Design view).

6. Double-click AlbumTitle and YearOfRelease in tblAlbums in the top pane of the query Design view.

AlbumTitle and YearOfRelease appear in the second and third columns of the QBE grid (in the lower pane of the query Design view).

7. In the QBE grid (in the lower pane of the query Design view), click in the Criteria row below YearOfRelease and type **2007**.

8. Click the Run command in the Results group on the (Query Tools) Design tab.

The query switches to Datasheet view, displaying the three records from 2007 that you want to copy to a new table.

9. Right-click the Query1 document tab and choose Design View from the pop-up menu that appears.

The query switches to Design view.

10. Click the Make Table command in the Query Type group on the (Query Tools) Design tab.

The Make Table dialog box appears (refer to Figure 13-1).

11. In the Make Table dialog box, type **tblAlbums2007** in the Table Name combo box.

12. In the Make Table dialog box, click OK.

The Make Table dialog box closes, and Access changes the query from a select query to a make table query (indicated by the now-highlighted Make Table command).

13. Click the Run command in the Results group on the (Query Tools) Design tab.

Access displays a confirmation dialog box telling you that you're about to paste three rows into a new table and you won't be able to undo the changes.

14. Click Yes in the dialog box.

The dialog box closes, and the make table query runs and creates the table. A new table named tblAlbums2007 appears in the Navigation pane.

15. Click the Save button on the Quick Access Toolbar.

The Save As dialog box appears.

16. Type **qryMakeAlbums2007** in the Save As dialog box.

17. Click OK.

Access saves the query and changes Query1 on the document tab to qryMakeAlbums2007. The query also appears in the Queries group in the Navigation pane.

18. Double-click tblAlbums2007 in the Navigation pane.

The table opens, and the three fields and three records from tblAlbums and tblArtists have been copied to the new table.

To create a quick archival routine, run a make table query against a table to create a table that contains data you want to archive (such as 2007 sales). Then, run a delete query against the original table with the same criteria as the make table query. This process essentially moves the data from one table to another instead of just copying it.

Part V
Building Forms

The 5th Wave   By Rich Tennant

"Yes, I know how to query information from the program, but what if I just want to leak it instead?"

In this part . . .

Forms let you view and edit data in a more user-friendly method than the row and column format of a datasheet. The chapters and exercises in Part V teach you how to build and use forms in Access. You start by creating a few simple forms to display and edit data and how to add, move, and size controls on a form. Then you learn how to set properties of the controls and the form itself. Finally, you create calculated fields to display information that's not in the database.

Chapter 14

Creating and Using Forms

• •

In This Chapter

▶ Making a new form

▶ Working with records in Form view

▶ Controlling your form's particulars by using the Form Wizard

• •

A *form* is a database object that presents data from a table or query in a structured view that makes data entry easier and more intuitive for the database users. Sure, you can enter and edit data in Datasheet view, but that can get tedious and downright boring. Instead, use forms to jazz up your database and make user-friendly applications.

In this chapter, you can create a new form with which you can view, edit, and add data. You can create forms that you can use to view either one record or multiple records at a time.

Creating a New Form

Just like when you create a new table or query, you start creating a new form by using the Create tab. Creating a new form lets you start from scratch to begin viewing your data in different ways.

Exercise 14-1: Creating a New Form

To create a new form that shows data from tblAlbums, continue working with the database from Exercise 13-3 or open the Exercise14-1.accdb file in the Chapter14 folder, then follow these steps:

1. In the Navigation pane, click tblAlbums.

tblAlbums appears highlighted in the Navigation pane. When you create forms, always select a table in the Navigation pane before you create the form. This table becomes the underlying table for the form. If you don't select a table or query in the Navigation pane, some commands on the Create tab are disabled.

2. Click the Form command in the Forms group on the Create tab (shown in Figure 14-1).

Form command

Create tab   Multiple Items command

Figure 14-1:
Creating a
new form.

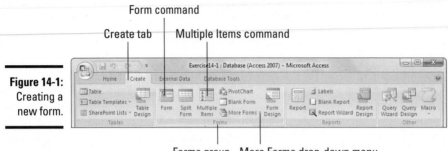

Forms group   More Forms drop-down menu

A new form opens in Layout view. In Layout view, you can make changes to the design of the form while you're viewing data on the form (which Chapter 15 covers).

3. Use one of the following methods to save your form:

• Click the Save button on the Quick Access Toolbar.

• Click the Microsoft Office Button and choose Save from the menu that appears.

• Right-click the tblAlbums tab and choose Save from the pop-up menu that appears.

The Save As dialog box appears.

4. Type **frmAlbums** in the Save As dialog box.

5. Click OK.

Access saves the form and changes tblAlbums on the document tab to frmAlbums. The form also appears in the Forms group in the Navigation pane.

6. Right-click the frmAlbums document tab and choose Close from the pop-up menu that appears.

The form closes.

By placing a prefix (frm) before the form name, you know this object is a form. When you create different database objects, adding a prefix lets you know whether an object is a form (frm), table (tbl), query (qry), report (rpt), or macro (mcr).

Manipulating Data in Form View

One of the main purposes of a form is to view, edit, and add data. Manipulating data in a form has many similarities to manipulating data in Datasheet view. You can change data, navigate between records, and add new records.

Editing data in Form view

Editing data can be less cumbersome in Form view than in a table's Datasheet view. In Form view, you can focus on one record at a time instead of trying to make sense of all those rows and columns, oh my!

Exercise 14-2: Editing Data in Form View

To view and edit data in frmAlbums, continue working with the database from Exercise 14-1 or open the `Exercise14-2.accdb` file in the Chapter14 folder, then follow these steps:

1. Double-click frmAlbums in the Navigation pane.

The form opens in Form view, displaying the first record in the underlying table (shown in Figure 14-2). Form view lets you manipulate data in the form's underlying table or query.

View command

Home tab

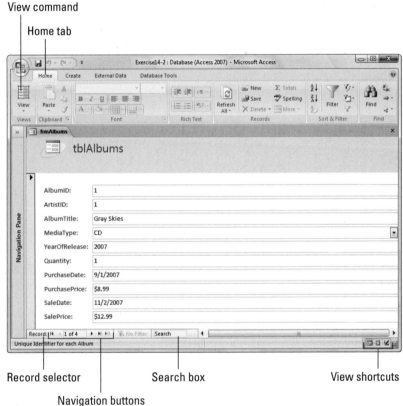

Figure 14-2: Viewing and editing data in Form view.

Record selector   Search box   View shortcuts

Navigation buttons

Many of the objects on the screen (such as the navigation buttons, Record Selector, Search box, and Home tab) work in the same way that they do in Datasheet view.

2. Change the value of AlbumTitle from Gray Skies to **Gray Skies Above**.

When you begin typing, a pencil appears in the Record Selector, replacing the arrow.

3. Change the value of SalePrice from $12.99 to **$14.99**.

4. Right-click the frmAlbums document tab and choose Close from the pop-up menu that appears.

The form closes and doesn't prompt you to save. When you edit data in your database, Access automatically saves the data when you leave the record or close the database object (table, query, or form) that you're using to edit the data.

5. Double-click tblAlbums in the Navigation pane.

The table opens in Datasheet view, displaying the changes you made on the form in Step 2 and Step 3 (to AlbumTitle and SalePrice).

Navigating data in Form view

Similar to navigating records in the table's Datasheet view, Access provides navigation buttons in Form view, which appear at the bottom of the form (refer to Figure 14-2). The navigation buttons allow you to navigate to the first, previous, next, or last record, or to add a new record (shown in Figure 14-3).

Figure 14-3:
Using the
Form view
navigation
buttons.

Current Record

First Record   Last Record   Search box

Next Record   New Record

Next Record

Exercise 14-3: Navigating Data in Form View

To practice navigating records by using the navigation buttons, continue working with the database from Exercise 14-2 or open frmAlbums in the `Exercise14-3.accdb` file in the Chapter14 folder, then practice these actions:

✔ Click the Last Record button.

The Current Record switches to 4 of 4.

✔ Click the Previous Record button.

The Current Record switches to 3 of 4.

✔ Click the First Record button.

The Current Record switches to 1 of 4.

✔ Click the Next Record button.

The Current Record switches to 2 of 4.

You can use the Search box, Find and Replace dialog box, and Spelling command just like you do in a table's Datasheet view. Refer to Chapter 4 to learn how to use these objects in Datasheet view, then apply the same techniques to a form.

Adding records in Form view

Instead of scrolling to the blank row at the bottom of a datasheet, you must navigate to a new record in Form view to add a new record to the database.

Exercise 14-4: Adding Records in Form View

To add a new record by using frmAlbums, continue working with the database from Exercise 14-3 or open the `Exercise14-4.accdb` file in the Chapter14 folder, then follow these steps:

1. Double-click frmAlbums in the Navigation pane.

   The form opens in Form view (refer to Figure 14-2).

2. Click the New (Blank) Record navigation button (refer to Figure 14-3).

   The form navigates to a new record (record 5 of 5) and displays (New) in the AlbumID field (an AutoNumber field).

3. Type **4** in the ArtistID field (the ID of the Left Sisters).

   The AlbumID field changes from (New) to 5 (since it's the fifth record), and a pencil appears in the Record Selector, replacing the arrow.

4. Press Tab.

   The cursor moves to the AlbumTitle field.

5. Enter the following information into the fields on the form:

FieldName	*Value*
AlbumTitle	Left at the Altar
MediaType	Vinyl Record
YearOfRelease	2004
Quantity	1
PurchaseDate	10/1/2007
PurchasePrice	$19.99
SaleDate	<leave blank>
SalePrice	<leave blank>

6. Click Save in the Records group on the Home tab.

   Access saves the record, and the arrow appears in the Record Selector, replacing the pencil.

TIP

To save a record without clicking the Save command, either navigate to a different record or close the form.

Using the Form Wizard

If you want to create a form that doesn't include all the fields from a table, or if you want to have a little more control over how the form looks, you can use the Form Wizard to create a form. The Form Wizard lets you select which fields you want on the form, choose a layout, select a style, and add a title. The Form Wizard takes more time than clicking the Form command, but with the wizard, you're making choices and clicking buttons — and who doesn't love doing that?

ON THE CD

Exercise 14-5: Using the Form Wizard

This exercise uses the Form Wizard to create a new form that displays data from tblArtists. Continue working with the database from Exercise 14-4 or open the `Exercise14-5.accdb` file in the Chapter14 folder, then follow these steps:

1. In the Navigation pane, click tblArtists.

   tblArtists becomes highlighted in the Navigation pane.

2. Click the arrow to the right of More Forms in the Forms group on the Create tab (refer to Figure 14-1), then select Form Wizard from the drop-down list that appears.

   The Form Wizard opens (shown in Figure 14-4). The first page of the wizard lets you select the form's underlying table or query, and you can choose the fields you want to add to the form. Because you selected tblArtists in Step 1, tblArtists appears in the Tables/Queries text box.

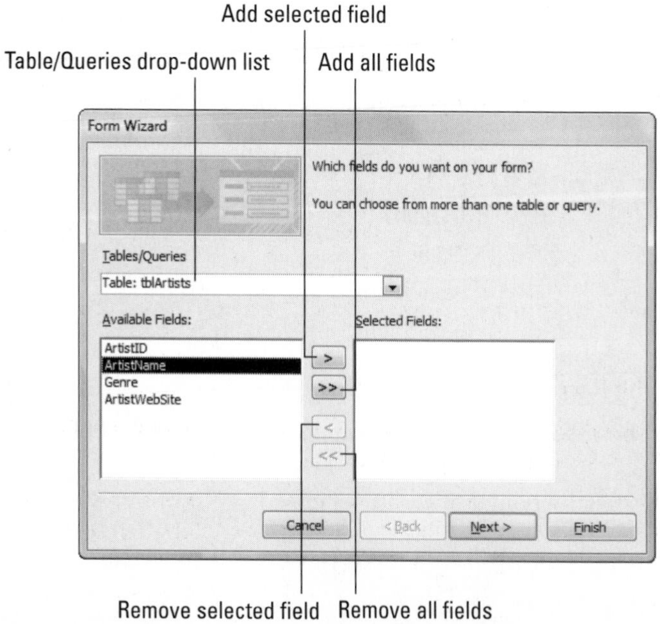

Add selected field

Table/Queries drop-down list   Add all fields

Figure 14-4:
Adding
fields to
your form in
the Form
Wizard.

> Form Wizard
>
> Which fields do you want on your form?
>
> You can choose from more than one table or query.
>
> Tables/Queries
>
> Table: tblArtists
>
> Available Fields: Selected Fields:
>
> ArtistID
> ArtistName
> Genre
> ArtistWebSite
>
> Cancel   < Back   Next >   Finish

Remove selected field   Remove all fields

3. Use one of the following methods to add ArtistName to the Selected Fields list on the form:

    • Click ArtistName in the Available Fields list, then click the Add Selected Field button (>).

    • Double-click ArtistName in the Available Fields list.

    ArtistName disappears from the Available Fields list and appears in the Selected Fields list.

4. Repeat Step 3 to add Genre and ArtistWebSite to the Selected Fields list.

5. Click Next.

    The next page of the wizard appears, asking you to choose a layout. A layout defines how the fields are arranged on the form — in a column, across the page, and so forth. When you click each option, the picture changes to show you a sample of that layout.

6. Select the Columnar layout option button.

7. Click Next.

    The next page of the wizard appears, asking you to choose a style. A style defines the look of the form and changes the colors and fonts. When you click each style in the list, the picture changes to show you a sample of that style.

8. Select the Flow style.

    You'll use the Flow style to apply a consistent look to your forms throughout this book.

9. Click Next.

    The next page of the wizard appears, asking you to choose a title for the form.

10. Type **Artists Form** in the text box for the title of the form.

    The title you enter here becomes the form's name in the Navigation pane, the text on the form's document tab, and as bold white text at the top of the form.

11. Select the Open the Form to View or Enter Information option button in the lower half of the Form Wizard.

12. Click Finish.

    Access creates the form and opens it in Form view, displaying the first record from tblArtists (shown in Figure 14-5). The title from Step 10 appears in the form's document tab, in bold white text at the top of the form, and as the form name in the Navigation Pane.

13. Right-click the Artists Form document tab and choose Close from the pop-up menu that appears.

    The form closes.

14. In the Forms group in the Navigation pane, right-click Artists Form and choose Rename from the pop-up menu that appears.

    The Artists Form text changes into a text box in the Navigation pane and appears highlighted and ready to edit. This is similar to renaming a file in Windows Explorer.

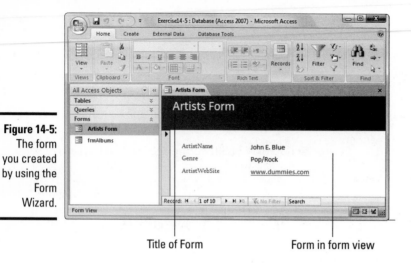

Figure 14-5:
The form
you created
by using the
Form
Wizard.

Title of Form   Form in form view

15. In the Navigation pane, type **frmArtists** in the text box.

16. Press Enter.

Access changes the name of the form to frmArtists.

When you create a form by using the Form Wizard, give the form a user-friendly title on the last page of the wizard, then change the name of the form in the Navigation pane, using the frm prefix. This way, the user doesn't see the prefix (frm) anywhere on the form. If you use the prefix with a descriptive name (such as frmArtists) as the title on the last page of the wizard, then the bold white text and the document tab show the name of the form with the prefix, instead of something more user-friendly (such as Artists Form).

Chapter 15

Basic Form Design

● ●

In This Chapter

▶ Working with a form in three different views

▶ Changing controls in Layout view

● ●

*F*orms are a great tool for entering and editing data. They're also easy to create — just a few button clicks, and you can create multiple forms that display your data in a variety of layouts and styles. But the form Access creates isn't always the form you want. You might want fields in a different order or to be larger or smaller. You're not stuck with what Access builds for you; you can go behind the scenes and change the design to reflect what the voices in your head are telling you it should look like.

In this chapter, you can modify the design of the forms that Access creates for you. You can use Layout view to change different aspects of the controls on your form. You can change the size and location of the controls on the form, and you can add and remove controls.

Switching Between Views on a Form

When you design forms, you routinely switch between three different views. Form view lets you modify data in the form's underlying table, and Design view and Layout view allow you to make design changes to the form. Design view is covered in Chapter 17.

Exercise 15-1: Switching Between Views on a Form

To practice switching between Form view, Layout view, and Design view, continue working with the database from Exercise 14-5 or open the Exercise15-1.accdb file in the Chapter15 folder, then follow these steps:

1. Double-click frmAlbums in the Navigation pane.

The form opens in Form view.

2. Use one of the following methods to switch to Layout view:

   • Click the arrow below View in the Views group on the Home tab, then select Layout View from the drop-down list that appears (shown in Figure 15-1).

   • Right-click the form's document tab and choose Layout View from the pop-up menu that appears.

   • Click the Layout View button in the view shortcuts at the bottom-right of the Access window.

3. Use one of the following methods to switch to Design view:

   • Click the arrow below View in the Views group on the Home tab, then select Design View from the drop-down list that appears (refer to Figure 15-1).

   • Right-click the form's document tab and choose Design View from the pop-up menu that appears.

   • Click the Design View button in the view shortcuts at the bottom-right of the Access window.

4. Use one of the following methods to switch to Form view:

   • Click the arrow below View in the Views group on the Home tab, then select Form View from the drop-down list that appears (refer to Figure 15-1).

   • Right-click the form's document tab and choose Form View from the pop-up menu that appears.

   • Click the Form View button in the view shortcuts at the bottom-right of the Access window.

Using Layout View

Layout view lets you make design changes while looking at the data in the form's under-lying table. Many changes to the form's design consist of manipulating the form's *controls* (objects on the form that display information, let you enter or change information, or perform some other action). Examples of controls include labels, text boxes, combo boxes, images, and buttons.

Sizing and moving controls

After you create a form, either by using the Form Wizard or a command on the Create tab, Access probably doesn't put all the controls exactly where you want them. Luckily, you have the power to resize and move every control on the form.

Exercise 15-2: Changing Control Sizes in Layout View

To change the size of the controls on frmAlbums, continue working with the database from Exercise 15-1 or open the `Exercise15-2.accdb` file in the Chapter15 folder, then follow these steps:

1. Right-click frmAlbums in the Navigation pane and choose Layout View from the pop-up menu that appears.

The form opens in Layout view (shown in Figure 15-2). Layout view contains some of the same elements as Form view (such as navigation buttons and Record Selectors), but Layout view doesn't let you change the data. Instead, clicking a control selects that control instead of placing the cursor inside the control in order to edit data. After you select a control, you can perform actions (such as moving, sizing, and changing other attributes) on that control.

Form Layout Tools contextual tab

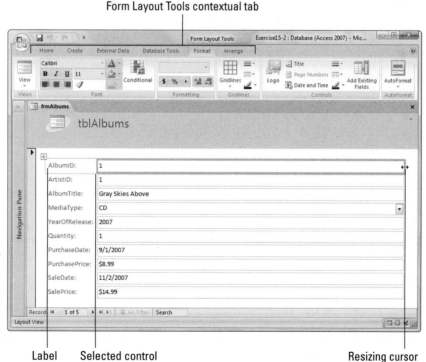

Figure 15-2:
Changing a
form in
Layout view.

Label   Selected control   Resizing cursor

2. Move the cursor to the right edge of the text box that contains the value AlbumID.

   The cursor changes to the resizing cursor, which is a double-headed arrow pointing left and right (refer to Figure 15-2).

3. When the resizing cursor appears, click and drag the right edge of the text box to the left until the text box is about half as wide as it was before.

   All the data controls on the form resize along with the AlbumID text box. When Access creates a form, the controls on the form are grouped together. When controls are grouped, you can make changes to the size and location of all the controls in a group at the same time. Chapter 20 shows you how to group and ungroup controls so you can manipulate them as a group or individually.

4. Move the cursor to the left edge of the text box that contains the value of AlbumID (or the right edge of the AlbumID label).

   The cursor changes to the resizing cursor.

5. When the resizing cursor appears, click and drag the left edge of the text box to the right, just enough to add a little more space between the YearOfRelease label and the text boxes (Access puts the labels and text boxes too close together).

   All of the controls on the form resize along with the AlbumID text box. The text box controls shrink, and the label controls get wider.

When you resize controls in Layout view, use the navigation buttons to look at data from other records and make sure you're not making the controls too small or too large; you want to be like Goldilocks and make them just right.

Exercise 15-3: Moving a Control in Layout View

To move the AlbumTitle control to the top of frmAlbums, continue working with the database from Exercise 15-2 or open the `Exercise15-3.accdb` file in the Chapter15 folder, then follow these steps:

1. Right-click frmAlbums in the Navigation pane and choose Layout View from the pop-up menu that appears.

   The form opens in Layout view (refer to Figure 15-2).

2. Move the cursor over the AlbumTitle text box.

   The cursor changes to the move cursor, which is a four-directional arrow below the standard cursor (shown in Figure 15-3).

3. When the move cursor appears, click and drag the AlbumTitle text box above the AlbumID text box.

   A line appears indicating the new location of the text box.

4. Release the mouse.

   The AlbumTitle text box moves above the AlbumID text box, and the AlbumID and ArtistID text boxes move down.

Selected control   Line of new location   Move cursor

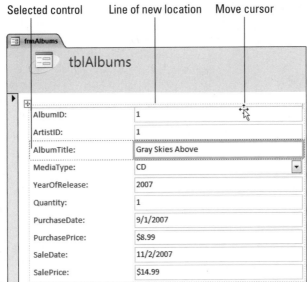

Figure 15-3:
Moving a
control in
Layout view.

To move all the controls in the group together, click the group selector in the top-right corner of the group (refer to Figure 15-3) and drag the group to its new location.

Adding and removing controls

In the process of creating the perfect form, you might find that you forgot to add a control or that Access added controls you don't need. You can add additional fields as controls from the table on which the form is based, or you can choose to add a field as a control from a related table. You can also remove unwanted controls from the form.

Exercise 15-4: Adding an Existing Field in Layout View

To add the ArtistName field to frmAlbums, continue working with the database from Exercise 15-3 or open the `Exercise15-4.accdb` file in the Chapter15 folder, then follow these steps:

1. Right-click frmAlbums in the Navigation pane and choose Layout View from the pop-up menu that appears.

The form opens in Layout view (refer to Figure 15-2).

2. Click the Add Existing Fields command in the Controls group on the (Form Layout Tools) Format tab.

The Field List pane opens (shown in Figure 15-4). The Field List pane usually appears docked on the right side of the Access window; depending on your configuration, the pane might appear undocked as a floating window.

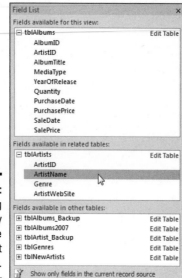

Figure 15-4:
Adding
fields by
using the
Field List
pane.

The Field List pane lets you add fields to your form from the current underlying table or from other tables in the database. You can add fields from any tables, whether those tables have a relationship to the form's underlying table or not.

You create relationships between tables in Chapter 6.

3. Click the plus sign (+) to the left of tblArtists in the middle section of the Field List pane.

   The Field List pane displays the fields in tblArtists.

4. Below tblArtists in the Field List pane, click and drag ArtistName onto the form above the AlbumTitle field.

   A line appears indicating the new location of the text box.

5. Release the mouse.

   Access creates an ArtistName combo box above AlbumTitle, and the other controls on the form move down. The combo box contains John E. Blue, which corresponds to the ArtistID 1.

6. Right-click the frmAlbums document tab and choose Form View from the pop-up menu that appears.

   The form opens in Form view.

7. Click the arrow in the ArtistName combo box.

   The drop-down list that appears includes all the artists from tblArtists. Adding a combo box for the ArtistName lets you select an artist from a list instead of making you remember the ArtistID for each artist.

Exercise 15-5: Deleting a Control in Layout View

Because you add the ArtistName field to the form in Exercise 15-4, you might not want users to see the ArtistID (to them, it's just a number). To delete the ArtistID text box from frmAlbums, continue working with the database from Exercise 15-4 or open the `Exercise15-5.accdb` file in the Chapter15 folder, then follow these steps:

1. Right-click frmAlbums in the Navigation pane and choose Layout View from the pop-up menu that appears.

The form opens in Layout view (refer to Figure 15-2).

2. Click the ArtistID text box.

The ArtistID text box becomes selected.

3. Press Delete.

The ArtistID text box disappears from the form, and the controls below it shift up to fill the empty space.

Formatting controls

Formatting a control refers to changing the font, font size and weight, and colors of the control, as well as how numbers and dates appear. Formatting controls let you make forms that are very pleasing to the eye, but don't get too carried away — your forms can end up looking like they were designed by a preschool student.

You might be tempted to change every color of every control, but don't do it unless you have a really good reason — like actually creating a database for pre-schoolers.

Exercise 15-6: Formatting Fonts and Colors in Layout View

To change fonts and colors on the controls for frmAlbums, continue working with the database from Exercise 15-5 or open the `Exercise15-6.accdb` file in the Chapter15 folder, then follow these steps:

1. Right-click frmAlbums in the Navigation pane and choose Layout View from the pop-up menu that appears.

The form opens in Layout view (refer to Figure 15-2).

2. Click the ArtistName combo box.

The ArtistName combo box becomes selected.

3. Click the Bold command in the Font group on the (Form Layout Tools) Format tab (shown in Figure 15-5).

The text in the ArtistName combo box switches to bold.

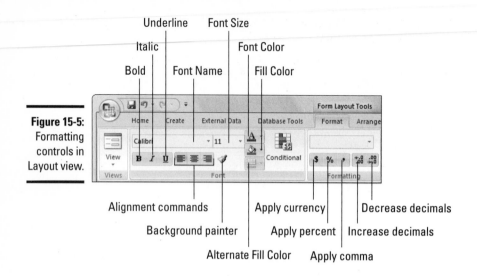

Figure 15-5:
Formatting
controls in
Layout view.

4. Click the AlbumTitle text box.

   The AlbumTitle text box becomes selected.

5. Click the Italic command in the Font group on the (Form Layout Tools) Format tab (refer to Figure 15-5).

   The text in the AlbumTitle text box switches to italic.

6. Click the arrow to the right of Font Color in the Font group on the (Form Layout Tools) Format tab, then select Dark Blue (in the bottom-right of the Standard Colors section) from the drop-down gallery that appears.

   The color of the text in the AlbumTitle text box switches to dark blue.

7. Click the arrow to the right of Font in the Font group on the (Form Layout Tools) Format tab, then select Comic Sans MS from the drop-down list that appears.

   The font in the AlbumTitle text box switches to Comic Sans MS.

Exercise 15-7: Using the Format Painter in Layout View

To copy fonts and colors from one control to other controls on frmAlbums, continue working with the database from Exercise 15-6 or open the `Exercise15-7.accdb` file in the Chapter15 folder, then follow these steps:

1. Right-click frmAlbums in the Navigation pane and choose Layout View from the pop-up menu that appears.

   The form opens in Layout view (refer to Figure 15-2).

2. Click the AlbumTitle text box.

   The AlbumTitle text box becomes selected.

3. Click the Format Painter command in the Font group on the (Form Layout Tools) Format tab (refer to Figure 15-5).

   The cursor changes to an arrow with a paint brush. The Format Painter lets you copy formatting from one area of the form and apply it to another.

4. Click the AlbumID text box.

   The text in the AlbumID text box changes to a blue, italic, Comic Sans MS font, matching the font in the AlbumTitle text box. The AlbumTitle text box remains selected.

5. Double-click the Format Painter command in the Font group on the (Form Layout Tools) Format tab (refer to Figure 15-5).

   The cursor changes to an arrow with a paint brush. Double-clicking the Format Painter command lets you apply the format from the selected control (AlbumTitle) to multiple controls.

6. Click the MediaType combo box and the YearOfRelease, Quantity, PurchaseDate, PurchasePrice, SaleDate, and SalePrice text boxes.

   The text in these controls changes to a blue, italic, Comic Sans MS font, matching the font in the AlbumTitle text box.

7. Click the Format Painter command in the Font group on the (Form Layout Tools) Format tab (refer to Figure 15-5).

   This step turns off the Format Painter, and the cursor changes to the normal cursor.

Exercise 15-8: Formatting Numbers and Dates in Layout View

To change the format of numbers and dates on frmAlbums, continue working with the database from Exercise 15-7 or open the `Exercise15-8.accdb` file in the Chapter15 folder, then follow these steps:

1. Right-click frmAlbums in the Navigation pane and choose Layout View from the pop-up menu that appears.

   The form opens in Layout view (refer to Figure 15-2).

2. Click the PurchaseDate text box.

   The PurchaseDate text box becomes selected.

3. Click the arrow to the right of Format in the Formatting group on the (Form Layout Tools) Format tab, then select Long Date from the drop-down list that appears (refer to Figure 15-5).

   The date in the PurchaseDate text box changes from a Short Date (9/1/2007) to a Long Date (Saturday, September 01, 2007).

4. Click the PurchasePrice text box.

   The PurchasePrice text box becomes selected.

5. Click the Increase Decimals command in the Formatting group on the (Form Layout Tools) Format tab twice.

The number in the PurchasePrice text box changes from two decimal places ($8.99) to four decimal places ($8.9900).

Changing label text

In addition to changing the fonts, colors, formatting, size, and location of the controls in Layout view, you can also change the text that appears on the form. No, you can't change the data that appears in the text boxes and combo boxes, but you can change the text in the labels to the left of those boxes, as well as the label at the top of the form.

Exercise 15-9: Changing Label Text in Layout View

To change the text of a label on frmAlbums, continue working with the database from Exercise 15-8 or open the `Exercise15-9.accdb` file in the Chapter15 folder, then follow these steps:

1. Right-click frmAlbums in the Navigation pane and choose Layout View from the pop-up menu that appears.

The form opens in Layout view (refer to Figure 15-2).

2. Click the text (tblAlbums) on the top of the form above the ArtistName text box.

The tblAlbums label becomes selected.

3. Click the label again.

The label switches to a control that you can edit. This process is similar to selecting a cell in Excel and clicking the cell again to edit the text in the cell.

4. Type **Albums Form** in the label (replacing tblAlbums).

5. Press Enter.

Access applies the changes to the label.

6. Follow Steps 2 through 5 to add spaces to the text on the labels to the left of each control on the form as follows:

Old Label Text	New Label Text
ArtistName:	Artist Name:
AlbumTitle:	Album Title:
AlbumID:	Album ID:
MediaType:	Media Type:
YearOfRelease:	Year Of Release:
PurchaseDate:	Purchase Date:
PurchasePrice:	Purchase Price:
SaleDate:	Sale Date:
SalePrice:	Sale Price:

Chapter 16

Changing Control Properties

• •

In This Chapter

▶ Working with the Property Sheet

▶ Making changes to a single control's properties

▶ Changing the properties of multiple controls at the same time

▶ Getting answers to your property questions

• •

A *property* is a setting that controls a particular attribute about an object. Properties can determine many characteristics of the object, such as how the content appears in the object and whether you can edit data in the object.

In this chapter, you can change properties of a form's controls. You can learn about the Property Sheet and how to change the properties of one or more controls. You can also find out where you can get help on a property — after all, this book can't cover every single property of every single control.

Using the Property Sheet

The *Property Sheet* is a window in which you can change the properties of objects in Access. You use the Property Sheet to view and change the properties of one or more controls on a form, or the properties of the form itself. Each control has its own set of properties that you can manipulate by using the Property Sheet.

Exercise 16-1: Displaying and Navigating the Property Sheet

To display and navigate the Property Sheet, continue working with the database from Exercise 15-9 or open the `Exercise16-1.accdb` file in the Chapter16 folder, then follow these steps:

1. Right-click frmAlbums in the Navigation pane and choose Layout View from the pop-up menu that appears.

The form opens in Layout view.

2. Click the Property Sheet command in the Tools group on the (Form Layout Tools) Arrange tab.

The Property Sheet window appears, displaying the properties for the selected control (shown in Figure 16-1). If the Field list window is open, the Property Sheet window replaces the Field List window on the screen (both windows can't be open at the same time).

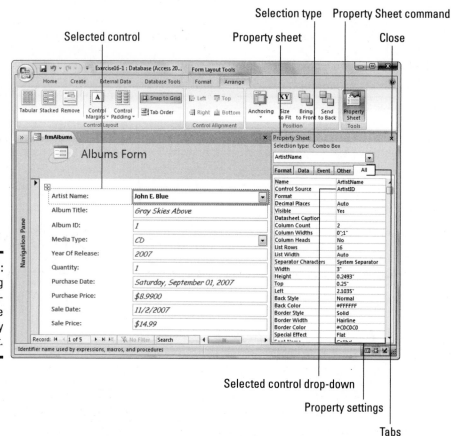

Figure 16-1: Displaying and navigating the Property Sheet.

3. Click the following tabs on the Property Sheet to view the available properties:

- **Format:** This tab displays the properties related to formatting the object, such as changing fonts and colors.

- **Data:** This tab displays the properties related to displaying data (such as which field from the database to display) and validating the data.

- **Event:** This tab displays the event properties of the object, which allows you to run procedures when you click or change the contents of a control. You can find more about events in Part VIII of this book.

- **Other:** This tab displays the properties that don't fit into the other categories, such as the name of the object and text on the controls tool tip and Status bar.

- **All:** This tab displays all the properties. Use this tab if you're not sure which tab has the property you're looking for.

4. (Optional) Use one of the following methods to close the Property Sheet:

   - Click the Close button in the top-right corner of the Property Sheet.

   - Click the Property Sheet command in the Tools group on the (Form Layout Tools) Arrange tab. This command toggles the Property Sheet on and off.

The Property Sheet usually appears docked on the right side of the Access window. You can undock the Property Sheet by clicking the title bar and dragging the window away from the right side of the screen. To re-dock the Property Sheet, drag it back to the right side of the Access window.

Exercise 16-2: Selecting Controls on a Form

To select different controls on frmAlbums, continue working with the database from Exercise 16-1 or open the `Exercise16-2.accdb` file in the Chapter16 folder, then follow these steps:

1. Right-click frmAlbums in the Navigation pane and choose Layout View from the pop-up menu that appears.

   The form opens in Layout view with the ArtistName combo box selected.

2. If the Property Sheet isn't displayed, click the Property Sheet command in the Tools group on the (Form Layout Tools) Arrange tab.

   The Property Sheet window appears (refer to Figure 16-1).

3. Use one of the following methods to select the AlbumTitle text box:

   - Click the AlbumTitle text box.

   - Click the arrow to the right of the Selected Control drop-down on the Property Sheet and select AlbumTitle from the drop-down list that appears.

   The Property Sheet displays the properties for the AlbumTitle text box.

4. Hold the Shift key and click the AlbumID text box.

   Both the AlbumTitle and AlbumID text boxes become selected, and the Property Sheet displays the common properties for both text boxes, along with Multiple Selection for the selection type (above the Selected Control drop-down which becomes blank). When you select multiple controls on a form, any properties that have the same setting display that setting; if the controls have different property settings, the property appears blank.

5. Hold the Shift key and click the AlbumID text box again.

   The AlbumID text box becomes deselected, and the Property Sheet displays only the properties for the AlbumTitle text box. Clicking a selected control while holding the Shift key deselects that control.

Unlike Windows Explorer and Excel, Access uses the Shift key to select multiple controls on a form. If you're used to using the Ctrl key to select multiple files in Windows Explorer or multiple cells in Excel, you have to un-train yourself and use Shift to select controls on an Access form.

Changing Single Control Properties

When you use the commands on the Ribbon to manipulate controls, you're simply changing the controls' properties. The Ribbon gives you access to some common properties, such as fonts and colors, but to change other characteristics of the controls, you must use the Property Sheet.

Exercise 16-3: Changing the Caption Property of a Label

The Caption property of a label sets the text that appears in the label. To change the Caption property of a label on frmAlbums, continue working with the database from Exercise 16-2 or open the `Exercise16-3.accdb` file in the Chapter16 folder, then follow these steps:

1. **Right-click frmAlbums in the Navigation pane and choose Layout View from the pop-up menu that appears.**

   The form opens in Layout view.

2. **If the Property Sheet isn't displayed, click the Property Sheet command in the Tools group on the (Form Layout Tools) Arrange tab.**

   The Property Sheet window appears.

3. **Click the Albums Form label at the top of the form.**

   The Property Sheet displays the properties for the label named Auto_Title0 (shown in Figure 16-2).

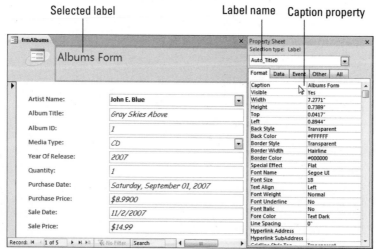

Figure 16-2: Changing a label's Caption property.

4. In the Property Sheet, click the Format tab.

   The Property Sheet displays the format properties.

5. In the Caption property, highlight the Albums Form text.

6. Press Delete.

   The Albums Form text disappears.

7. In the Caption property, type **Albums**.

8. Press Enter.

   The text in the label at the top of the form changes to Albums.

When you change properties in the Property Sheet, the new setting doesn't take effect until you press Enter or click another property.

Exercise 16-4: Formatting Numbers and Dates

To change the format of numbers and dates on frmAlbums, continue working with the database from Exercise 16-3 or open the `Exercise16-4.accdb` file in the Chapter16 folder, then follow these steps:

1. Right-click frmAlbums in the Navigation pane and choose Layout View from the pop-up menu that appears.

   The form opens in Layout view.

2. If the Property Sheet isn't displayed, click the Property Sheet command in the Tools group on the (Form Layout Tools) Arrange tab.

   The Property Sheet window appears.

3. Click the SaleDate text box.

   The Property Sheet displays the properties for the SaleDate text box.

4. In the Property Sheet, click the Format tab.

   The Property Sheet displays the format properties.

5. Change the Format property to Long Date using the drop-down list for this property.

   The date in the SaleDate text box changes from a Short Date (11/2/2007) to a Long Date (Friday, November 02, 2007).

6. Click the SalePrice text box.

   The Property Sheet displays the properties for the SalePrice text box.

7. Change the Decimal Places property from 2 to **4**.

   The number in the SalePrice text box changes from two decimal places ($14.99) to four decimal places ($14.9900).

Changing number and date formats in Exercise 16-4 gives you the same results as using the Ribbon in Exercise 15-8.

Changing Multiple Control Properties

If you're going to change the properties of more than one control to the same value, you can change them by selecting all the controls you want to change and changing their properties on the Property Sheet. This approach is much more efficient than changing the properties of each control individually.

Exercise 16-5: Changing Multiple Control Properties

To change the properties of multiple controls on frmAlbums, continue working with the database from Exercise 16-4 or open the `Exercise16-5.accdb` file in the Chapter16 folder, then follow these steps:

1. Right-click frmAlbums in the Navigation pane and choose Layout View from the pop-up menu that appears.

The form opens in Layout view.

2. If the Property Sheet isn't displayed, click the Property Sheet command in the Tools group on the (Form Layout Tools) Arrange tab.

The Property Sheet window appears.

3. Hold the Shift key and click the following controls:

ArtistName combo box	Quantity text box
AlbumTitle text box	PurchaseDate text box
AlbumID text box	PurchasePrice text box
MediaType combo box	SaleDate text box
YearOfRelease text box	SalePrice text box

The controls become selected, and the Property Sheet displays the common properties for all the selected controls.

4. In the Property Sheet, click the Format tab.

The Property Sheet displays the format properties.

5. Change the following properties in the Property Sheet:

Property Name	*New Setting*
Font Name	Calibri
Font Size	11
Font Weight	Bold
Font Underline	No
Font Italic	No
Font Color	Text Black

The text in the selected controls changes to match the property settings.

Getting Help on Properties

Many properties appear on the Property Sheet, and it's not always clear what each property does. You might find yourself changing property settings and then trying to figure out what exactly changes because not all properties affect something you can see. This book doesn't have enough pages to define every property for each and every object, so you need to know how to get help in figuring out the effects of changing a certain property.

Exercise 16-6: Getting Help on Properties

To view the help file for a property, continue working with the database from Exercise 16-5 or open the `Exercise16-6.accdb` file in the Chapter16 folder, then follow these steps:

1. Right-click frmAlbums in the Navigation pane and choose Layout View from the pop-up menu that appears.

The form opens in Layout view.

2. If the Property Sheet isn't displayed, click the Property Sheet command in the Tools group on the (Form Layout Tools) Arrange tab.

The Property Sheet window appears.

3. Click the ArtistName combo box.

The Property Sheet displays the properties for the ArtistName combo box.

4. In the Property Sheet, click the Format tab.

The Property Sheet displays the format properties.

5. In the Property Sheet, click the Format property.

6. Press F1.

The Access Help window appears, giving you two hyperlink suggestions: ComboBox.Format Property and TextBox.Format Property. Because the Format property exists for each of these types of controls, the Help window displays all the controls that have a Format property (text boxes and combo boxes).

7. In the Access Help window, click TextBox.Format Property.

The Access Help window displays the help for the Format property (shown in Figure 16-3). In this window, you can read the purpose of the Format property and any additional remarks on the property. The Help entry for the Format property includes additional hyperlinks that show you different ways to format Date/Time Data Types, Number and Currency Data Types, Text and Memo Data Types, and Yes/No Data Types by using the predefined format settings or creating custom formats.

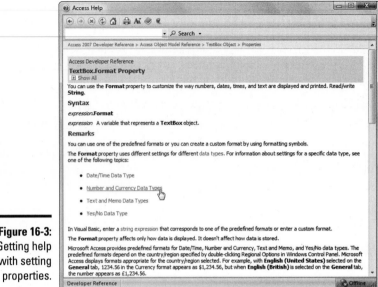

Figure 16-3:
Getting help
with setting
properties.

Chapter 17

Changing Form Properties

. . . .

In This Chapter

▶ Adjusting your form's appearance in Design view

▶ Changing how your form operates

▶ Making different views available to users

▶ Creating a pop-up form

. . . .

*J*ust like each control on a form has properties, the form itself has its own set of properties. By changing properties of the form, you control how the form looks and operates, and what data you're allowed to modify.

In this chapter, you can change the necessary form properties to prohibit users from using a particular view and limit the data that users can add, edit, and delete. You also can learn how to show and hide different elements of the form, depending on what you want to display.

Using Design View

Although you can use Layout view to make most kinds of changes to a form, Design view gives you a more detailed view of the structure of your form. You can perform most design changes in either Design view or Layout view, but certain tasks are easier to perform in Design view, such as

- ✔ Adding additional controls, such as labels, images, lines, and rectangles
- ✔ Editing text box and combo box control sources directly in the control, without using the Property Sheet
- ✔ Resizing the form sections, such as the Form Header and Detail sections

You can also change some form properties in Design view that you can't alter in Layout view.

ON THE CD

Exercise 17-1: Selecting the Form

To select the form as the object on which you want to change properties, continue working with the database from Exercise 16-6 or open the `Exercise17-1.accdb` file in the Chapter17 folder, then follow these steps:

1. Right-click frmAlbums in the Navigation pane and choose Design View from the pop-up menu that appears.

The form opens in Design view (shown in Figure 17-1).

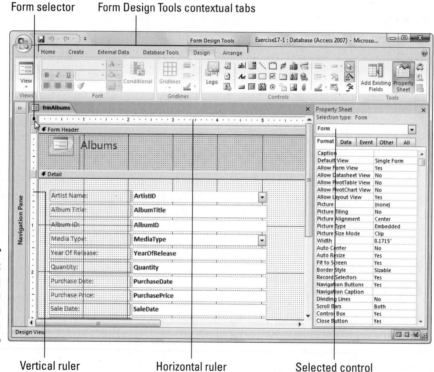

2. If the Property Sheet isn't displayed, click the Property Sheet command in the Tools group on the (Form Design Tools) Design tab.

The Property Sheet window appears.

3. Use one of the following methods to select the form:

- Click the Form Selector in the top-left corner of the form's Design view (where the horizontal and vertical rulers meet).

- Click the arrow on the right of the Selected Control drop-down on the Property Sheet and select Form from the drop-down list that appears.

- Click the gray area below the Form Footer section at the bottom of the form's Design view. (You might have to scroll down to see this area.)

The Property Sheet displays the properties of the form.

Changing the form's caption

The value in the Caption property of the form appears in the form's document tab in both Form view and Layout view. If the Caption property setting is blank, the document tab displays the name of the form.

Exercise 17-2: Changing the Form's Caption Property

To change the Caption property of frmAlbums, either use the database from Exercise 17-1 or open the `Exercise17-2.accdb` file in the Chapter17 folder, then follow these steps:

1. Right-click frmAlbums in the Navigation pane and choose Design View from the pop-up menu that appears.

The form opens in Design view (refer to Figure 17-1).

2. If the Property Sheet isn't displayed, click the Property Sheet command in the Tools group on the (Form Design Tools) Design tab.

The Property Sheet window appears.

3. Select the form (refer to Exercise 17-1).

4. In the Property Sheet, click the Format tab.

The Property Sheet displays the format properties for the form.

5. Change the Caption property to **Albums Form**.

6. Press Enter.

Access accepts the change to the Caption property.

7. Right-click the form's document tab and choose Form View from the pop-up menu that appears.

The form switches to Form view, with the document tab displaying Albums Form as the new caption (shown in Figure 17-2).

Figure 17-2:
Viewing the caption in Form view.

The form's caption appears in all other form views except Design view. In Design view, the document tab always shows the name of the form.

Showing and hiding form elements

You might want to omit certain form elements (such as the Record Selector and navigation buttons shown in Figure 17-2) from your form. To get rid of these elements (or bring them back), change the Record Selectors and Navigation Buttons properties on the form.

Exercise 17-3: Showing and Hiding Form Elements

To remove the Record Selector and navigation buttons from frmAlbums, continue working with the database from Exercise 17-2 or open the Exercise17-3.accdb file in the Chapter17 folder, then follow these steps:

1. Right-click frmAlbums in the Navigation pane and choose Design View from the pop-up menu that appears.

   The form opens in Design view (refer to Figure 17-1).

2. If the Property Sheet isn't displayed, click the Property Sheet command in the Tools group on the (Form Design Tools) Design tab.

   The Property Sheet window appears.

3. Select the form (refer to Exercise 17-1).

4. In the Property Sheet, click the Format tab.

   The Property Sheet displays the format properties for the form.

5. Change the Record Selectors property to No.

6. Change the Navigation Buttons property to No.

7. Right-click the form's document tab and choose Form View from the pop-up menu that appears.

   The form switches to Form view, displaying frmAlbums without the Record Selector and navigation buttons.

8. Right-click the form's document tab and choose Design View from the pop-up menu that appears.

   The form switches to Design view.

9. In the Property Sheet, change the Navigation Buttons property back to Yes.

   For this form, the navigation buttons let you move between records, so you want to keep them on the form.

You can also use the Scroll Bars, Control Box, Close Button, and Min Max Buttons properties to show and hide additional elements on the form. For more information on these properties and what they control, select a property on the Property Sheet and press F1 to open Access Help.

Changing Data Entry Properties

In addition to changing how the elements of the form appear, you can change the operation of the form. With a few property settings, you can control whether or not users can add, edit, or delete data on the form. You can even remove the filtering capabilities from the form if you don't want users to drill-down into the information being displayed.

Exercise 17-4: Changing Data Entry Properties

To prevent users from editing and filtering data on frmAlbums, you need to change the data entry properties. To make these changes, continue working with the database from Exercise 17-3 or open the `Exercise17-4.accdb` file in the Chapter17 folder, then follow these steps:

1. Right-click frmAlbums in the Navigation pane and choose Design View from the pop-up menu that appears.

The form opens in Design view (refer to Figure 17-1).

2. If the Property Sheet isn't displayed, click the Property Sheet command in the Tools group on the (Form Design Tools) Design tab.

The Property Sheet window appears.

3. Select the form (refer to Exercise 17-1).

4. In the Property Sheet, click the Data tab.

The Property Sheet displays the data properties for the form.

5. Change the following properties in the Property Sheet:

Property Name	*New Setting*
Allow Additions	No
Allow Deletions	No
Allow Edits	No
Allow Filters	No

6. Right-click the form's document tab and choose Form View from the pop-up menu that appears.

The form switches to Form view.

7. Try to perform the following operations in Form view:

- Click the New button in the navigation buttons at the bottom of the form.

  Nothing happens because setting the Allow Additions property to No prevents you from moving to a new record.

- Click the arrow to the right of Delete in the Records group on the Home tab, then select Delete Record from the drop-down list that appears.

  You can't delete a record because setting the Allow Deletions property to No prevents it.

- Click in any text box or combo box on the form and try editing data.

  Access doesn't let you! Setting the Allow Edits property to No prevents you from changing data on the form.

- Click any of the filtering commands in the Sort & Filter group on the Home tab.

  The buttons aren't available. Setting the Allow Filters property to No prevents you from filtering the data on the form — however, you can still sort the data by using the Sort Ascending and Sort Descending commands.

8. Change each property that you changed to No in Step 5 back to Yes, then repeat Step 6 and Step 7 to see the effect of changing each property setting.

Allowing Different Views

You can view each form in different views, such as Form view, Design view, and Layout view. You can make additional views (Datasheet view, PivotTable view, and PivotChart view) available to users, depending on the data displayed on the form.

Exercise 17-5: Allowing Different Views

To allow different views on frmAlbums, continue working with the database from Exercise 17-4 or open the `Exercise17-5.accdb` file in the Chapter17 folder, then follow these steps:

1. Right-click frmAlbums in the Navigation pane and choose Design View from the pop-up menu that appears.

  The form opens in Design view (refer to Figure 17-1).

2. If the Property Sheet isn't displayed, click the Property Sheet command in the Tools group on the (Form Design Tools) Design tab.

  The Property Sheet window appears.

3. Select the form (refer to Exercise 17-1).

4. In the Property Sheet, click the Format tab.

  The Property Sheet displays the format properties for the form.

5. Change or verify the following properties in the Property Sheet:

Property Name	New Setting
Allow Form View	Yes
Allow Datasheet View	Yes
Allow PivotTable View	No
Allow PivotChart View	No
Allow Layout View	No

6. Right-click the form's document tab and choose Datasheet View from the pop-up menu that appears.

   The form switches to Datasheet view. A form's Datasheet view lets you view the form's data in a row and column format, similar to Datasheet view of a table or query. Before you changed settings in Step 5, Datasheet view wasn't available on the pop-up menu.

7. Right-click the form's document tab and choose Form View from the pop-up menu that appears.

   The form switches to Form view.

8. Right-click the form's document tab and choose Design View from the pop-up menu that appears.

   The form switches to Design view.

9. Change the form's Allow Layout View property back to Yes.

10. Right-click the form's document tab and choose Layout View (which is now available) from the pop-up menu that appears.

    The form switches to Layout view.

The form has no Allow Design View property. Without Design view, you wouldn't be able to allow or not allow the additional views.

Exercise 17-6: Changing the Default View

A form opens in its default view when you double-click the form in the Navigation pane. To set the default view for frmAlbums, continue working with the database from Exercise 17-5 or open the `Exercise17-6.accdb` file in the Chapter17 folder, then follow these steps:

1. Double-click frmAlbums in the Navigation pane.

   The form opens in Form view.

2. Right-click the form's document tab and choose Design View from the pop-up menu that appears.

   The form switches to Design view.

3. If the Property Sheet isn't displayed, click the Property Sheet command in the Tools group on the (Form Design Tools) Design tab.

   The Property Sheet window appears.

4. Select the form (refer to Exercise 17-1).

5. In the Property Sheet, click the Format tab.

   The Property Sheet displays the Format properties for the form.

6. Change the Default View property to Datasheet.

7. Click the Save button on the Quick Access Toolbar.

   Access saves the design changes to the form.

8. Right-click the form's document tab and choose Close from the pop-up menu that appears.

   The form closes.

9. Double-click frmAlbums in the Navigation pane.

   The form opens in Datasheet view with the new value in the Default View property.

10. Right-click the form's document tab and choose Design View from the pop-up menu that appears.

    The form switches to Design view.

11. Change the Default View property back to Single Form.

Creating a Modal Pop-Up Form

Many times when you run an application, you want to work with a form without that form showing up as a document tab in the Access window. Instead, you want this form to show up on top of the other form(s), and you might not want to allow users to switch between forms until they close the pop-up form. You can create this type of pop-up form by changing the Modal and Pop Up properties on the form.

Exercise 17-7: Creating a Modal Pop-Up Form

To turn frmArtists into a pop-up form that the user must close before he or she can use another database object, continue working with the database from Exercise 17-6 or open the `Exercise17-7.accdb` file in the Chapter17 folder, then follow these steps:

1. Double-click frmArtists in the Navigation pane.

   The form opens in Form view, displaying Artists Form in the document tab.

2. Right-click the form's document tab and choose Design View from the pop-up menu that appears.

   The form switches to Design view.

3. If the Property Sheet isn't displayed, click the Property Sheet command in the Tools group on the (Form Design Tools) Design tab.

   The Property Sheet window appears.

4. Select the form (refer to Exercise 17-1).

5. In the Property Sheet, click the Other tab.

   The Property Sheet displays the Other properties.

6. Change the Pop Up property to Yes.

7. Change the Modal property to Yes.

8. Right-click the form's document tab and choose Form View from the pop-up menu that appears.

The form switches to Form view and appears on top of the Access window (shown in Figure 17-3) rather than inside the window with a document tab. (This form appears as a separate window because you set the Pop Up property to Yes in Step 6.) You also can't perform any other operations in Access (clicking the Ribbon or opening another form by using the Navigation pane) until you close frmArtists (because you set the Modal property to Yes in Step 7).

Figure 17-3: Viewing a modal pop-up form.

9. On Artists Form, click the Close button in the top-right corner of the window.

A dialog box appears, asking if you want to save changes to frmArtists.

10. In the dialog box, click Yes.

Access saves the changes to frmArtists and closes the form.

You can set the Pop Up and Modal properties independent of each other, so you can create a pop-up form that lets you perform other operations or a modal form that appears with a document tab but doesn't let you perform other operations until you close that tab.

Chapter 18

Creating Calculated Controls

· ·

In This Chapter

▶ Determining a control's value with the Control Source property

▶ Using Access's built-in functions

· ·

*W*hen you build forms, you can easily add a control that displays data from one of the tables; you simply drag a field from the field list onto the form (see Chapter 15). But sometimes, you want to display a calculated field that isn't stored in the database. By using calculated controls, you can display these values.

In this chapter, you can create calculated controls that show mathematical calculations between fields, as well as concatenate text fields. You also can add controls that show information and totals by using some built-in functions.

Changing the Control Source

The Control Source property of a control usually determines which field's data appears in the control. For example, if you have a field's Control Source property set to AlbumTitle, that field displays the AlbumTitle field from the form's underlying table. You can also use the Control Source property to create calculated controls by setting the property to a valid expression.

Exercise 18-1: Adding a Text Box to Display a Mathematical Calculation

To display the difference between the Sale Price and Purchase Price in frmAlbums, you can add a text box. Continue working with the database from Exercise 17-7 or open the `Exercise18-1.accdb` file in the Chapter18 folder, then follow these steps:

1. Right-click frmAlbums in the Navigation pane and choose Design View from the pop-up menu that appears.

The form opens in Design view.

2. Click the Text Box command in the Controls group on the (Form Design Tools) Design tab (shown in Figure 18-1).

The cursor changes to a crosshair with the Text Box icon in the lower-right. The Controls group lets you add controls (such as combo boxes, labels, images, and check boxes) to the form. The text box is the most common choice for displaying a calculated value because you can set the Control Source to display a variety of information.

Form Design Tools contextual tabs   Controls group

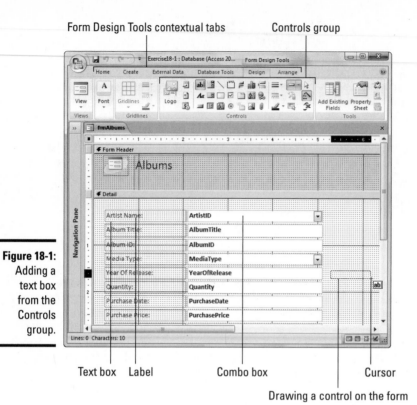

Figure 18-1:
Adding a
text box
from the
Controls
group.

Text box   Label   Combo box   Cursor

Drawing a control on the form

3. On a blank area of the form, draw a rectangle by clicking and dragging the mouse diagonally across the form (refer to Figure 18-1).

Access creates a text box on the form the same size as the rectangle you draw. The text box contains the word Unbound, indicating it doesn't display a field from the form's underlying table. Access also creates a label to the left of the text box. The label's caption is set to Text followed by a number (such as Text25:). The cursor changes from the Text Box cursor to the standard cursor.

4. Place the standard cursor over the edge of the text box until the cursor changes to the move cursor (the standard arrow cursor with a crosshair with an arrow on each end).

5. Click and drag the cursor below the SalePrice text box, until you see a line indicating to where the text box will move to (shown in Figure 18-2).

6. Release the mouse button.

Access moves the text box, resizes the text box and the label to match the other controls in the group, and aligns them with the other controls in the group.

7. Click the label to the left of the new text box.

The label becomes selected.

8. Click the label again.

The label switches to an editable control.

9. Type **Profit:** in the label (replacing the existing text).

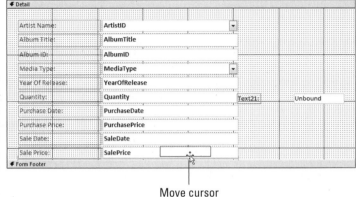

Figure 18-2:
Dragging a
text box to
the group of
controls.

Move cursor

10. Press Enter.

Access applies the changes to the label.

11. If the Property Sheet isn't displayed, click the Property Sheet command in the Tools group on the (Form Design Tools) Design tab.

The Property Sheet window appears.

12. Click the new text box.

The text box becomes selected.

13. In the Property Sheet, click the All tab.

The Property Sheet displays all the properties for the new text box.

14. Change the Name property from the name Access assigned (such as Text25) to **Profit** and press Enter.

15. Change the Control Source property from blank to **=[SalePrice]-[PurchasePrice]** and press Enter.

The text inside the new text box changes to the value of the Control Source property. Starting the expression with an equal sign (=) indicates this is a calculated field. The value that's displayed in the calculated field is the value in the SalePrice field minus the value in the PurchasePrice field.

16. Change the Format property to Currency.

17. Right-click the form's document tab and choose Form View from the pop-up menu that appears.

The form switches to Form view and displays the new text box, which shows the difference between the Sale Price and Purchase Price.

In Design view, combo boxes and text boxes show the value of the Control Source property in the combo/text box itself. You can edit this text directly in the combo/text box instead of changing it on the Property Sheet.

Exercise 18-2: Concatenating Text Fields into One Text Box

To add a single text box to the top of frmAlbums that displays the year of release followed by the album title, continue working with the database from Exercise 18-1 or open the `Exercise18-2.accdb` file in the Chapter18 folder, then follow these steps:

1. Right-click frmAlbums in the Navigation pane and choose Design View from the pop-up menu that appears.

   The form opens in Design view.

2. Click the Text Box command in the Controls group on the (Form Design Tools) Design tab (refer to Figure 18-1).

   The cursor changes to a crosshair with the Text Box icon in the lower-right.

3. On a blank area of the form header to the right of the Albums label, draw a rectangle.

   Access creates a text box on the form the same size as the rectangle you draw. Access also creates a label to the left of the text box. The label's caption is set to Text followed by a number (such as Text27:).

4. Click the label to the left of the new text box.

   The label becomes selected.

5. Press Delete.

   The label disappears.

6. Click the new text box.

   The text box becomes selected.

7. Click the new text box again.

   The text box switches to an editable control.

8. Type =[YearOfRelease] & " - " & [AlbumTitle] in the text box.

9. Press Enter.

   Access accepts the new value for the Control Source property.

10. In the form header, click the Albums label.

    The label becomes selected.

11. Click the Format Painter command (the command that looks like a paint brush) in the Font group on the (Form Design Tools) Design tab.

    The cursor changes to an arrow with a paint brush. The Format Painter lets you copy formatting from one place and apply it to another.

12. Click the new text box.

    The format of the text (font, color, size) in the new text box changes to match the format of the text in the Albums label.

13. Click and drag the new text box to the right of the word Albums.

14. Right-click the form's document tab and choose Form View from the pop-up menu that appears.

    The form switches to Form view and displays the new text box, which shows the year of release and the album title in the form's header (shown in Figure 18-3).

    If the new text box shows #Name? Instead of the year of release and the album title, you made a mistake when entering the value of the Control Source property. Switch back to Design view and return to Step 6.

Figure 18-3:
Displaying
the results
of concate-
nating text
fields.

Albums Form

Albums   2007 - Gray Skies Above

To prevent users from clicking in a calculated control, set the Enabled property of the calculated control to No and the Locked property to Yes. If you set the Enabled property to No without setting the Locked property to Yes, the text appears gray, regardless of the fore color setting. Setting the Locked property to Yes after you set the Enabled property to No restores the fore color. For more information on these properties and what they control, click a property on the Property Sheet and press F1 to open Access Help.

Using Built-In Functions

Access contains many built-in functions that let you get data from the database and information from the system. You can also perform other operations, such as calculating totals. By using these functions, you can add calculated controls that display anything from the system date to the sum of values for a particular field or fields on the form.

Exercise 18-3: Showing the Date on a Form

To add a control to frmAlbums that displays the system date, continue working with the database from Exercise 18-2 or open the Exercise18-3.accdb file in the Chapter18 folder, then follow these steps:

1. Right-click frmAlbums in the Navigation pane and choose Design View from the pop-up menu that appears.

The form opens in Design view.

2. Click the Date & Time command in the Controls group on the (Form Design Tools) Design tab (refer to Figure 18-1).

The Date and Time dialog box appears. The default setting for the date is Long Date (Wednesday, December 26, 2007).

3. In the Date and Time dialog box, uncheck the Include Time check box.

4. In the Date and Time dialog box, click OK.

The Date and Time dialog box disappears, and Access adds a text box to the top-right of the form header with the Control Source set to =Date(). The Date() function displays the current date.

5. Right-click the form's document tab and choose Form View from the pop-up menu that appears.

The form switches to Form view and displays the current date in the top-right corner of the form.

Exercise 18-4: Creating a Multiple Items Form with Totals

To create a form that displays a list of albums with counts and totals, continue working with the database from Exercise 18-3 or open the `Exercise18-4.accdb` file in the Chapter18 folder, then follow these steps:

1. In the Navigation pane, click qryAlbumPrices.

   qryAlbumPrices appears highlighted in the Navigation pane. You can create a form based on a query, as well as a table. You create qryAlbumPrices in Exercise 9-1.

2. Click the Multiple Items command in the Forms group on the Create tab.

   Access creates a Multiple Items form based on qryAlbumPrices and opens it in Layout view (shown in Figure 18-4). A Multiple Items form shows multiple records at the same time with each record on its own row.

3. Right-click the form's document tab and choose Design View from the pop-up menu that appears.

   The form opens in Design view.

4. Move the cursor just below the form footer section until the standard cursor changes to the resize cursor (shown in Figure 18-5).

5. Click and drag the resize cursor down.

   The form footer increases in size and the cursor changes back to the standard cursor.

Multiple Items command   Multiple records displayed

Figure 18-4: Creating a Multiple Items form.

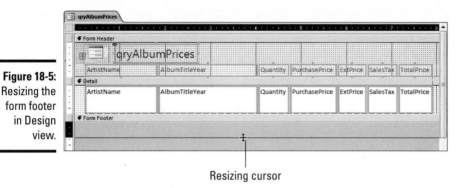

Figure 18-5:
Resizing the
form footer
in Design
view.

Resizing cursor

6. Click the Text Box command in the Controls group on the (Form Design Tools) Design tab (refer to Figure 18-1).

   The cursor changes from the standard cursor to a crosshair with the Text Box icon in the lower-right.

7. On a blank area of the form footer below the AlbumTitleYear text box, draw a rectangle.

   Access creates a text box and a label in the form footer.

8. Change the caption of the label to **Total Unique Albums:**.

9. Click the new text box.

   The text box becomes selected.

10. Click the new text box again.

    The text box switches to an editable control.

11. Type =**Count([AlbumTitleYear])** in the text box.

12. Press Enter.

    Access accepts the new value for the Control Source property. The Count( ) function counts the number of times AlbumTitleYear appears on the form.

13. If the Property Sheet isn't displayed, click the Property Sheet command in the Tools group on the (Form Design Tools) Design tab.

    The Property Sheet window appears.

14. In the Property Sheet, click the All tab.

    The Property Sheet displays all the properties for the new text box.

15. Change the Name property to **CountOfAlbums** and press Enter.

16. Follow Step 6 through Step 15 to create four new text boxes.

17. Set the Control Source (Step 11) and Name (Step 15) properties for the new text boxes as follows:

Under Control	*Control Source*	*Name*
Quantity	=Sum([Quantity])	SumOfQuantity
ExtPrice	=Sum([ExtPrice])	SumOfExtPrice
SalesTax	=Sum([SalesTax])	SumOfSalesTax
TotalPrice	=Sum([TotalPrice])	SumOfTotalPrice

The Sum() function adds the numbers for the control contained in the parentheses.

18. Hold the Shift key and click the SumOfExtPrice, SumOfSalesTax, and SumOfTotalPrice text boxes.

The text boxes appear selected, and the Property Sheet displays the common properties for the multiple selection.

19. In the Property Sheet, change the Format property to Currency and press Enter.

20. Click the qryAlbumPrices label in the form header section.

The label becomes selected.

21. In the Property Sheet, change the Caption property of the label to **Album Prices** and press Enter.

The text in the label changes to Album Prices.

22. Click the Save button on the Quick Access Toolbar.

The Save As dialog box appears.

23. Type **frmAlbumPrices** in the Save As dialog box.

24. Click OK.

Access saves the form and changes qryAlbumPrices on the document tab to frmAlbumPrices. The form also appears in the Forms group in the Navigation pane.

25. Right-click the form's document tab and choose Form View from the pop-up menu that appears.

The form switches to Form view and displays all the records in the underlying query and the totals at the bottom of the form (shown in Figure 18-6).

ArtistName	AlbumTitleYear	Quantity	PurchasePrice	ExtPrice	SalesTax	TotalPrice
John E. Blue	Gray Skies Above (2007)	1	$8.99	$8.99	0.5394	$9.53
Christy Aguadilla	Sucio (2007)	2	$8.99	$17.98	1.0788	$19.06
Gnu Farm	Gnu World Order (2006)	1	$9.99	$9.99	0.5994	$10.59
Gnu Farm	Start Spreading the Gnus (2007)	1	$9.99	$9.99	0.5994	$10.59
Left Sisters	Left at the Alter (2004)	1	$19.99	$19.99	1.1994	$21.19
Total Unique Albums:		5	6		$66.94	$4.02	$70.96

Figure 18-6: Showing totals on a Multiple Items form.

Form footer

Text boxes for totals

TIP

Using built-in functions, such as Count() and Sum(), on a form gives the same results as using the Total row to calculate totals in select queries (refer to Chapter 9).

Part VI
Advanced Form Design

The 5th Wave
By Rich Tennant

"I couldn't get this 'job skills' program to work on my PC, so I replaced the mother-board, upgraded the BIOS and wrote a program that links it to my personal database. It told me I wasn't technically inclined and should pursue a career in sales."

In this part . . .

Creating easy to use forms is an art form that requires you to know and understand the tools available to you. The chapters and exercises in Part VI show you how to format your forms to give them a consistent look and feel. Then you ungroup controls and move them to any position on the screen. You learn how to create and customize combo boxes and list boxes to make data entry easy for the users. Finally, you learn about split forms and subforms that provide alternative views of your data.

Chapter 19

Formatting a Form

●●●

In This Chapter

▶ Applying a format to your form by using AutoFormat

▶ Customizing the look of your form's controls

▶ Determining a control's look by using conditional formatting

▶ Adding a logo or graphic to your form

●●●

*W*hen you create forms, the forms will probably look a little different from one another. Forms you create by using the Form command on the Create tab look different than forms you create by using the Form Wizard. The commands on the Create tab let you quickly create a form, but after the form's been created, you might have to tweak each form to make them appear exactly how you want.

In this chapter, you can change the formatting of the three forms you created in earlier chapters. You also can adjust the spacing between the controls and where the text appears in the controls. You can even change the format of a control based on the value in that control.

Using AutoFormat

The AutoFormat options let you quickly apply a new look to your form. Access provides a variety of formats that you can apply to one or more forms in your database. Experiment with the different formats until you find the one that suits your database. Unfortunately, you can't create your own custom formats, so you're stuck with what Access offers.

Exercise 19-1: Using AutoFormat

To apply a consistent format to all three forms in the database, continue working with the database from Exercise 18-4 or open the `Exercise19-1.accdb` file in the Chapter19 folder, then follow these steps:

1. Right-click frmAlbumPrices in the Navigation pane and choose Layout View from the pop-up menu that appears.

   The form opens in Layout view.

2. Click the arrow below the AutoFormat command in the AutoFormat group on the (Form Layout Tools) Format tab.

   The AutoFormat gallery appears (shown in Figure 19-1). Depending on your screen resolution, the AutoFormat choices might appear directly in the AutoFormat group.

AutoFormat command

Form Layout Tools contextual tabs

AutoFormat gallery

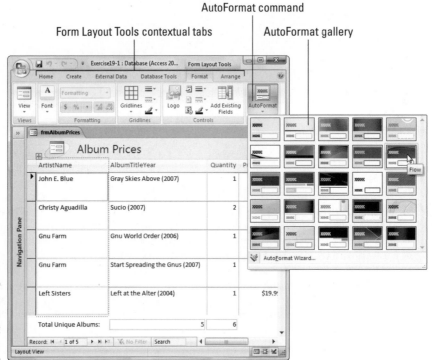

Figure 19-1:
Using the
AutoFormat
gallery.

3. In the AutoFormat gallery, select Flow (refer to Figure 19-1). The appearance of the form changes to the fonts, colors, and background associated with the Flow option.

4. Repeat Step 1 through Step 3 for frmAlbums and frmArtists.

   The appearance of all three forms is consistent.

Adjusting Control Padding and Margins

When Access creates a new form, it groups the controls together to allow you to easily resize and move controls. If you don't like how close the controls are to each other or where the text appears in the control, you can change this setup by adjusting the padding and margins of the controls in the group.

Exercise 19-2: Adjusting Control Padding and Margins

To adjust the control padding and margins on frmAlbums, continue working with the database from Exercise 19-1 or open the `Exercise19-2.accdb` file in the Chapter19 folder, then follow these steps:

1. Right-click frmAlbums in the Navigation pane and choose Layout View from the pop-up menu that appears.

The form opens in Layout view.

2. Click the control group selector (a four-pointed arrow inside a square) in the top-left corner of the control group (shown in Figure 19-2).

Control group selector

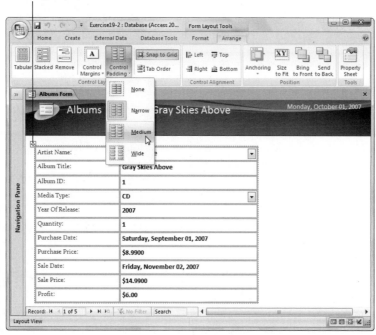

Figure 19-2:
Selecting a
control
group to
adjust
padding and
margins.

All the controls in the group appear selected.

3. Click the Control Padding command in the Control Layout group on the (Form Layout Tools) Arrange tab.

The Control Padding gallery appears (refer to Figure 19-2). Setting the Control Padding adjusts the spacing between controls.

4. In the Control Padding gallery, click Wide.

The spacing between the controls increases.

5. In the Control Padding gallery, click Medium.

The spacing between the controls decreases.

6. Click the Control Margins command in the Control Layout group on the (Form Layout Tools) Arrange tab.

   The Control Margins gallery appears. Setting the Control Margins adjusts the position of the text inside each control.

7. In the Control Margins gallery, click None.

   The text in each control shifts to the upper-left corner of the control.

8. In the Control Margins gallery, click Medium.

   The text in each control moves more towards the center of the control.

Using Conditional Formatting

Conditional formatting lets you change the fonts and colors of a control based on the value of the control. You can test up to three conditions to change the way the control appears.

Exercise 19-3: Using Conditional Formatting

To change the text in the TotalPrice field on frmAlbumPrices if the value is less than $10 or more than $20, continue working with the database from Exercise 19-2 or open the `Exercise19-3.accdb` file in the Chapter19 folder, then follow these steps:

1. Right-click frmAlbumPrices in the Navigation pane and choose Layout View from the pop-up menu that appears.

   The form opens in Layout view.

2. Click the TotalPrice text box for the first record.

   The text box becomes selected.

3. Click the Conditional command in the Font group on the (Form Layout Tools) Format tab.

   The Conditional Formatting dialog box appears (shown in Figure 19-3). The Default Formatting section sets the fonts and colors if no conditions are met. The Condition 1 section lets you set the fonts and colors for a particular condition.

Set condition   Set font characteristics

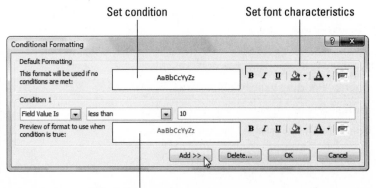

Figure 19-3:
Using the
Conditional
Formatting
dialog box.

Preview box

4. In the Condition 1 section, don't change the first drop-down setting from Field Value Is. Click the arrow to the right of between in the second drop-down and choose Less Than from the drop-down list that appears.

5. In the Condition 1 section, type **10** in the text box.

6. In the Condition 1 section, click the Bold button.

   The text in the Condition 1 preview box changes to bold.

7. In the Condition 1 section, click the arrow to the right of Font Color and choose Red from the drop-down gallery that appears.

   The text in the Condition 1 preview box changes to red.

8. Click the Add button.

   A Condition 2 section appears.

9. In the Condition 2 section, click the arrow to the right of between and choose Greater Than or Equal To from the drop-down list that appears.

10. In the Condition 2 section, type **20** in the text box.

11. In the Condition 2 section, click the Bold button.

    The text in the Condition 2 preview box changes to bold.

12. In the Condition 2 section, click the arrow to the right of Font Color and choose Green from the drop-down gallery that appears.

    The text in the Condition 2 preview box changes to green.

13. Click the OK button.

    The Conditional Formatting dialog box closes. The text in the TotalPrice text box containing $9.53 appears red and in boldface, and the text in the TotalPrice text box containing $21.19 appears green and in boldface.

One option in the first drop-down list in each section of the Conditional Formatting dialog box lets Access change the format of the control when the control gets the focus (a user tabs to or clicks in the control). Use this option if you have trouble determining which control contains the cursor.

Adding a Picture

A picture or logo can really personalize a form to your company or what you're using the database for. Access adds its own picture to the forms when you use the Create tab, but you don't have to live with the choice Access makes. Customize your forms by adding a graphic of your own.

Exercise 19-4: Adding a Picture

To add a picture to frmArtists, continue working with the database from Exercise 19-3 or open the Exercise19-4.accdb file in the Chapter19 folder, then follow these steps:

1. Right-click frmArtists in the Navigation pane and choose Layout View from the pop-up menu that appears.

The form opens in Layout view.

2. Click the Logo command in the Controls group on the (Form Layout Tools) Format tab.

3. Click the TotalPrice text box for the first record.

The Insert Picture dialog box opens.

4. In the Insert Picture dialog box, navigate to the Chapter19 folder and click the CD_Logo.bmp file.

5. In the Insert Picture dialog box, click OK.

The Insert Picture dialog box closes, and the CD logo appears in the form header section covering the words Artist Form.

6. Click and drag the Artist Form label to the right, away from the logo, until the logo no longer covers the text.

Exercise 19-5: Changing an Existing Graphic

To change the picture in the header of frmAlbums, continue working with the database from Exercise 19-4 or open the Exercise19-5.accdb file in the Chapter19 folder, then follow these steps:

1. Right-click frmAlbums in the Navigation pane and choose Layout View from the pop-up menu that appears.

The form opens in Layout view.

2. If the Property Sheet isn't displayed, click the Property Sheet command in the Tools group on the (Form Layout Tools) Arrange tab.

The Property Sheet window appears.

3. Click the picture (which looks like an Access form icon) in the form header to the left of the word Albums.

The Property Sheet displays the properties for the image.

4. In the Property Sheet, click the Format tab.

The Property Sheet displays the format properties for the image.

5. In the Property Sheet, click the Picture property.

A button with an ellipsis appears in the Picture property.

6. In the Property Sheet, click the ellipsis button in the Picture property.

The Insert Picture dialog box opens.

7. In the Insert Picture dialog box, navigate to the Chapter19 folder and click the CD_Logo.bmp file.

8. In the Insert Picture dialog box, click OK.

The Insert Picture dialog box closes, and the CD logo replaces the default graphic.

Chapter 20

Arranging and Sizing Controls on a Form

*W*hen you build a form, you might not always want the controls in a column aligned down the page (such as the controls in frmAlbums) or in a row across the page (such as the controls in frmAlbumPrices). When Access creates a form, it groups the controls together, and you move and resize all the controls in a group at the same time (refer to Chapter 15). If you like to have more control over exactly where you put each control, you can ungroup the controls and move them wherever you want.

In this chapter, you can ungroup controls, then resize and move them individually around the form. You can learn the techniques for keeping controls the same size and lined up without having them in a group. Finally, you can learn the effect on the tab order when you use feng shui and start moving things around.

Grouping and Ungrouping Controls

When Access creates a new form, it groups the controls together to allow you to easily resize and move them. If you want to move the controls around individually, you have to remove them from the group.

Exercise 20-1: Grouping and Ungrouping Controls

ON THE CD

To remove the controls on frmAlbums from the group, continue working with the database from Exercise 19-5 or open the `Exercise20-1.accdb` file in the Chapter20 folder, then follow these steps:

1. Right-click frmAlbums in the Navigation pane and choose Layout View from the pop-up menu that appears.

   The form opens in Layout view.

2. Click the control group selector (a four-pointed arrow inside a square) in the top-left corner of the control group (shown in Figure 20-1).

Control group selector   Form Layout Tools contextual selector

Figure 20-1:
Selecting
and remov-
ing a control
group.

All the controls in the group appear selected.

3. Click the Remove command in the Control Layout group on the (Form Layout Tools) Arrange tab.

All the controls still appear selected, but the control group selector and dotted line surrounding the controls disappear, indicating the controls are no longer grouped.

4. Click the Stacked command in the Control Layout group on the (Form Layout Tools) Arrange tab.

All the controls are still selected, and the control group selector and dotted line surrounding the controls appear, indicating the controls are grouped together. The Stacked command arranges the controls in a column down the form, and the Tabular command arranges the controls in a row across the form.

5. Click the Remove command in the Control Layout group on the (Form Layout Tools) Arrange tab.

The control group is removed from the controls.

Sizing and Moving Controls

After you ungroup the controls on frmAlbums, you can resize and move them individu-ally without changing the other controls in the group. But you don't have to size and move the controls individually; you can select multiple controls, then size and move them together.

Exercise 20-2: Sizing Controls

To size some of the controls on frmAlbums, continue working with the database from Exercise 20-1 or open the `Exercise20-2.accdb` file in the Chapter20 folder, then follow these steps:

1. Right-click frmAlbums in the Navigation pane and choose Design View from the pop-up menu that appears.

   The form opens in Design view.

2. Click the Profit text box at the bottom of the form.

   The text box becomes selected with squares on each corner and in the center of each line surrounding the control (shown in Figure 20-2).

Figure 20-2: Sizing a single control.

The squares surrounding the control are called *handles,* and they operate as follows:

- **Move handle:** Click and drag the square in the top-left corner of the selected control to move the control.

- **Size handles:** Click and drag each square in the other three corners and on each line to resize the selected control.

3. Move the cursor to the right edge of the selected text box.

   The cursor changes to the resizing cursor, which is a double-headed arrow pointing left and right (refer to Figure 20-2).

4. When the resizing cursor appears, click and drag the right edge of the text box to the left.

   The selected control gets smaller, and none of the other controls change.

5. Hold the Shift key and click the SalePrice and PurchasePrice text boxes.

   The Profit, SalePrice, and PurchasePrice text boxes appear selected (shown in Figure 20-3).

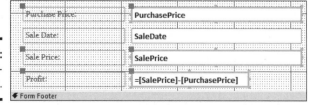

Figure 20-3: Sizing multiple controls.

6. Click the To Narrowest command in the Size group on the (Form Design Tools) Arrange tab.

The PurchasePrice and SalePrice text boxes shrink to match the width of the Profit text box.

When you select multiple controls, you can resize them all at the same time by using the commands in the Size group on the (Form Design Tools) Arrange tab. Choose from the following commands:

- **To Fit:** Resizes all the selected controls to match their contents, judged by the font size or pictures they contain

- **To Tallest:** Resizes the height of all the selected controls to the control with the largest height in the selection

- **To Shortest:** Resizes the height of all the selected controls to the control with the smallest height in the selection

- **To Grid:** Resizes the height and width of all the selected controls to line up with the grid

- **To Widest:** Resizes the width of all the selected controls to the control with the largest width in the selection

- **To Narrowest:** Resizes the width of all the selected controls to the control with the smallest width in the selection

When you select multiple controls to size, you can drag the sizing handle of one of the selected controls, and the other selected controls also resize.

Exercise 20-3: Moving and Aligning Controls

To move some of the controls on frmAlbums, continue working with the database from Exercise 20-2 or open the `Exercise20-3.accdb` file in the Chapter20 folder, then follow these steps:

1. Right-click frmAlbums in the Navigation pane and choose Design View from the pop-up menu that appears.

The form opens in Design view.

2. Click and drag the PurchasePrice text box to the right of the PurchaseDate text box.

When you click and drag a control that's not selected, you can move that control. The Purchase Price label moves along with the PurchasePrice text box (shown in Figure 20-4).

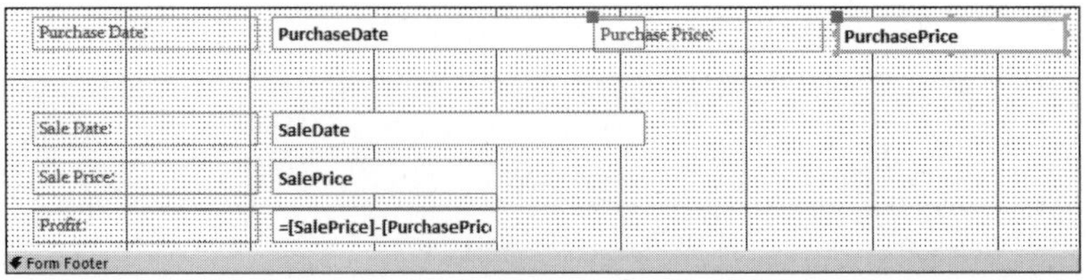

Figure 20-4:
Moving a
control.

Purchase Date:	PurchaseDate	Purchase Price:	PurchasePrice
Sale Date:	SaleDate		
Sale Price:	SalePrice		
Profit:	=[SalePrice]-[PurchasePric		

◀ Form Footer

3. (Optional) If the Purchase Price label covers part of the PurchaseDate text box, follow these steps to resize the label:

    a. Click the Purchase Price label.

       The label becomes selected with the move and resize handles displayed (refer to Figure 20-2).

    b. Click and drag the left edge of the Purchase Price label to the right until the text in the label no longer covers the PurchaseDate text box.

       The selected control gets smaller, and the text in the Purchase Price label moves right, getting closer to the PurchasePrice text box.

4. Hold the Shift key and click the PurchaseDate and PurchasePrice text boxes and the Purchase Date and Purchase Price labels.

   The four controls appear selected.

5. Click the Top command in the Control Alignment group on the (Form Design Tools) Arrange tab.

   Two of the controls shift upwards and align their top edges with the other two controls. Which controls move depends on whether you placed the PurchasePrice text box slightly above or slightly below the PurchaseDate text box in Step 2. If you aligned the tops in Step 2, none of the controls move.

   When you select multiple controls, you can align them with each other by using the commands in the Control Alignment group on the (Form Design Tools) Arrange tab. Choose from the following commands:

     • **Grid:** Moves all the selected controls to align with the grid

     • **Left:** Moves all the selected controls so their left edges align with the left-most selected control

     • **Right:** Moves all the selected controls so their right edges align with the right-most selected control

     • **Top:** Moves all the selected controls so their top edges align with the highest selected control.

     • **Bottom:** Moves all the selected controls so their bottom edges align with the lowest selected control.

6. Use the techniques in Exercises 20-2 and 20-3 to size and arrange the controls so they look like Figure 20-5.

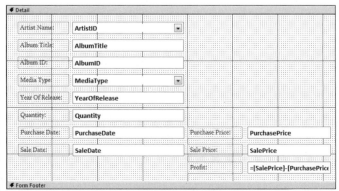

Figure 20-5: Moving and sizing the controls on frmAlbums.

When you size and align controls by using the mouse or commands on the Ribbon, you're simply setting the Top, Left, Width, and Height properties of the controls. You can edit these properties in the Property Sheet instead of using the other methods described in this chapter.

Setting the Tab Order

If you open a form to enter or edit data, you expect the cursor to be in the first control on the form. And when you press Tab, you expect the cursor to move to the following control on the form. The *tab order,* the order in which pressing Tab moves from control to control, is determined by the order in which you add the controls to the form. If you move the controls around, the tab order can appear random, but you can fix it.

Exercise 20-4: Setting the Tab Order

To change the tab order of the controls on frmAlbums, continue working with the database from Exercise 20-3 or open the `Exercise20-4.accdb` file in the Chapter20 folder, then follow these steps:

1. Double-click frmAlbums in the Navigation pane.

   The form opens in Form view with the cursor in the AlbumTitle text box, the second control on the form.

2. Press Tab.

   The cursor moves up to the ArtistName combo box, the first control on the form.

3. Press Tab.

   The cursor moves down to the AlbumID text box, skipping over the AlbumTitle text box.

4. Right-click the Albums Form document tab and choose Design View from the pop-up menu that appears.

   The form opens in Design view.

5. Click the Tab Order command in the Control Layout group on the (Form Design Tools) Arrange tab.

   The Tab Order dialog box opens (shown in Figure 20-6), displaying the names of the controls in the current tab order.

6. In the Tab Order dialog box, click the gray box to the left of ArtistName.

   The ArtistName row becomes selected.

7. Click and drag the ArtistName row above the AlbumTitle row.

   The ArtistName row moves to the top of the list.

Drag the selected row up or down to change tab order

Click here to select row

Figure 20-6:
Setting the
tab order.

8. Repeat Step 6 and Step 7 to change the tab order as follows:

   Custom Order
   ArtistName
   AlbumTitle
   AlbumID
   MediaType
   YearOfRelease
   Quantity
   PurchaseDate
   SaleDate
   PurchasePrice
   SalePrice
   Profit

9. In the Tab Order dialog box, click OK.

   The Tab Order dialog box closes.

10. Right-click the frmAlbums document tab and choose Form View from the pop-up menu that appears.

    The form opens in Form view with the cursor in the ArtistName combo box, the first control on the form.

11. Press Tab repeatedly.

The cursor moves down the first column of controls, then switches to the second column of controls.

The Tab Order dialog box sets the Tab Index property of each control. If you don't want to tab to a particular control, set that control's Tab Stop property to No. For more information on setting control properties, refer to Chapter 16.

Chapter 21

Using Combo Boxes and List Boxes

In This Chapter

▶ Putting your choices in a combo box drop-down list

▶ Leaving your choices out in the open with a list box

▶ Getting your boxes just right with the Property Sheet

C ombo boxes and list boxes are two controls that make data entry as simple as selecting a value from a list. Each control displays a list of values from which you can choose a predefined value. A *combo box* displays the current selected value, and you have to click the down arrow to the right of the display to see the full list of values; a *list box* displays all the possible values in the control, with the current value highlighted. A list box takes up more room than a combo box, but it allows you to see more values without additional clicks.

In this chapter, you can add a combo box and a list box to a form by using wizards. You can also explore the properties that make these controls function.

Adding a Combo Box to a Form

When you create a lookup column in a table (refer to Chapter 3) and create a form based on that table, Access automatically adds a combo box for that lookup field to the form. If you build forms without setting the lookup columns in the tables, or you decide later that you want to add a combo box to a form, I have good news for you — you can.

Exercise 21-1: Adding a Combo Box to a Form

To replace the existing ArtistName combo box on frmAlbums with a combo box that displays the artist name and the genre of music in the combo box's drop-down list, continue working with the database from Exercise 20-4 or open the `Exercise21-1.accdb` file in the Chapter21 folder, then follow these steps:

1. Right-click frmAlbums in the Navigation pane and choose Design View from the pop-up menu that appears.

   The form opens in Design view.

2. Make sure the Use Control Wizards command (the magic wand) is selected in the Controls group on the (Form Design Tools) Design tab (shown in Figure 21-1).

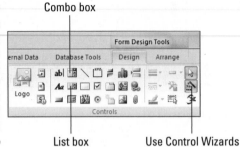

Combo box

Figure 21-1:
Adding
combo
boxes and
list boxes by
using the
control
wizards.

List box   Use Control Wizards

Selecting the Use Control Wizards command starts a wizard when you add certain types of controls (such as combo boxes and list boxes) to the form.

3. Click the Combo Box command in the Controls group on the (Form Design Tools) Design tab (refer to Figure 21-1).

   The cursor changes to a crosshair with the Combo Box icon in the lower-right.

4. On a blank area of the form to the right of the ArtistID combo box, draw a rectangle.

   The Combo Box Wizard starts, displaying a page asking if you want the combo box to look up the values in a table or query, or if you want to type the values you want.

5. Select the I Want the Combo Box to Look Up the Values in a Table or Query option button.

6. Click Next.

   The wizard displays the next page, asking which table or query should provide the values for your combo box.

7. Select Table: tblArtists from the list box of tables.

8. Click Next.

   The wizard displays the next page, asking which fields you want to include in your combo box.

9. Double-click ArtistName in the Available Fields list.

   ArtistName disappears from the Available Fields list and appears in the Selected Fields list.

10. Double-click Genre in the Available Fields list.

    Genre disappears from the Available Fields list and appears in the Selected Fields list.

11. Click Next.

    The wizard displays the next page, asking which fields you want to sort on in the drop-down list in the combo box.

12. Click the arrow on the right of the first sort field and select Genre from the drop-down list that appears.

13. Click the arrow on the right of the second sort field and select ArtistName from the drop-down list that appears.

14. Click Next.

The wizard displays the next page, asking how wide you want each column in the combo box (shown in Figure 21-2). The Hide Key Column check box is automatically selected, indicating you want to hide the primary key column from the list. The data is sorted by Genre, then by ArtistName.

Figure 21-2: Setting the column width.

15. (Optional) To adjust the width of a column, drag its right edge to the width you want or double-click the right edge of the column heading to get the best fit (the column sizes to accommodate the longest value in the column).

16. Click Next.

The wizard displays the next page, asking if you want to remember the value for later use or store that value in a field.

17. Select the Store That Value in This Field option button.

18. Click the arrow on the right of the drop down to the right of the Store That Value In This Field option button and select ArtistID from the drop-down list that appears.

19. Click Next.

The wizard displays the next page, asking what label you want for your combo box.

20. Type **Artist Name:** in the text box.

21. Click Finish.

The wizard creates a combo box on the form with a label to its left.

22. Click the old ArtistID combo box.

The combo box becomes selected.

23. Click the Format Painter command in the Font group on the (Form Design Tools) Design tab.

The cursor changes to an arrow with a paint brush.

24. Click the new ArtistID combo box.

The text in this control changes to match the text in the old ArtistID combo box.

25. Click the old ArtistID combo box.

The combo box becomes selected.

26. Press Delete.

The old ArtistID combo box disappears.

27. Move and size the new ArtistID combo box into the same position as the old combo box.

28. Click the new ArtistID combo box.

The combo box becomes selected.

29. If the Property Sheet isn't displayed, click the Property Sheet command in the Tools group on the (Form Design Tools) Design tab.

The Property Sheet window appears.

30. In the Property Sheet, click the Other tab.

The Property Sheet displays the other properties.

31. Change the Name property to **ArtistName**.

32. Change the Tab Index property to 0.

When you change the Tab Index property manually (instead of using the Tab Order dialog box described in Chapter 20), all the other Tab Index properties of the controls greater than or equal to the number you assign increase by one. Setting the Tab Index property to 0 makes the ArtistID combo box the first control on the form where the cursor appears.

33. Right-click the form's document tab and choose Form View from the pop-up menu that appears.

The form switches to Form view.

34. Click the arrow on the right of the Artist Name combo box.

The drop-down list that appears displays two columns, sorted by Genre, then by ArtistName.

Adding a List Box to a Form

A list box is useful if you have only a few items to include on the list — and the real estate to put that list on the form. When you use a list box to make a selection, you can easily see more than one choice without having to click a button.

Exercise 21-2: Adding a List Box to a Form

To replace the existing Media Type combo box on frmAlbums with a list box, continue working with the database from Exercise 21-1 or open the `Exercise21-2.accdb` file in the Chapter21 folder, then follow these steps:

1. Right-click frmAlbums in the Navigation pane and choose Design View from the pop-up menu that appears.

The form opens in Design view.

2. Make sure the Use Control Wizards command (the magic wand) is selected in the Controls group on the (Form Design Tools) Design tab (refer to Figure 21-1).

3. Click the List Box command in the Controls group on the (Form Design Tools) Design tab (refer to Figure 21-1).

   The cursor changes to a crosshair with the List Box icon in the lower-right.

4. On a blank area of the form to the right of the AlbumTitle text box, draw a rectangle.

   The List Box Wizard opens, displaying a page asking if you want the list box to look up the values in a table or query, or if you want to type the values you want.

5. Select the I Will Type in the Values That I Want option button.

6. Click Next.

   The wizard displays the next page, asking you to specify the number of columns (it defaults to one, which is what you want in this example) and type the values you want in your lookup column.

7. Type the following values in each row of the grid, pressing Tab after each entry to move to the following row:

   CD

   Cassette

   DVD-Audio

   SA-CD (Super Audio)

   Vinyl Record

8. Click Next.

   The wizard displays the next page, asking if you want to remember the value for later use or store that value in a field.

9. Select the Store That Value in This Field option button.

10. Click the arrow on the right of the drop down to the right of the Store That Value In This Field option button and select MediaType from the drop-down list that appears.

11. Click Next.

    The wizard displays the next page, asking what label you want for your combo box.

12. Type **Media Type:** in the text box.

13. Click Finish.

    The wizard creates a list box on the form with a label to its left.

14. Click the Media Type label to the left of the list box.

    The label becomes selected.

15. Click and drag the move handle in the top-left corner of the Media Type label and move the label above the list box.

    When you move a control by using the move handle, only that control moves. If you click and drag the control without the move handle, the control and associated label move together.

16. Click the Media Type combo box.

The combo box becomes selected. This is the combo box that you're replacing with the list box.

17. Press Delete.

The Media Type combo box disappears.

18. Click the list box.

The list box becomes selected.

19. If the Property Sheet isn't displayed, click the Property Sheet command in the Tools group on the (Form Design Tools) Design tab.

The Property Sheet window appears.

20. In the Property Sheet, click the Format tab.

The Property Sheet displays the format properties.

21. Change the Border Style property to Solid.

22. Click the arrow in the Border Color property and select Borders/Gridlines from the drop-down list that appears.

The drop-down list displays a list of system colors that changes as you change the formatting of the form. If you always wanted the border to be a certain color, click the ellipsis in the Border Color property and select a color from the gallery that appears.

23. In the Property Sheet, click the Other tab.

The Property Sheet displays the other properties.

24. Change the Name property to **MediaType**.

25. Click the Tab Order command in the Control Layout group on the (Form Design Tools) Arrange tab.

The Tab Order dialog box opens, displaying the names of the controls in the current tab order, with MediaType at the bottom because it's the last control you added.

26. In the Tab Order dialog box, click and drag MediaType above PurchasePrice, then release the mouse.

27. In the Tab Order dialog box, click OK.

The Tab Order dialog box closes.

28. Size and arrange the controls to take up the empty space left by the deleted MediaType combo box.

29. Right-click the form's document tab and choose Form View from the pop-up menu that appears.

The form switches to Form view and shows the MediaType list box, which displays all the values you can choose from (shown in Figure 21-3).

Whenever you add a new control to a form, you should check the tab order to make sure the cursor moves from control to control in a logical order.

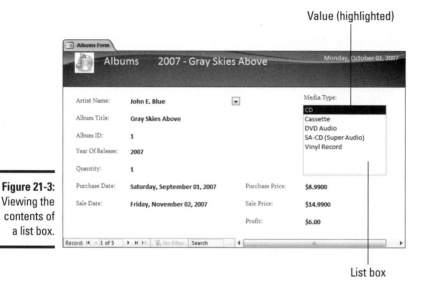

Value (highlighted)

List box

Figure 21-3: Viewing the contents of a list box.

Exploring the Property Sheet

Even though Access's wizards do a pretty good job of creating combo boxes and list boxes, you might need to change the characteristics of these controls after you put them on the form. Combo boxes and list boxes have similar properties that tell Access where to get the data to populate the list and what the list looks like. The combo box has a few extra properties because its list appears only when you click the drop-down arrow.

Exercise 21-3: Exploring the Property Sheet for Combo Boxes and List Boxes

To explore the properties specific to combo boxes and list boxes, continue working with the database from Exercise 21-2 or open the `Exercise21-3.accdb` file in the Chapter21 folder, then follow these steps:

1. Right-click frmAlbums in the Navigation pane and choose Design View from the pop-up menu that appears.

   The form opens in Design view.

2. Click the ArtistID combo box.

   The combo box becomes selected.

3. If the Property Sheet isn't displayed, click the Property Sheet command in the Tools group on the (Form Design Tools) Design tab.

   The Property Sheet window appears.

4. In the Property Sheet, click the Data tab.

   The Property Sheet displays the combo box's data properties (shown in Figure 21-4).

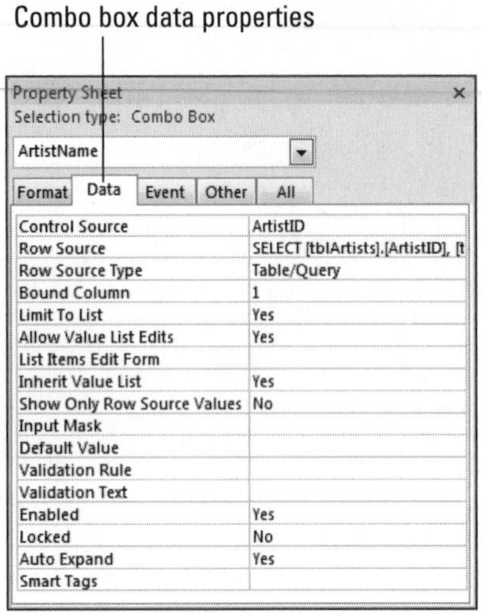

Combo box data properties

Figure 21-4:
Exploring
combo box
and list box
properties.

The properties that control the data for combo boxes and list boxes are as follows:

- **Row Source:** Specifies where to get the data to display in the list. This property can be a list of values, the name of a table or query, or a SQL statement.

- **Row Source Type:** Specifies how to get the data to display in the list. You can choose from Table/Query, Value List, or Field List.

- **Bound Column:** Specifies which column's value to use as the value of the control.

- **Limit To List:** Set this property, which applies to combo boxes only, to Yes if you want to select only values from the list. Set it to No if you also want to be able to type values in the box that aren't in the list.

- **Allow Value List Edits:** Specifies whether you can use the Edit List Items command when you right-click the control.

- **List Items Edit Form:** Specifies which form to open when you click the Edit List Items command (if you allow the command to be displayed with the Allow Value List Edits property).

- **Inherit Value List:** Specifies whether to use the value list from the control's underlying field.

- **Show Only Row Source Values:** Tells Access whether the control can display values that aren't specified by the Row Source property.

5. In the Property Sheet, click the Format tab.

The Property Sheet displays the format properties. The properties that control the formatting for combo boxes and list boxes are as follows:

- **Column Count:** Specifies the number of columns displayed in the control's list.

- **Column Widths:** Specifies the width of each column (separated by semicolons). To hide a column, set the width of the column to 0.

- **Column Heads:** Specifies whether to display headings.

- **List Rows:** This combo-box-only property specifies the maximum number of rows you want to display in the drop-down list.

- **List Width:** This property (which also applies only to combo boxes) specifies the width of the drop-down list. Set the width to the sum of the values in the Column Widths property so the entire drop-down list displays.

6. For more information on these properties, click a property in the Property Sheet and press F1 to open Access Help.

After you become familiar with setting the properties of combo boxes and list boxes, you can turn existing controls into combo boxes or list boxes. If you right-click a text box, you can choose Change To → Combo Box or Change To → List Box from the pop-up menu that appears. Similarly, you can right-click a combo box and change the combo box into a list box or right-click a list box and change the list box into a combo box. If you're not comfortable changing the properties of these controls, you can always create these controls by using the control wizards.

Chapter 22

Using Split Forms and Subforms

● ●

In This Chapter

▶ Creating a split form

▶ Adding a subform to a form

▶ Looking into subform properties

● ●

*I*n addition to viewing a single record at a time on a form (like in frmArtists) and viewing multiple records at a time (like in frmAlbumPrices), you can create forms that display a list of records and a single record at the same time. You can also place the contents of one form on another form.

In this chapter, you can create a *split form,* which shows a table's records in a list and shows the current record in a form. You can also create a *subform,* which displays the contents of one form inside of a control on another form.

Using Split Forms

If you're torn between using Form view and Datasheet view to view and edit records on a form, don't be. Why choose when you can create a split form? A split form lets you see all the records in a datasheet while simultaneously displaying the data on a form.

Exercise 22-1: Creating a Split Form

To create a new split form based on tblArtists, continue working with the database from Exercise 21-3 or open the `Exercise22-1.accdb` file in the Chapter22 folder, then follow these steps:

1. In the Navigation pane, click tblArtists.

tblArtists appears highlighted in the Navigation pane.

2. Click the Split Form command in the Forms group on the Create tab.

A new split form opens in Layout view (shown in Figure 22-1). A split form contains a form section and a datasheet section.

3. In the datasheet section, click the Farm Gals record.

The data in the form portion changes to display the Farm Gals record.

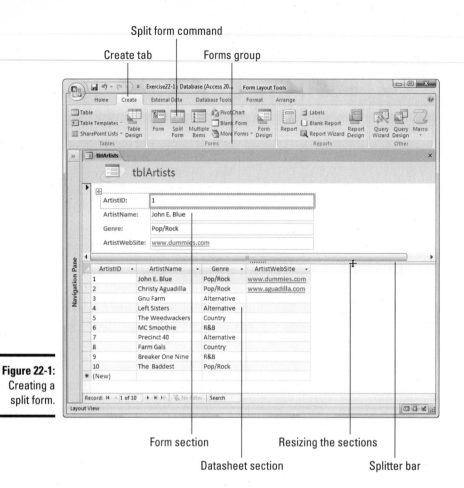

Split form command

Create tab

Forms group

Form section

Datasheet section

Resizing the sections

Splitter bar

Figure 22-1:
Creating a
split form.

4. Click and drag the splitter bar (between the form section and datasheet section) up to just under the ArtistWebSite text box.

The datasheet section gets larger, and the form section gets smaller.

5. Click the arrow below the AutoFormat command in the AutoFormat group on the (Form Layout Tools) Format tab.

The AutoFormat gallery appears. Depending on your screen resolution, the AutoFormat choices might appear directly in the AutoFormat group.

6. In the AutoFormat gallery, select Flow.

The appearance of the form changes with the fonts, colors, and background for the Flow option. This option matches the other forms in your database.

7. Click the Save button on the Quick Access Toolbar.

The Save As dialog box appears.

8. Type **frmArtistsSplit** in the Save As dialog box.

9. Click OK.

Access saves the query and changes tblArtists on the document tab to frmArtistsSplit. The form also appears in the Forms group in the Navigation pane.

By default, you can modify data in both the datasheet section and the form section. The changes don't show up as you make them, only after you move to another control in the form section or another record in the datasheet section.

Exercise 22-2: Changing the Look of a Split Form

To change the look of the split form frmArtistsSplit, continue working with the database from Exercise 22-1 or open the `Exercise22-2.accdb` file in the Chapter22 folder, then follow these steps:

1. Right-click frmArtistsSplit in the Navigation pane and choose Design View from the pop-up menu that appears.

The form opens in Design view.

2. If the Property Sheet isn't displayed, click the Property Sheet command in the Tools group on the (Form Design Tools) Design tab.

The Property Sheet window appears.

3. On the Property Sheet, click the arrow to the right of the Selected Control drop down and select Form from the drop-down list that appears.

The Property Sheet displays the form's properties.

4. In the Property Sheet, click the Format tab.

The Property Sheet displays the format properties. The properties that control the split form are as follows:

- **Default View:** Set to Split Form to show the form in Split Form view.

- **Split Form Size:** Specifies the size of the form when it's displayed in Split Form view.

- **Split Form Orientation:** Specifies where the datasheet appears in relation to the form. You can display the datasheet on the bottom, top, left, or right of the form.

- **Split Form Splitter Bar:** Specifies whether you want the splitter bar to appear between the sections. Without the splitter bar, you can't resize the sections.

- **Split Form Datasheet:** Specifies whether you want to allow edits in the datasheet or make it read-only.

- **Split Form Printing:** Specifies which section prints when you print the form.

- **Save Splitter Bar Position:** Specifies whether to save the splitter bar location when you close the form.

5. Change the Split Form Orientation property to Datasheet on Top.

6. Change the Split Form Datasheet property to Read Only.

7. Right-click the form's document tab and choose Form View from the pop-up menu that appears.

The form switches to Form view and shows the read-only datasheet section at the top of the Access window. You can still edit data in the form section.

Using Subforms

You use subforms to display data from a related table on a form. For instance, if you want to display the artist's information and see only the albums for that artist, you add a subform that displays albums for that artist. Subforms are useful for displaying data between related tables since you can link the subform to the main form.

Exercise 22-3: Adding a Subform to a Form

To create a new form based on tblArtists that includes a subform showing data from tblAlbums, continue working with the database from Exercise 22-2 or open the Exercise22-3.accdb file in the Chapter22 folder, then follow these steps:

1. In the Navigation pane, right-click frmArtists and choose Copy from the pop-up menu that appears.

2. Right-click a blank area of the Navigation pane below the list of forms and choose Paste from the pop-up menu that appears.

The Paste As dialog box appears.

3. In the Paste As dialog box, type **frmArtistsAndAlbums** in the Form Name text box.

4. Click OK.

The Paste As dialog box disappears, and Access creates a form called frmArtistsAndAlbums, which is a copy of frmAlbums.

5. Right-click frmArtistsAndAlbums in the Navigation pane and choose Design View from the pop-up menu that appears.

The form opens in Design view.

6. If the Property Sheet isn't displayed, click the Property Sheet command in the Tools group on the (Form Design Tools) Design tab.

The Property Sheet window appears.

7. On the Property Sheet, click the arrow to the right of the Selected Control drop down and select Form from the drop-down list that appears.

The Property Sheet displays the properties of the form.

8. In the Property Sheet, click the All tab.

The Property Sheet displays all the form's properties.

9. Change the following properties in the Property Sheet:

Property Name	*New Setting*
Caption	Artists and Albums
Pop Up	No
Modal	No

10. Click just above the form footer (where the cursor changes to the resizing cursor which looks like a horizontal line with arrows pointing up and down) and drag down to make some room at the bottom of the form (about double the original size).

The detail section gets larger.

11. Make sure the Use Control Wizards command (the magic wand) is selected in the Controls group on the (Form Design Tools) Design tab (shown in Figure 22-2).

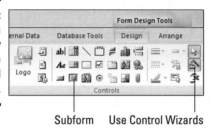

Subform   Use Control Wizards

12. Click the Subform/Subreport command in the Controls group on the (Form Design Tools) Design tab (refer to Figure 22-2).

The cursor changes to a crosshair with the Subform/Subreport icon in the lower-right.

13. On a blank area of the form below the ArtistWebSite text box, draw a rectangle.

The Subform Wizard starts, displaying a page asking if you want to use existing tables and queries, or an existing form.

14. Select the Use Existing Tables and Queries option button.

15. Click Next.

The wizard displays the next page, asking which fields to include in your subform.

16. Click the arrow to the right of the Tables/Queries drop down and select Table: tblAlbums from the drop-down list that appears.

The Available Fields list box displays the values from tblAlbums.

17. In the Available Fields list box, double-click the AlbumTitle, MediaType, and YearOfRelease fields.

The AlbumTitle, MediaType, and YearOfRelease fields disappear from the Available Fields list box and appear in the Selected Fields list box after you double-click them.

18. Click Next.

The wizard displays the next page, asking how to link the main form to the sub-form. The *main form* is the form to which you're adding the subform.

19. Click Show tblAlbums for Each Record in tblArtists Using ArtistID from the list box.

Because a relationship exists between tblArtists and tblAlbums, the wizard assumes you want the forms linked on the ArtistID field.

20. Click Next.

The wizard displays the next page, asking what you want to name the subform.

21. Type **subfrmAlbums** in the text box.

22. Click Finish.

Access creates the subform (subfrmAlbums, shown in Figure 22-3) on the main form (frmArtistsAndAlbums) based on the choices you make in the wizard. Access adds the subform to the Forms group in the Navigation pane.

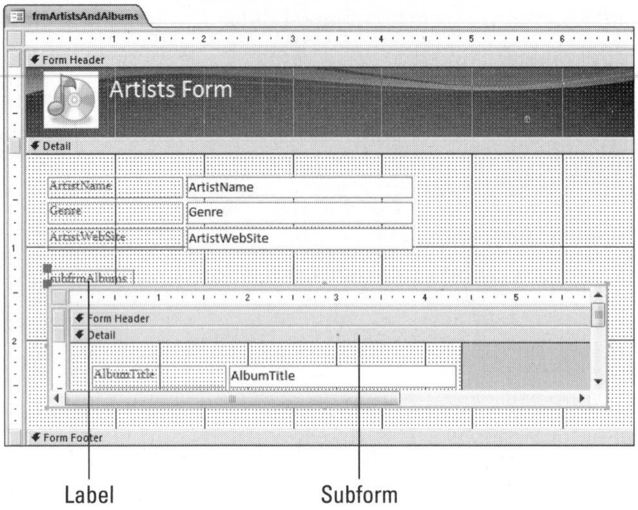

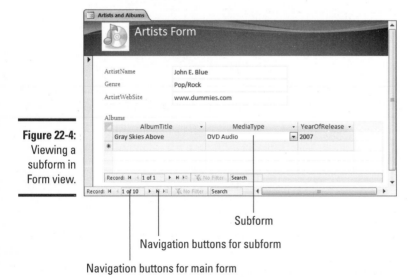

Figure 22-3:
Viewing a subform in Design view.

Label   Subform

In Design view, the subform control displays another form (also in Design view). Two forms are displayed at the same time.

23. Change the subform's label caption to **Albums**.

24. Right-click the form's document tab and choose Form View from the pop-up menu that appears.

The form switches to Form view, displaying the first artist in tblArtists on the main form and only the albums for that artist in the subform (shown in Figure 22-4).

Figure 22-4:
Viewing a subform in Form view.

Subform

Navigation buttons for subform

Navigation buttons for main form

25. Click the Next navigation button for the main form.

The main form moves to the next artist record, and the subform changes to display only the albums for the displayed artist.

By default, the subform appears in Datasheet view. You can change this behavior by opening the subform in Design view and changing the Default View property to Single Form or Continuous Forms (which looks like a Multiple Items form). For more information on changing the Default View property, see Chapter 17.

Exercise 22-4: Using an Existing Form as a Subform

To create a form based on tblArtists that includes a subform showing data from the existing form frmAlbums, continue working with the database from Exercise 22-3 or open the `Exercise22-4.accdb` file in the Chapter22 folder, then follow these steps:

1. Right-click frmArtistsAndAlbums in the Navigation pane and choose Design View from the pop-up menu that appears.

The form opens in Design view.

2. Click the Microsoft Office Button and choose Save As from the menu that appears.

The Save As dialog box appears.

3. Type **frmArtistsAndAlbumsDetailed** in the Save 'frmArtistsAndAlbums' To: text box.

4. Click OK.

The Save As dialog box closes, and the form's document tab changes to frmArtistsAndAlbumsDetailed. The new form also appears in the Forms group in the Navigation pane.

5. In the Detail section of frmArtistsAndAlbumsDetailed, click subfrmAlbums.

The subform becomes selected.

6. Press Delete.

The subform and its label disappear from the screen.

7. From the Navigation pane, click and drag frmAlbums to the Detail section of frmArtistsAndAlbumsDetailed.

When you move the cursor over the Detail section, it changes to look like the Subform/Subreport icon.

8. With the cursor near the left edge of the Detail section, release the mouse button.

Access creates a subform control on frmArtistsAndAlbumsDetailed that displays the Design view of frmAlbums inside the subform control.

9. Right-click the form's document tab and choose Form View from the pop-up menu that appears.

The form switches to Form view, displaying the first artist in tblArtists on the main form and the artist's related albums from frmAlbums in the subform (shown in Figure 22-5).

Figure 22-5:
Using an
existing
form as a
subform.

Exploring Subform Properties

When you add subforms to main forms, a few properties of the subform/subreport control determine how the forms link together. These properties of the subform/subreport
control are different from the subform's Form properties, which determine how the form
looks and operates inside the subform/subreport control.

Exercise 22-5: Exploring Subform Properties

To explore the properties of the subform/subreport control, continue working with the
database from Exercise 22-4 or open the `Exercise22-5.accdb` file in the Chapter22
folder, then follow these steps:

1. Right-click frmArtistsAndAlbums in the Navigation pane and choose Design View
from the pop-up menu that appears.

The form opens in Design view.

2. In the Detail section of frmArtistsAndAlbums, click subfrmAlbums.

The subform becomes selected.

3. If the Property Sheet isn't displayed, click the Property Sheet command in the
Tools group on the (Form Design Tools) Design tab.

The Property Sheet window appears.

4. In the Property Sheet, click the Data tab.

   The Property Sheet displays the data properties. The properties that control how the subform links to the main form to display data are as follows:

   - **Source Object:** Specifies the form that appears within the contents of the subform/subreport control.

   - **Link Master Fields:** Specifies the field(s) on the main form that link to the subform.

   - **Link Child Fields:** Specifies the field(s) on the subform that link to the main form.

   - **Filter On Empty Master:** Specifies whether to show all the records in the subform when the master field is Null.

5. For more information on these properties, click a property in the Property Sheet and press F1 to open Access Help.

If you add a subform to the main form, and the data in the subform doesn't change when you navigate from record to record in the main form (or doesn't show any data at all), check the Link Master Fields and Link Child Fields properties to make sure they contain fields that should link together.

Part VII
Building Reports

The 5th Wave   By Rich Tennant

"Look-what if we just increase the size of the charts?"

In this part . . .

Reports let you view information from your database in a printed format. The chapters and exercises in Part VII teach you how to build and use reports in Access. You start by creating a few simple reports including labels and learn to use the different reporting views. Then you change the look of the report by arranging and formatting the report, changing properties, and adding additional elements. Finally, you group and sort data on the report and learn about the different report sections.

Chapter 23

Creating Simple Reports

· ·

· ·

A report is a database object that presents information from your database in a printed format. Although you don't have to print a report, doing so gets the information from the database onto paper. Reports can include information from one or more tables or queries, and you have full control over how the data appears on the page.

In this chapter, you can create a report that shows data from tables in your database. You also can create a report that prints labels (you can pick up blank labels at an office supply store). You also can use the different views of a report to interact with the data on the screen or send it to your trusty printer.

Creating a New Report

Just like creating a new form, creating a new report starts with the Create tab. Creating a new report lets you turn that blank piece of paper into art that you can hang on your refrigerator.

Exercise 23-1: Creating a New Report

To create a new report that shows data from tblArtists, continue working with the database from Exercise 22-5 or open the `Exercise23-1.accdb` file in the Chapter23 folder, then follow these steps:

1. In the Navigation pane, click tblArtists.

tblArtists becomes highlighted in the Navigation pane. When you create reports, always select the table in the Navigation pane before creating the report. This table becomes the underlying table for the report.

2. Click the Report command in the Reports group on the Create tab (shown in Figure 23-1).

Report in Layout view   Reports group

Create tab   Report command

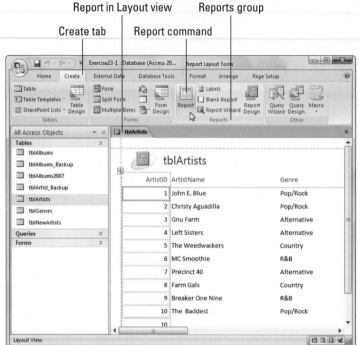

A new report opens in Layout view, displaying data from tblArtists. Layout view lets you make changes to the design of the report while viewing data on the report.

3. Use one of the following methods to save your report:

   • Click the Save button on the Quick Access Toolbar.

   • Click the Microsoft Office Button and choose Save from the menu that appears.

   • Right-click the tblArtists tab and choose Save from the pop-up menu that appears.

   The Save As dialog box appears.

4. Type **rptArtists** in the Save As dialog box.

5. Click OK.

   Access saves the report and changes tblArtists on the document tab to rptArtists. The report also appears in the Reports group in the Navigation pane.

6. Right-click the rptArtists document tab and choose Close from the pop-up menu that appears.

   The report closes.

By placing a prefix (rpt) before the report name, you know this object is a report. When you create different database objects, adding a prefix lets you know if an object is a table (tbl), query (qry), form (frm), report (rpt), or macro (mcr).

Using Report View

Report view lets you interact with the data on the report. By using Report view, you can filter the data to narrow the results so you can print only a selection of that data. You can't make any changes to the report's design (such as fonts, colors, and sorting) or the individual fields of data on the report.

Exercise 23-2: Using Report View

To view and interact with rptArtists in Report view, continue working with the database from Exercise 23-1 or open the `Exercise23-2.accdb` file in the Chapter23 folder, then follow these steps:

1. Double-click rptArtists in the Navigation pane.

  The report opens in Report view. Report view shows the data from the report's underlying table. It doesn't present any contextual tabs, so you can't change the design of the report.

2. Right-click the Pop/Rock genre (next to the John E. Blue artist name) on the report and choose Equals "Pop/Rock" from the pop-up menu that appears (shown in Figure 23-2).

  The report changes so that it displays only the three artists in the Pop/Rock genre, and the right side of the Status bar displays the word Filtered.

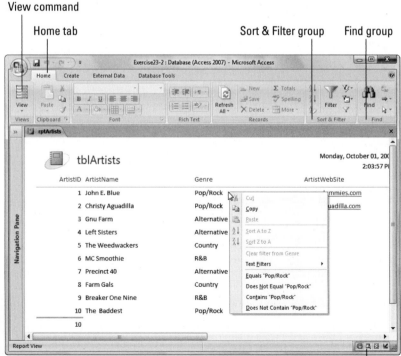

Figure 23-2: Filtering Data in Report View.

3. Click the Toggle Filter command in the Sort & Filter group on the Home tab.

   The report changes to show all the records, and the word Filtered disappears from the Status bar. The Toggle Filter command works in the same manner when you're filtering tables (refer to Chapter 5).

4. Use one of the following methods to display the Find dialog box:

   • Click Find in the Find group on the Home tab.

   • Press Ctrl+F.

   The Find dialog box appears.

5. Type **farm** in the Find What text box.

6. Click the arrow to the right of Look In and select rptArtists from the drop-down list that appears.

7. Click the arrow to the right of Match and select Any Part of Field from the drop-down list that appears.

8. In the Find dialog box, click Find Next.

   The Farm in Gnu Farm (row 3) becomes highlighted. You might have to move the Find dialog box to see the value highlighted on the report.

9. In the Find dialog box, click Find Next.

   The Farm in Farm Gals (row 8) becomes highlighted and the Farm in Gnu Farm is no longer highlighted.

10. In the Find dialog box, click Find Next.

    A message box appears, stating that Access searched the records and didn't find the search item. All instances of farm in rptArtists were found.

Use the Find dialog box if you need to find a particular value in a report that has a lot of pages.

Print Previewing a Report

Print Preview lets you look at the report as it would appear on a piece of paper. Print Preview also lets you zoom in and out of the report, navigate between pages, adjust the margins, and print the report.

Exercise 23-3: Print Previewing a Report

To Print Preview rptArtists, continue working with the database from Exercise 23-2 or open the `Exercise23-3.accdb` file in the Chapter23 folder, then follow these steps:

1. Double-click rptArtists in the Navigation pane.

   The report opens in Report view.

2. Use one of the following methods to switch the report to Print Preview view:

   • Click the arrow below View in the Views group on the Home tab (refer to Figure 23-2), then select Print Preview from the drop-down list that appears.

- Right-click the rptArtists document tab and choose Print Preview from the pop-up menu that appears.
- Click the Print Preview button in the view shortcuts at the bottom-right of the Access window.

The report opens in Print Preview view (shown in Figure 23-3).

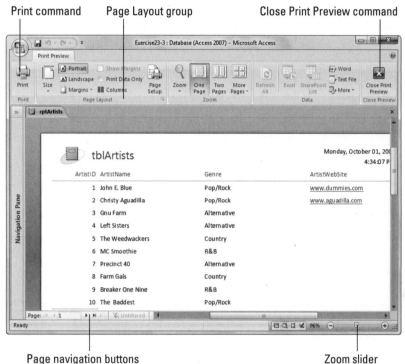

Print command   Page Layout group   Close Print Preview command

Page navigation buttons   Zoom slider

Figure 23-3:
Using Print
Preview.

3. In the Page Layout group on the Print Preview tab, click the Margins command and select Narrow from the drop-down gallery that appears.

   The report's margins change to 0.25 inches on each edge of the page.

4. Move the cursor over the report.

   The cursor changes to a magnifying glass with a minus sign.

5. Click anywhere on the report.

   The report zooms out, displaying more of the page, and the cursor changes to a magnifying glass with a plus sign.

6. Click the area of the report that you want to zoom in on.

   The report zooms in on the area on which you click.

7. Drag the Zoom Slider — in the bottom right of the Access window (refer to Figure 23-3) — to the left until the number to the left of the Zoom Slider is 50%.

   The report zooms out, showing more of the page. The *Zoom Slider* lets you change the zooming level in Print Preview view.

8. On the Page navigation buttons — in the bottom-left of the reports document window (refer to Figure 23-3) — click the Next Page button.

   The report moves to Page 2. Page 2 contains no data, but it does contain a line and part of the date because the design of the report is larger than the printed page.

9. Click the Two Page command in the Zoom group on the Print Preview tab.

   The Print Preview view displays two pages at the same time (side by side).

10. (Optional) To send the report to the printer, click the Print command in the Print group on the Print Preview tab.

    The Print dialog box opens, and you can select which printer prints the report, as well as the page range that prints.

11. Click the Close Print Preview command in the Close Preview group on the Print Preview tab.

    The report switches to Report view — the view that the report was in prior to switching to Print Preview view.

To customize the layout of the page beyond what the commands on the Ribbon allow, click the Page Setup command in the Page Layout group. The Page Setup dialog box appears. This dialog box lets you set custom values for the margins, change the orientation and paper size, select a specific printer, and change the number of columns.

Using the Report Wizard

By using the Report Wizard, you can create a report that doesn't include all the fields from a table, and you have much more control over how the report looks. You can even add fields from multiple tables to the same report.

Exercise 23-4: Using the Report Wizard

To use the Report Wizard to create a new report that shows data from tblArtists and tblAlbums, continue working with the database from Exercise 23-3 or open the `Exercise23-4.accdb` file in the Chapter23 folder, then follow these steps:

1. In the Navigation pane, click tblArtists.

   tblArtists becomes highlighted in the Navigation pane.

2. Click the Report Wizard command in the Reports group on the Create tab.

   The Report Wizard opens. The first page of the wizard lets you select the report's underlying table or query, and you can choose the fields you want to add to the report. Because you select tblArtists in Step 1, tblArtists appears in the Tables/Queries drop down.

3. Double-click ArtistName and Genre in the Available Fields list.

   ArtistName and Genre disappear from the Available Fields list and appear in the Selected Fields list.

4. Click the arrow to the right of Table: tblArtists and select Table: tblAlbums from the drop-down list that appears.

The Available Fields list changes to show the fields from tblAlbums.

5. Double-click AlbumTitle and YearOfRelease in the Available Fields list.

AlbumTitle and YearOfRelease disappear from the Available Fields list and appear in the Selected Fields list (shown in Figure 23-4).

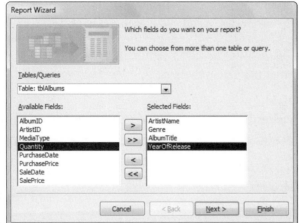

Figure 23-4:
Using the
Report
Wizard.

6. Click Next.

The wizard displays the next page, asking how you want to view your data, By tblArtists or By tblAlbums. Because you created a one-to-many relationship from tblArtists to tblAlbums, By tblArtists is the default selection which you don't want to change since you normally want to view the data by tblArtists (the one side of the relationship). The right pane of this wizards page shows the fields from tblArtists grouped at the top of the page and the fields from tblAlbums indented below the fields from tblArtists.

7. Click Next.

The wizard displays the next page, asking if you want to add any grouping levels. Because you're viewing the data in the report by artists, you don't have to add additional grouping levels.

8. Click Next.

The wizard displays the next page, asking how you want to sort the information in the detail records.

9. Click the arrow to the right of the first drop down (which is blank) and select AlbumTitle from the drop-down list that appears.

10. Click Next.

The wizard displays the next page, asking you to choose a layout for the report. You can choose from a Stepped, Block, or Outline layout in a Portrait or Landscape orientation. Clicking each option changes the associated graphics to indicate how the new option affects the report.

11. In the Layout option group, select the Block option button.

The preview graphic on the left side of the wizard changes to show a preview of the Block layout.

12. In the Orientation option group, select the Portrait option button.

Portrait orientation looks like a standard letter with the short side at the top. *Landscape* orientation has the long side of the paper at the top. You may prefer to use landscape orientation if your report contains many fields going across the page.

13. Click Next.

The wizard displays the next page, asking you to choose the style for the report. A *style* defines the look of the report and changes the colors and fonts. As you click each style in the list, the picture changes to show you a sample of that style.

14. Select the Flow style from the list box.

15. Click Next.

The wizard displays the next page, asking you to choose a title for the report.

16. Type **rptArtistsAndAlbums** in the text box underneath What Title Do You Want For Your Report?

The title of the report now appears as the report name in the Navigation pane and on top of the report.

17. Select the Preview the Report option button.

18. Click Finish.

Access creates the report and opens it in Print Preview view, displaying the data from tblAlbums and tblArtists (shown in Figure 23-5).

Figure 23-5:
Viewing the
Report
Wizard's
results.

Creating Labels

The Label Wizard lets you create labels based on data in your database. By using the Label Wizard, you can easily create mailing labels based on addresses in your database or CD/DVD labels for your collection.

Exercise 23-5: Creating Labels

To use the Label Wizard to create CD labels that display artist and album information, continue working with the database from Exercise 23-4 or open the `Exercise23-5.accdb` file in the Chapter23 folder, then follow these steps:

1. In the Navigation pane, click qryArtistsAndAlbums.

qryArtistsAndAlbums becomes highlighted in the Navigation pane.

2. Click the Labels command in the Reports group on the Create tab.

The Label Wizard opens (shown in Figure 23-6). The first page of the wizard lets you select the type of labels you want to print. Prior to printing labels, you should know the manufacturer of the blank labels you plan to print on and the product number.

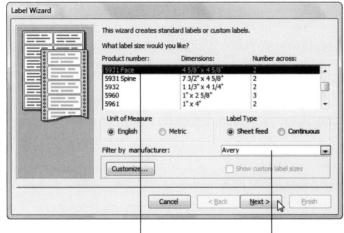

Figure 23-6:
Using the
Label
Wizard.

Manufacturer's product   Selected manufacturer

3. Click the arrow to the right of Filter by Manufacturer and select Avery from the drop-down list that appears.

The label-size list box displays labels manufactured by Avery.

4. In the label-size list box, select 5931 Face.

This label is 4⅝ inches by 4⅝ inches (the size of a CD), and two labels on each page.

5. Click Next.

The wizard displays the next page, asking what fonts and colors you want on your labels.

6. Click the arrow to the right of Font Name and select Comic Sans MS from the drop-down list that appears.

7. Click the arrow to the right of Font Size and select 12 from the drop-down list that appears.

8. Click the arrow to the right of Font Weight and select Bold from the drop-down list that appears.

9. Click Next.

   The wizard displays the next page, asking which fields you want on your label.

10. Double-click ArtistName in the Available Fields list.

    ArtistName disappears from the Available Fields list and appears on the Prototype Label in braces.

11. Click to the right of {ArtistName} in the Prototype Label.

    The cursor appears to the right of {ArtistName}.

12. Press Enter.

    A new line appears in the Prototype Label under {ArtistName} with the cursor at the beginning of the line.

13. Double-click AlbumTitle in the Available Fields list.

    AlbumTitle disappears from the Available Fields list and appears below {ArtistName} on the Prototype Label in braces.

14. Press Enter.

    A new line appears in the Prototype Label under {AlbumTitle} with the cursor at the beginning of the line.

15. Type **My Collection** on the new line in the Prototype Label.

16. Click Next.

    The wizard displays the next page, asking which fields you want to sort by.

17. Double-click ArtistName and AlbumTitle in the Available Fields list.

    ArtistName and AlbumTitle disappear from the Available Fields list and appear in the Sort By list.

18. Click Next.

    The wizard displays the next page, asking you to choose a name for the report.

19. Type **rptCDLabels** in the text box underneath What Title Do You Want For Your Report?

20. Select the See the Labels as They Will Look Printed option button.

21. Click Finish.

    Access creates the label report and opens it in Print Preview view, displaying the labels as they'll look printed. It might look like this report wastes a lot of blank space, but when you print the report on the selected label, the printed data should fit perfectly on the blank CD labels.

When you print labels for the first time, print them on a regular piece of paper, then hold the paper up to the labels to make sure the printed text appears within the borders of the labels.

Chapter 24

Changing Report Design

●●●

In This Chapter

▶ Changing the size of your controls

▶ Adjusting control properties

▶ Tweaking report properties

▶ Altering your report's appearance

●●●

*R*eports differ from forms because you use reports primarily when you want to print data, and reports don't allow you to edit the table's or query's underlying data. However, designing a report is almost the same as designing a form. You can move and manipulate controls and properties on a report in much the same way you do on a form.

In this chapter, you can resize controls on a report to fit them onto one page. You also can set properties of both the controls on the report and properties of the report itself. You also can customize the page numbers for the report.

Layout view lets you make design changes while looking at the data in the report's underlying table or query. Many changes to the report's design consist of manipulating the report's controls and properties, as well as manipulating the report itself.

Sizing Controls

After you create a report, either by using the Report Wizard or a command on the Create tab, you probably find that Access doesn't size the controls to properly fit your data — especially if you're working within the confines of an 8.5-x-11-inch sheet of paper.

Exercise 24-1: Sizing Controls

ON THE CD

To size controls on rptArtists to fit in the width of one 8.5-x-11-inch page, continue working with the database from Exercise 23-5 or open the `Exercise24-1.accdb` file in the Chapter24 folder, then follow these steps:

1. Right-click rptArtists in the Navigation pane and choose Layout View from the pop-up menu that appears.

The report opens in Layout view (shown in Figure 24-1). The report shows the margins of the paper, as well as the controls that fall outside the margins.

Grouped controls

Margins

Figure 24-1:
Sizing con-
trols in
Layout view.

2. Click the ArtistName column heading label.

The ArtistName column heading label becomes selected, and a dotted line appears around the ArtistName text boxes below the column heading because the controls are grouped together.

3. Move the cursor to the right edge of the ArtistName column heading label.

The cursor changes to the resizing cursor, which is a double-headed arrow pointing left and right.

4. When the resizing cursor appears, click and drag the right edge of the label to the left until the column is just wider than the longest Artist Name.

All of the ArtistName text boxes on the report resize, along with the ArtistName column heading label.

5. Repeat Step 2 through Step 4 on the other columns until they all fit within the margins of the page.

6. Click the text box containing the date that appears in the top-right of the report.

The text box becomes highlighted.

7. Hold Shift and click the text box containing the time (below the date text box).

Both the date and time text boxes become highlighted.

8. Click and drag the right edge of the text boxes to the left until the edge is to the left of the right margin line.

Both the date and time text boxes shrink in size, and the top margin line disappears to the right of the right margin line, indicating that all of the controls on the page are to the left of the right margin line.

You can also move controls in a control group by clicking a column and dragging it and its grouped controls left or right into their new position. This process is similar to moving controls on a form (refer to Chapter 15).

Setting Control Properties

The controls on reports have properties, just like the controls on forms. You can use the Property Sheet to change a report's controls in the same way you can change the control properties on a form (refer to Chapter 16).

Exercise 24-2: Setting Control Properties

To set control properties on rptArtists, continue working with the database from Exercise 24-1 or open the `Exercise24-2.accdb` file in the Chapter24 folder, then follow these steps:

1. Right-click rptArtists in the Navigation pane and choose Layout View from the pop-up menu that appears.

The report opens in Layout view (refer to Figure 24-1).

2. If the Property Sheet isn't displayed, click the Property Sheet command in the Tools group on the (Report Layout Tools) Arrange tab.

The Property Sheet window appears (shown in Figure 24-2).

3. Click the text box containing the ArtistName John E. Blue.

The text box becomes selected, and the Property Sheet displays the properties for the John E. Blue ArtistName text box. The text boxes below the John E. Blue text box also become selected with a lighter-colored box around each of them. All these text boxes become selected because you're changing the properties for all the text boxes, not just John E. Blue. You're not changing multiple controls, you're just changing one control that's duplicated down the page for each record.

Property sheet

Report Layout Tools contextual tab

Property sheet command

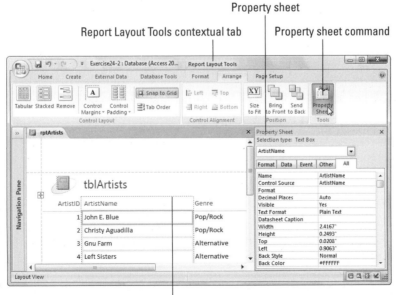

Figure 24-2:
Displaying
the Property
Sheet.

Selected control

4. In the Property Sheet, click the Format tab.

   The Property Sheet displays the format properties.

5. Change the Font Weight property from Normal to Bold.

   All the text in the ArtistName text boxes changes to boldface type.

6. Click the label containing tblArtists (which Access names Auto_Title0) that appears at the top of the report.

   The label becomes selected, and the Property Sheet displays the properties for the Auto_Title0 label.

7. Change the Caption property to **Artists Report**.

8. Press Enter.

   The text in the label at the top of the report changes to Artists Report.

9. Change the Width property to 3".

10. Press Enter.

    The width of the label increases to the value you enter in Step 9, which accommodates the new text in the label. Changing the Width property in the Property Sheet is equivalent to resizing the control.

11. Follow Step 6 through Step 8 to add spaces to the text on the column heading labels as follows:

Old Label Caption	*New Label Caption*
ArtistID	Artist ID
ArtistName	Artist Name
ArtistWebSite	Artist Web Site

You can also use the commands on the (Report Layout Tools) Format tab to change the fonts and colors of the controls on the report.

Exercise 24-3: Formatting Page Numbers

To format the page numbers on rptArtists, continue working with the database from Exercise 24-2 or open the `Exercise24-3.accdb` file in the Chapter24 folder, then follow these steps:

1. Right-click rptArtists in the Navigation pane and choose Layout View from the pop-up menu that appears.

   The report opens in Layout view.

2. If the Property Sheet isn't displayed, click the Property Sheet command in the Tools group on the (Report Layout Tools) Arrange tab.

   The Property Sheet window appears (refer to Figure 24-2).

3. Click the Page 1 of 1 text box that appears below the list of artists.

   The text box becomes selected, and the Property Sheet displays the properties for that text box.

4. In the Property Sheet, click the Data tab.

The Property Sheet displays the data properties. The Control Source property is set as follows:

```
="Page " & [Page] & " of " [Pages]
```

This calculated control concatenates multiple values together to display Page 1 of 1. The string concatenation displays the values in quotation marks exactly as they appear and uses the values in brackets as follows:

- **[Page]:** Shows the current page.
- **[Pages]:** Shows the total number of pages.

5. Change the Control Source property to =**"Page " & [Page]**.

6. Press Enter.

The page number text box changes from Page 1 of 1 to Page 1.

Setting Report Properties

Just like each control on a report has properties, the report itself has its own set of properties. By changing the properties of the report, you control how the report looks and prints.

Exercise 24-4: Setting Report Properties

To set properties of rptArtists, continue working with the database from Exercise 24-3 or open the Exercise24-4.accdb file in the Chapter24 folder, then follow these steps:

1. Right-click rptArtists in the Navigation pane and choose Layout View from the pop-up menu that appears.

The report opens in Layout view.

2. If the Property Sheet isn't displayed, click the Property Sheet command in the Tools group on the (Report Layout Tools) Arrange tab.

The Property Sheet window appears (refer to Figure 24-2).

3. On the Property Sheet, click the arrow to the right of the Selected Control drop down and select Report from the drop-down list that appears.

The Property Sheet displays the properties of the report.

4. In the Property Sheet, click the Format tab.

The Property Sheet displays the format properties.

5. Change the Caption property to **Artists Report**.

6. Press Enter.

The report's document tab changes from rptArtists to Artists Report.

You can change only some report properties in Design view. To get information on a particular report property, click the property in the Property Sheet and press F1 to start Access Help.

Formatting a Report

The AutoFormat options let you quickly apply a new look to your report. Access provides a variety of formats that you can apply to one or more reports in your database.

Exercise 24-5: Formatting a Report

To apply the Flow format to rptArtists, continue working with the database from Exercise 24-4 or open the `Exercise24-5.accdb` file in the Chapter24 folder, then follow these steps:

1. Right-click rptArtists in the Navigation pane and choose Layout View from the pop-up menu that appears.

   The report opens in Layout view (refer to Figure 24-1).

2. In the AutoFormat group on the (Report Layout Tools) Format tab, click the arrow below the AutoFormat command.

   The AutoFormat gallery appears. Depending on your screen resolution, the AutoFormat choices might appear directly in the AutoFormat group.

3. In the AutoFormat gallery, select Flow (shown in Figure 24-3).

   The report's appearance changes to the fonts, colors, and background for the Flow option.

TIP

You can use many of the same form design techniques covered in Parts V and VI when you're creating and designing reports. Review the exercises in Chapter 15 through Chapter 22 and work through the exercises on a report rather than a form. After you learn shortcuts in form design, you can apply those same techniques when you design reports.

AutoFormat command   AutoFormat gallery

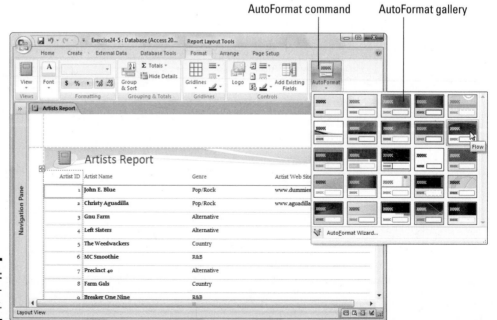

Figure 24-3:
AutoFormat-
ting a Report.

Chapter 25

Grouping and Sorting Reports

● ●

In This Chapter

▶ Grouping data in a report so you can sort and total it

▶ Moving controls from one section to another

▶ Putting page breaks where you want them

▶ Making section changes in the Property Sheet

● ●

Reports are a powerful tool for summarizing data. By adding groups and sorts to a report, you can summarize data by each section, as well as summarizing the entire report. You can also decide where you want a new page to begin and what sections should display totals.

In this chapter, you can explore the various grouping levels of a report and how to add and remove these grouping levels. You can learn how to sort the data in each group, as well as how to set the section properties to start new pages. You can also learn how to use the Property Sheet to control when and where these report sections appear.

Just like a form's Design view, a report's Design view gives you a more detailed view of the report's structure. In Design view, you see the different sections of the report and move controls between those sections. You can also change some report properties in Design view that you can't change in Layout view.

Adding Groups, Sorts, and Totals to a Report

When you create a report by using the Report Wizard, you can choose the grouping levels you want on your report. These grouping levels appear as sections on the report and allow you to sort and add totals to each section.

Exercise 25-1: Adding a Grouping and Totals to a Report

To add a grouping level on Genre that includes a total field to rptArtistsAndAlbums, continue working with the database from Exercise 24-5 or open the `Exercise25-1.accdb` file in the Chapter25 folder, then follow these steps:

1. Right-click rptArtistsAndAlbums in the Navigation pane and choose Design View from the pop-up menu that appears.

   The report opens in Design view (shown in Figure 25-1), which shows the structure of the sections of the report.

Group & Sort

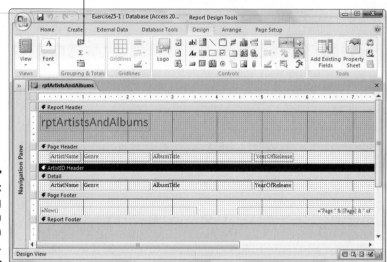

The sections of the report print out in the following order:

- **Report Header:** Appears on the first page of the report, above the Page Header section.

- **Page Header:** Appears at the top of each page of the report.

- **ArtistID Header:** Appears when a new ArtistID appears in the report. This header appears for each grouping level added to the report, regardless of the field on which the grouping level is set.

- **Detail:** Appears for each record in the report.

- **ArtistID Footer:** Appears after the Detail section if the following record has a different ArtistID. Each grouping level's Footer section appears in reverse order of the grouping levels. (This footer isn't shown in Figure 25-1.)

- **Report Footer:** Appears on the last page after all the records in the report have been printed.

- **Page Footer:** Appears at the bottom of each page of the report, below the Report Footer, even though the Report Footer appears at the bottom of the report's Design view.

2. Click the Group & Sort command in the Grouping & Totals group on the (Report Design Tools) Design tab.

   The Group, Sort, and Total pane appears docked at the bottom of the report's Design view window (shown in Figure 25-2). The Group, Sort, and Total pane lets you add and remove sorts and grouping levels.

3. In the Group, Sort, and Total pane, click the Add a Group box.

   A new section appears below the Sort by AlbumTitle section that includes a list of fields on the report.

First grouping level

Sort within first grouping level

Click to add more groups and sorts

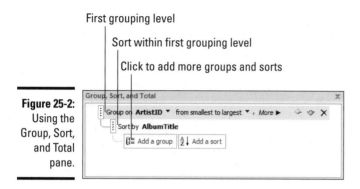

Figure 25-2:
Using the
Group, Sort,
and Total
pane.

4. In the list of available fields, click Genre.

The name of the new section changes to Group on Genre. The sort order appears to the right of the name, and the word More appears to the right of the sort order. The Add a Group and Add a Sort boxes reappear below the new group. The Genre Header section appears in the report's Design view below the ArtistID Header section.

5. In the Group on Genre section, click More.

The group expands, displaying all the options for the group (shown in Figure 25-3).

Sort order   Totals

Field name   Interval   Title

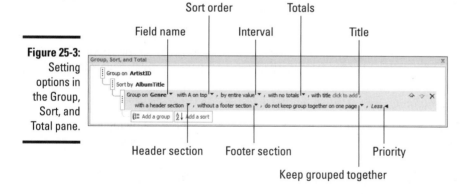

Figure 25-3:
Setting
options in
the Group,
Sort, and
Total pane.

Header section   Footer section   Priority

Keep grouped together

6. Set the values in the Group on Genre section as follows:

- **Field Name:** Set to Genre. The drop-down list lets you select the field in the grouping level.

- **Sort Order:** Set to With A on Top. The drop-down list lets you select the sort order for this grouping level.

- **Group Interval:** Set to By Entire Value. The drop-down list lets you select if you want to sort by the entire value or some other subsets, such as the first letter (if you're printing an address book, for example).

- **Totals:** The drop-down gallery lets you select a field on which to display totals. Click the arrow to the right of Totals and set the values as follows:

- Click the arrow to the right of Total On and select AlbumTitle from the drop-down list that appears.

- Click the arrow to the right of Type and select Count Values from the drop-down list that appears.

- Select the Show Grand Total check box.

- Select the Show in Group Footer check box.

  The Genre Footer section appears in the report's Design view below the Detail section. The Genre Footer section contains a text box below the AlbumTitle text box in the Detail section that has the Control Source property set to =Count([AlbumTitle]). Another text box with the same setting in the Control Source property appears in the Report Footer section.

- **Title:** Don't set this value. The Click to Add link lets you set the title for the grouping level.

- **Header Section:** Set to With a Header Section. The drop-down list lets you select if you want a Header section for this grouping level.

- **Footer Section:** Set to With a Footer Section. The drop-down list lets you select if you want a Footer section for this grouping level.

- **Keep Grouped Together:** Set to Keep Whole Group Together on One Page. The drop-down list lets you select how to display the records in the group when a page break occurs in the group. You can split the group, keep the group together on one page, or keep the header with the first detail record on one page.

7. In the Group on Genre section, click Less.

   The group contracts, displaying only the Field Name and Sort Order options (the other options disappear).

8. In the Group on Genre section, click the up arrow to the right of the group.

   The Group on Genre section moves above the Sort by Album Title section.

9. In the Group on Genre section, click the up arrow to the right of the group.

   The Group on Genre section moves above the Group on ArtistID section, and the Genre Header section moves above the ArtistID Header section in the report's Design view.

10. Right-click the report's document tab and choose Print Preview from the pop-up menu that appears.

   The report opens in Print Preview view, displaying the total number of albums for each genre, as well as the total for the report (shown in Figure 25-4).

 To sort by a field within each group, make sure the Sort By section in the Group, Sort, and Total pane appears below the Group On section. For instance, in Figure 25-2, the data on the report is sorted and grouped by ArtistID, then sorted within each ArtistID by AlbumTitle.

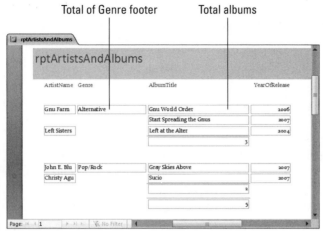

Total of Genre footer   Total albums

Figure 25-4:
Viewing
groups and
totals.

Moving Controls Between Sections

When you create Header and Footer sections, you can place controls in those sections to build reports that show a hierarchy of data without repeating a field within the Detail section. When a control appears in a Header or Footer section, it's only displayed once for the grouping level for that Header or Footer.

Exercise 25-2: Moving Controls Between Sections

To move controls from one section to another on rptArtistsAndAlbums, continue working with the database from Exercise 25-1 or open the `Exercise25-2.accdb` file in the Chapter25 folder, then follow these steps:

1. Right-click rptArtistsAndAlbums in the Navigation pane and choose Design View from the pop-up menu that appears.

The report opens in Design view (refer to Figure 25-1).

2. Click the ArtistName label in the Page Header section.

The label becomes highlighted, and a dotted line appears around the ArtistName text box in the Detail section. The control group selector (a four-pointed arrow inside a square) also appears in the top-left corner of the control group.

3. Click the control group selector in the top-left corner of the control group.

All the controls in the group become selected.

4. Click the Remove command in the Control Layout group on the (Report Design Tools) Arrange tab.

All the controls are still selected, but the control group selector and dotted line surrounding the controls disappear, indicating the controls are no longer grouped. In order to move controls between sections, you must remove them from a control group.

5. Click a blank area of the report.

All the controls formerly in the group become unselected. If you want to select a single control, that control can't be part of a multiple selection.

6. Click the Genre text box in the Detail section and drag it to the left side of the Genre Header section.

   The Genre text box moves to the Genre Header section.

7. Click the Genre label in the Page Header section.

   The Genre label becomes selected.

8. Press Delete.

   The Genre label disappears.

9. Resize the ArtistName text box and label, and the AlbumTitle text box and label, making them fill the space left vacant by the deletion of the Genre text box and label.

10. Right-click the report's document tab and choose Print Preview from the pop-up menu that appears.

   The report opens in Print Preview view, displaying the Genre in the Genre Header (shown in Figure 25-5), rather than to the right of each ArtistName (refer to Figure 25-4).

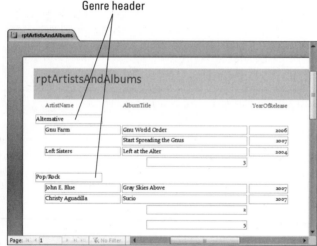

Genre header

Figure 25-5:
Viewing
data in the
Genre
Header
section.

Adding Page Breaks

You might not want to let Access decide at what point in the data it prints a new page in your report. Instead, you can place page breaks in your reports so that a new page starts in a logical breaking point. Typically, you place page breaks at the end of a section if you want to start the following section on a new page.

Exercise 25-3: Adding Page Breaks

To add page breaks to rptArtistsAndAlbums, continue working with the database from Exercise 25-2 or open the Exercise25-3.accdb file in the Chapter25 folder, then follow these steps:

1. Right-click rptArtistsAndAlbums in the Navigation pane and choose Design View from the pop-up menu that appears.

The report opens in Design view (refer to Figure 25-1).

2. Click the Genre Footer section on the report.

The Genre Footer section becomes selected.

3. If the Property Sheet isn't displayed, click the Property Sheet command in the Tools group on the (Report Design Tools) Design tab.

The Property Sheet window appears, displaying the properties for the Genre Footer section.

4. In the Property Sheet, click the All tab.

The Property Sheet displays all the properties for the Genre Footer.

5. Change the Force New Page property to After Section.

The values for the Force New Page property are as follows:

- **None:** No page breaks.
- **Before Section:** A page break occurs before this section prints.
- **After Section:** A page break occurs after this section prints.
- **Before & After:** A page break occurs before and after this section prints.

6. Right-click the report's document tab and choose Print Preview from the pop-up menu that appears.

The report opens in Print Preview view, displaying each Genre on its own page (shown in Figure 25-6). The report footer also appears on its own page (Page 3).

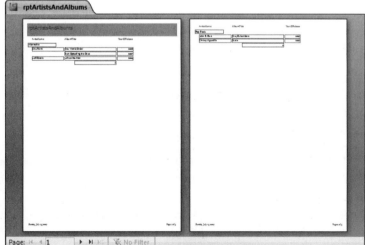

Figure 25-6:
Viewing multiple pages after adding page breaks.

Exploring Other Section Properties

Like the other controls on forms and reports, each section has its own set of properties. You don't have to scroll through quite as many properties for sections as you do for some objects, but the section properties control when and where each section prints. So if your sections aren't showing up on the paper where you expect, dig in to the Property Sheet and explore.

Exercise 25-4: Exploring Section Properties

To explore section properties for rptArtistsAndAlbums, continue working with the database from Exercise 25-3 or open the `Exercise25-4.accdb` file in the Chapter25 folder, then follow these steps:

1. Right-click rptArtistsAndAlbums in the Navigation pane and choose Design View from the pop-up menu that appears.

The report opens in Design view (refer to Figure 25-1).

2. Click the Genre Header section on the report.

The Genre Header section becomes selected.

3. If the Property Sheet isn't displayed, click the Property Sheet command in the Tools group on the (Report Design Tools) Design tab.

The Property Sheet window appears, displaying the properties for the Genre Header section.

4. In the Property Sheet, click the All tab.

The Property Sheet displays all the properties for the Genre Header section. The properties that control when the section prints are as follows:

- **Force New Page:** Specifies whether you want a page break to occur before the section prints, after the section prints, or before and after the section prints.

- **New Row or Col:** In a multiple-column report, specifies where you want the section to print.

- **Keep Together:** Specifies whether you want to keep the entire section together on one page. Select Yes if you want the section to print on the following page if the entire section doesn't fit on the page that includes the preceding section; select No if you want the section to simply print immediately after the preceding section. If the entire section spans more than one page, the data will print out on multiple pages.

- **Visible:** Specifies whether the section is visible on the printout.

- **Can Grow:** Specifies whether the section grows so that all the data the section contains can be printed. This is useful if you have controls that might contain a lot of data, but you don't want to have a lot of white space when the controls don't contain a lot of data.

- **Can Shrink:** Specifies whether the section shrinks so that all the data the section contains can be printed without leaving blank lines.

- **Repeat Section:** Specifies whether you want the Header or Footer section to repeat at the top of the following page when the data in a section spans multiple pages. Set this to Yes if you have column headings you'd like repeated on the next page.

5. For more information on these properties, click a property in the Property Sheet and press F1 for Access Help.

Part VIII
Automating Access

The 5th Wave   By Rich Tennant

"You know kids — you can't buy them just any database creation software."

In this part . . .

*A*ccess contains many built in functions accessible from the various tabs on the Ribbon and other places within the Access interface. If you're creating an Access application for others, you might want to provide easier methods for using the program than training your users how to use Access. The chapters and exercises in Part VIII teach you how to automate Access. You start by adding buttons to your forms. Then you learn how to edit and build simple macros. You also create a switchboard to open forms and print reports in your database. Finally, you learn to import and export data from Excel and other sources.

Chapter 26

Adding Buttons to Forms

. . . .

. . . .

*W*hen you create a form in Access, you can use objects within the Access interface to close the form, navigate records, and perform other operations on your data. Some of these operations require multiple clicks, and you can't always easily find the commands on the screen. If you're building a database for other users, or you just want to simplify your daily activities, you can add buttons to your forms.

In this chapter, you can add command buttons to your forms that perform the operations of other components in Access. You can create a close button that you can use to close the form and navigation buttons that you can use to navigate between records. Finally, you can create a button that opens a specific record in another form.

Using the Command Button Wizard

The Command Button Wizard is similar to the Combo Box Wizard (which I talk about in Chapter 21) and Subform Wizard (refer to Chapter 22) in that it walks you through the steps to create a control on a form. The Command Button Wizard asks you what you want the button to do, then it creates a button that can perform that task.

Adding a close button

You can't always easily find the X that appears to the far right of the document tabs used to close the form, especially if you don't know what you're looking for. Including a close button on the form makes closing that form simple for you and any other database application users.

Exercise 26-1: Adding a Close Button

To add a close button to frmAlbums, continue working with the database from Exercise 25-4 or open the `Exercise26-1.accdb` file in the Chapter26 folder, then follow these steps:

1. Right-click frmAlbums in the Navigation pane and choose Design View from the pop-up menu that appears.

The form opens in Design view.

2. Make sure the Use Control Wizards command (the magic wand) is selected in the Controls group on the (Form Design Tools) Design tab (shown in Figure 26-1).

Use Control Wizards

Figure 26-1:
Adding a
button by
using the
Control
Wizard.

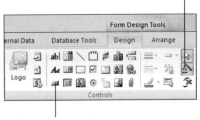

Button command

3. Click the Button command in the Controls group on the (Form Design Tools) Design tab (refer to Figure 26-1).

The cursor changes to a crosshair with the Button icon in the lower-right.

4. On a blank area of the form header below the date text box, draw a rectangle.

The Command Button Wizard opens, displaying a page that asks what action you want to occur when you click the button (shown in Figure 26-2).

Figure 26-2:
In the
Command
Button
Wizard,
select the
action you
want your
button to
take when
pressed.

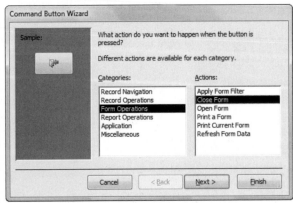

5. In the Categories list box, select Form Operations.

   Form Operations becomes highlighted in the Categories list box, and the Actions list box displays actions relating to form operations.

6. In the Actions list box, select Close Form.

7. Click Next.

   The wizard displays the next page, asking if you want to display text or a picture on the button. The sample area on the left side of the wizard displays the default selection (the Exit Doorway picture) on a button.

8. Select the Text radio button.

   The button in the sample area on the left side of the wizard changes to display the words Close Form.

9. Click the text box to the right of the Text radio button and type **Close Albums Form**.

   The button in the sample area on the left side of the wizard changes to display the words Close Albums Form.

10. Click Next.

    The wizard displays the next page, asking what you want to name the button.

11. Click the text box asking for a meaningful name and type **cmdClose**.

    In addition to using a naming convention for the database objects (such as tables, queries, forms, and reports), you should use a naming convention for naming controls. When you start a control's name with a three-letter prefix (such as cmd for a command button), that name immediately tells you what type of control it is.

12. Click Finish.

    In the header of frmAlbums (where you draw the rectangle in Step 4), Access creates a button that includes the caption Close Albums Form.

13. Click the Save button on the Quick Access Toolbar.

    Access saves the form.

14. Right-click the form's document tab and choose Form View from the pop-up menu that appears.

    The form switches to Form view, displaying the Close Albums Form button in the form header section below the date (shown in Figure 26-3).

15. Click the Close Albums Form button.

    The form frmAlbums closes.

Creating navigation buttons

Users unfamiliar with Access might not instinctively know the navigation buttons at the bottom of the form let them move between records. Adding navigation buttons to the form itself can help novice users more easily navigate the records on the form.

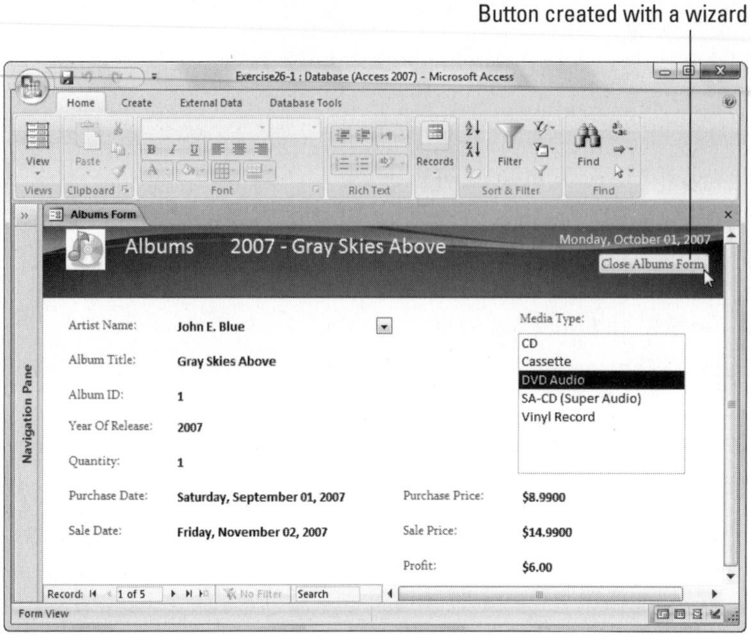

Button created with a wizard

Figure 26-3:
Clicking a
button in
Form view.

Exercise 26-2: Creating Navigation Buttons

To create navigation buttons that appear in the header of frmAlbums, continue working with the database from Exercise 26-1 or open the `Exercise26-2.accdb` file in the Chapter26 folder, then follow these steps:

1. Right-click frmAlbums in the Navigation pane and choose Design View from the pop-up menu that appears.

The form opens in Design view.

2. Make sure the Use Control Wizards command (the magic wand) is selected in the Controls group on the (Form Design Tools) Design tab (refer to Figure 26-1).

3. Click the Button command in the Controls group on the (Form Design Tools) Design tab (refer to Figure 26-1).

The cursor changes to a crosshair with the Button icon in the lower-right.

4. On a blank area of the form header below the Albums label, draw a rectangle.

The Command Button Wizard opens, displaying a page that asks what action you want to occur when you click the button (refer to Figure 26-2).

5. In the Categories list box, select Record Navigation.

Record Navigation appears highlighted in the Categories list box, and the Actions list box displays actions relating to record navigation.

6. In the Actions list box, select Go To First Record (shown in Figure 26-4).

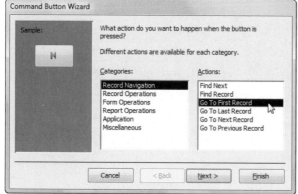

Figure 26-4:
Creating
navigation
buttons
using the
Command
Button
Wizard.

7. Click Next.

The wizard displays the next page, asking if you want to display text or a picture on the button. The sample area on the left side of the wizard displays the default selection (the Go To First picture) on a button. For this exercise, use the default picture.

8. Click Next.

The wizard displays the next page, asking what you want to name the button.

9. Click the text box asking for a meaningful name and type **cmdFirst**.

10. Click Finish.

In the header of frmAlbums (where you draw the rectangle in Step 4), Access creates a button that features the Go To First picture.

11. Repeat Step 3 through Step 10 to create the following buttons (in the order they appear in the following table), placing each button to the right of the preceding button.

Action (Step 6)	Name (Step 9)
Go To Previous Record	cmdPrevious
Go To Next Record	cmdNext
Go To Last Record	cmdLast

Access creates the buttons where you draw the rectangles on the form each time you repeat Step 4.

12. (Optional) If the buttons aren't aligned, move them in the form header so they appear aligned and spaced evenly (as shown in Figure 26-5). For more information on moving controls, see Chapter 20.

13. Click the Save button on the Quick Access Toolbar.

Access saves the form.

14. Right-click the form's document tab and choose Form View from the pop-up menu that appears.

The form switches to Form view, displaying the first, previous, next, and last buttons in the form header.

cmdFirst cmdNext

Figure 26-5:
Lining up
your custom
navigation
buttons.

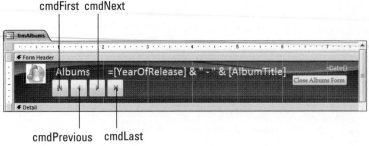

cmdPrevious cmdLast

15. Click the last button.

The form displays the last record (5 of 5).

16. Click the previous button.

The form displays the previous record (4 of 5). If you click the previous button when you're on the first record, a message appears stating you can't go to the specific record.

17. Click the first button.

The form displays the first record (1 of 5).

18. Click the next button.

The form displays the next record (2 of 5). If you click the next button when you're on a new record, a message appears stating you can't go to the specific record (since you can't go beyond the new record until you add information to that record).

Opening a form

If users know how to use Access, you can instruct them in how to open a form by using the Navigation pane and filter the form to display certain records. Or you can add a button that opens another form and displays records that are related to the record on the original form. The button method saves everyone time, especially if you have a lot of data in the database.

Exercise 26-3: Opening a Form

To add a button to frmArtists that opens frmAlbums and displays only albums for the current artist, continue working with the database from Exercise 26-2 or open the `Exercise26-3.accdb` file in the Chapter26 folder, then follow these steps:

1. Right-click frmArtists in the Navigation pane and choose Design View from the pop-up menu that appears.

The form opens in Design view.

2. If the Field List window isn't displayed, click the Add Existing Fields command in the Tools group on the (Form Design Tools) Design tab.

The Field List window appears.

3. In the Field List pane, double-click ArtistID.

Access adds an ArtistID text box and label to the form. In order to open a form that shows specific records from another form, the primary key field (ArtistID) must be on the form.

4. Click the Property Sheet command in the Tools group on the (Form Design Tools) Design tab.

The Property Sheet window appears, displaying the properties of the ArtistID text box. (The text box's properties appear in the Property Sheet window because it's still selected after you add it to the form in Step 3.)

5. In the Property Sheet, click the Format tab.

The Property Sheet displays the format properties.

6. Set the Visible property of the ArtistID text box to No.

Setting the Visible property to No allows you to use the control, but you can't see it in Form view or Layout view.

7. Make sure the Use Control Wizards command (the magic wand) is selected in the Controls group on the (Form Design Tools) Design tab (refer to Figure 26-1).

8. Click the Button command in the Controls group on the (Form Design Tools) Design tab (refer to Figure 26-1).

The cursor changes to a crosshair with the Button icon in the lower-right.

9. On a blank area of the form header below the Artists Form label, draw a rectangle.

The Command Button Wizard opens, displaying a page that asks what action you want to occur when you click the button (refer to Figure 26-2).

10. In the Categories list box, select Form Operations.

Form Operations becomes highlighted in the Categories list box, and the Actions list box displays actions relating to form operations.

11. In the Actions list box, select Open Form.

12. Click Next.

The wizard displays the next page, asking which form you want the button to open.

13. In the form's list box, select frmAlbums.

14. Click Next.

The wizard displays the next page, asking if you want to display specific data or show all the records in the form.

15. Select the Open the Form and Find Specific Data to Display option button.

16. Click Next.

The wizard displays the next page, asking which fields contain matching data the button can use to look up information (shown in Figure 26-6).

17. In the frmArtists list box, select ArtistID (which you added in Step 3).

18. In the frmAlbums list box, select ArtistID.

Field in form containing the button   <-> button

Matching fields

Fields in form being opened

19. Click the <-> button that appears between the text boxes.

The Matching Fields text box that appears below the list boxes displays ArtistID <-> ArtistID, indicating Access will compare those fields when you click the button you're creating.

20. Click Next.

The wizard displays the next page, asking if you want to display text or a picture on the button. The sample area on the left side of the wizard displays the default selection (the MS Access Form picture) on a button.

21. Select the Text radio button.

The button in the sample area on the left side of the wizard changes to display the words Open Form.

22. Click the Text radio button's text box and type **Show Albums**.

The button in the sample area on the left side of the wizard changes to display the words Show Albums.

23. Click Next.

The wizard displays the next page, asking what you want to name the button.

24. Click the text box asking for a meaningful name and type **cmdShowAlbums**.

25. Click Finish.

In the header of frmArtists (where you draw the rectangle in Step 9), Access creates a button that includes the caption Show Albums.

26. Click the Save button on the Quick Access Toolbar.

Access saves the form.

27. Right-click the form's document tab and choose Form View from the pop-up menu that appears.

    The form switches to Form view, displaying the Show Albums button in the form header.

28. Click the Show Albums button.

    The frmAlbums form opens, showing only records for artist displayed on frmArtists. Because you set frmAlbums to be a modal pop-up form in Chapter 17, it stays on top of frmAlbums.

 Using the Command Button Wizard to create buttons that open, print, or preview a report is similar to using the wizard to create a button that opens a form. On the first page of the Command Button Wizard, select Report Operations from the list of Categories and select Open Report, Preview Report, or Print Report from the list of Actions, then follow the remaining steps to create the button.

Reusing Buttons

If you create buttons on one form and want to create a similar set of buttons on another form, you don't have to run through the wizard again. Instead, you can copy and paste the buttons from one form to another.

Exercise 26-4: Reusing Buttons

To reuse the navigation buttons you create on frmAlbums in Exercise 26-2 on frmArtistsAndAlbums, continue working with the database from Exercise 26-3 or open the `Exercise26-4.accdb` file in the Chapter26 folder, then follow these steps:

1. Right-click frmAlbums in the Navigation pane and choose Design View from the pop-up menu that appears.

   The form opens in Design view.

2. Hold the Shift key and click cmdFirst, cmdPrevious, cmdNext, and cmdLast.

   The buttons become highlighted.

3. Click the Copy command in the Clipboard group on the Home tab.

   Access copies the controls to the Windows Clipboard.

4. Right-click frmAlbums's document tab and choose Close from the pop-up menu that appears.

   The frmAlbums form closes.

5. Right-click frmArtistsAndAlbums in the Navigation pane and choose Design View from the pop-up menu that appears.

   The form opens in Design view.

6. Click a blank area of the form header to the right of the Artists Form label.

The form header becomes selected.

7. Click the Paste command in the Clipboard group on the Home tab.

Access pastes the buttons from the Windows Clipboard to frmArtistsAndAlbums. The buttons appear in the top-left corner of the form header section.

8. Click and drag the buttons below the Artists Form label.

9. Click the Save button on the Quick Access Toolbar.

Access saves the form.

10. Right-click fromArtistsAndAlbums's document tab and choose Form View from the pop-up menu that appears.

The form switches to Form view, displaying the first, previous, next, and last buttons in the form header.

11. Click the last button.

The form displays the last record (10 of 10). This button (along with the other buttons you paste in Step 7) works in the same way that the navigation buttons on frmAlbums do.

When you reuse buttons, use only buttons that don't refer to specific controls on a form. Operations such as navigating records and closing forms can be applied to all forms. If you copy the Show Albums button that you create in Exercise 26-3 and paste it onto another form, it might not work properly because the original button links the forms in a certain way. If you copy and paste a button and it's not working properly, delete the copied button from the form and create a new button by using the Command Button Wizard.

Chapter 27

Editing and Building Simple Macros

In This Chapter

▶ Making changes to an embedded macro

▶ Creating a macro without using a wizard

▶ Deciding how to run a macro

▶ Using the Navigation pane to edit a macro

A macro is an action or set of actions that performs operations on your database. You use macros to open and close forms, navigate records, print reports, and manipulate data. In fact, when you run the Command Button Wizard (which you can read about in Chapter 26), you're actually building a macro.

In this chapter, you can learn about Access macros. You can modify a macro that you created by using the Command Button Wizard in Chapter 26. Then, you can create a new macro that appears in the Navigation pane. You can learn how to run macros when you click a button and when other events occur in Access (such as opening a form).

Editing a Macro Created with a Wizard

When you create a command button by using the wizard, Access creates an embedded macro that runs when you click the button. An *embedded macro* is part of the control and isn't visible in the Navigation pane. If you create a copy of a control that contains an embedded macro, the macro is copied along with the control.

Exercise 27-1: Editing a Macro Created with a Wizard

To edit the embedded macro on frmArtists that closes frmArtists after opening frmAlbums, continue working with the database from Exercise 26-4 or open the `Exercise27-1.accdb` file in the Chapter27 folder, then follow these steps:

1. Right-click frmArtists in the Navigation pane and choose Design View from the pop-up menu that appears.

   The form opens in Design view.

2. Click the Show Albums button (cmdShowAlbums) in the form header section.

   The Show Albums button becomes selected.

3. If the Property Sheet isn't displayed, click the Property Sheet command in the Tools group on the (Form Design Tools) Design tab.

The Property Sheet window appears, displaying the properties for cmdShowAlbums.

4. In the Property Sheet, click the Event tab.

The Property Sheet displays the event properties. The On Click event property is set to [Embedded Macro] (shown in Figure 27-1).

Figure 27-1:
Viewing the event properties.

5. In the Property Sheet, click the On Click event property.

An arrow and a builder button (the button featuring an ellipsis) appear to the right of [Embedded Macro].

6. Click the builder button to the right of the On Click event property (refer to Figure 27-1).

A new document window opens, displaying the embedded macro's design for the On Click event property on cmdShowAlbums (shown in Figure 27-2).

The macro design window is broken into two panes:

- **The Actions pane:** At the top of the macro window, this pane contains the actions for the macro. Macro *actions* are predefined tasks that perform specific operations within Access. To perform multiple tasks, you can select multiple actions.

- **The Action Arguments pane:** This pane, at the bottom of the macro window, contains the arguments for the selected macro action in the top pane. Action arguments specify attributes for each macro action, such as which form to open.

Builder button   Event tab   Actions pane

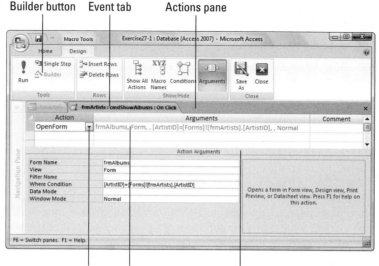

Figure 27-2:
Opening the
embedded
macro.

Drop-down arrow   Event properties   Action Arguments pane

7. Click the cell in the Action column below the OpenForm macro action.

   An arrow appears in the Action column.

8. Click the arrow in the Action column and select Close from the drop-down list that appears.

   The Action Arguments pane displays the arguments for the Close action. You can edit these arguments in the Action Arguments pane. The Arguments column in the Action pane also displays the arguments, so you can see the arguments for each macro action without clicking that macro action.

9. Set the Action Arguments in the bottom pane as follows (setting Action Arguments is similar to setting properties in the Property Sheet, which is covered in Chapter 16):

   • **Object Type: Form** — This argument specifies the type of object you want to close.

   • **Object Name: frmArtists** — This argument specifies the name of the object you want to close.

   • **Save: Prompt** — This argument specifies how to save changes to the form if you edit the form's design and then run this macro. You can choose Yes to save the form, No to discard any changes, or Prompt to display a message box asking if you want to save changes.

10. Click the Close command in the Close group on the (Macro Tools) Design tab.

    A message box appears, asking if you want to save the changes made to the macro and update the property.

11. Click Yes.

    The macro document window closes, and the frmAlbums Design view appears.

12. Click the Save button on the Quick Access Toolbar.

    Access saves the form.

13. Right-click the form's document tab and choose Form View from the pop-up menu that appears.

    The form switches to Form view.

14. Click the Show Albums button.

    The frmAlbums form opens, displaying only records for artists displayed on frmArtists. frmArtists closes because you added the Close macro action to the embedded macro in Step 8.

Creating a New Macro

If you want to create macros to perform actions on your database, and the Command Button Wizard doesn't walk you through the steps properly, you can create your own macro from scratch. You can create macros to open database objects, run action queries, or perform quite a few other operations.

Exercise 27-2: Creating a New Macro

To create a new macro that runs the action query that backs up tblArtists, continue working with the database from Exercise 27-1 or open the `Exercise27-2.accdb` file in the Chapter27 folder, then follow these steps:

1. Click the Macro command in the Other group on the Create tab.

   The macro design window opens, displaying a new macro with no actions.

2. Click the arrow in the Action column and select OpenQuery from the drop-down list that appears.

   The Action Arguments pane displays the arguments for the OpenQuery action. The OpenQuery action opens a select query in Datasheet view, Design view, or Print Preview, or runs an action query.

3. Set the action arguments in the bottom pane as follows:

   • **Query Name: qryMakeArtistBackup** — This argument specifies the name of the query you want to open/run.

   • **View: Datasheet** — This argument specifies the view in which the query opens. For an action query, setting the View argument to Datasheet runs the action query.

   • **Data Mode: Edit** — This argument specifies the data entry mode for the query. For select queries, you can set this to Add, Edit, or Read Only. You don't need to set this for an action query since running an action query doesn't open a datasheet.

4. Click the Save button on the Quick Access Toolbar.

   The Save As dialog box opens. You must always save a macro prior to running the macro.

5. Type **mcrRunMakeArtistBackup** in the Save As dialog box.

6. Click OK.

Access saves the macro and changes Macro1 on the document tab to mcrRunMakeArtistBackup. The macro also appears in the Macros group in the Navigation pane.

7. Click the Run command in the Tools group on the (Macro Tools) Design tab.

A message box appears, stating that you're about to run a make table query that will modify data and asking if you're sure you want to run the query.

8. Click Yes.

A message box appears, stating that the existing table, tblArtist_Backup, will be deleted before you run the query and asking if you want to continue anyway.

9. Click Yes.

A message box appears, stating that you're about to paste ten rows into a new table and asking if you want to create a new table containing the selected records.

10. Click Yes.

The macro runs and creates the tblArtist_Backup table containing ten records.

11. Right-click the mcrRunMakeArtistBackup document tab and choose Close from the pop-up menu that appears.

The macro Design view closes.

If you click the Run command and nothing happens, your database might not be trusted or isn't in a trusted location. You can tell when Access doesn't trust your database because a security warning appears in the Message bar below the Ribbon. Click the Options button in the Message bar and select the Enable This Content radio button to enable macros to run. For more information on trusted locations and enabling database content, refer to Chapter 2.

Running a Macro

After you create macros in your database, you don't want to have to open one of those macros in Design view and click the Run command. You can either run macros directly from the Navigation pane or when a particular event occurs on a control (such as when you click a button).

Exercise 27-3: Running a Macro from the Navigation Pane

To run the mcrRunMakeArtistBackup macro from the Navigation pane, continue working with the database from Exercise 27-2 or open the `Exercise27-3.accdb` file in the Chapter27 folder, then follow these steps:

1. Double-click mcrRunMakeArtistBackup in the Navigation pane.

The macro runs, and a message box appears, stating that you're about to run a make table query that will modify data and asking if you're sure you want to run the query (shown in Figure 27-3).

Double-click the macro to run

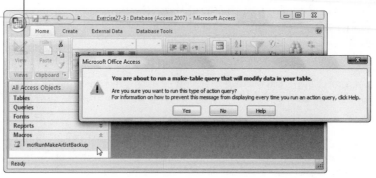

Figure 27-3:
Running a
macro from
the
Navigation
pane.

2. Follow Step 8 through Step 10 in Exercise 27-2 to confirm the prompts and run the macro.

The macro runs and creates the tblArtist_Backup table containing ten records.

Exercise 27-4: Running a Macro from a Command Button

To run the mcrRunMakeArtistBackup macro from a command button on frmArtists, continue working with the database from Exercise 27-3 or open the `Exercise27-4.accdb` file in the Chapter27 folder, then follow these steps:

1. Right-click frmArtists in the Navigation pane and choose Design View from the pop-up menu that appears.

The form opens in Design view.

2. Make sure the Use Control Wizards command (the magic wand) isn't selected in the Controls group on the (Form Design Tools) Design tab.

In this exercise, you create a button without using the Command Button Wizard.

3. Click the Button command in the Controls group on the (Form Design Tools) Design tab.

The cursor changes to a crosshair with the Button icon in the lower-right.

4. On a blank area of the form header to the right of the Show Albums button, draw a rectangle.

A command button appears on the form with a caption of Command followed by a number (such as Command11).

5. If the Property Sheet isn't displayed, click the Property Sheet command in the Tools group on the (Form Design Tools) Design tab.

The Property Sheet window appears, displaying the properties for the new command button.

6. In the Property Sheet, click the All tab.

The Property Sheet displays all the properties.

7. Set the Name property to cmdCreateArtistBackup.

8. Set the Caption property to Create Artist Backup.

9. In the Property Sheet, click the Event tab.

The Property Sheet displays the event properties.

10. Click the arrow to the right of the On Click event property and select mcrRunMakeArtistBackup from the drop-down list that appears.

This drop-down list contains the macros that appear in the Navigation pane.

11. Click the Save button on the Quick Access Toolbar.

Access saves the form.

12. Right-click the form's document tab and choose Form View from the pop-up menu that appears.

The form switches to Form view, displaying the Create Artist Backup button in the form header (shown in Figure 27-4).

Click to run the macro

Figure 27-4:
Viewing the
button in
Form view.

13. Click the Create Artist Backup button.

The mcrRunMakeArtistBackup macro runs, and a message box appears, stating that you're about to run a make table query that will modify data and asking if you're sure you want to run the query.

14. Click No.

The macro stops running.

You can run a macro when any events occur while you're using an Access database. On the Property Sheet for each control, section, form, or report, click the Event tab and explore the different events. To run a macro when a form opens, use the On Open or On Load event property of the form. Use the On Got Focus event property to run a macro when you press Tab or click a control. To get additional information about when an event occurs, click the event property and press F1 to start Access Help.

Editing a Macro from the Navigation Pane

One reason to create macros is to automate tasks in your database. When you run a macro that runs an action query, message boxes appear, asking for your permission to update data. You can turn these message boxes off for the entire database by using the

Access Options window. If you turn these messages off and accidentally double-click an action query in the Navigation pane, the query runs, and you don't have a chance to stop it. Instead of turning these messages off for the entire database, you can just turn the messages off while the macro runs.

Exercise 27-5: Editing a Macro from the Navigation Pane

To edit the mcrRunMakeArtistBackup macro so it doesn't display messages asking for permission to execute the action query, continue working with the database from Exercise 27-4 or open the `Exercise27-5.accdb` file in the Chapter27 folder, then follow these steps:

1. Right-click mcrRunMakeArtistBackup in the Navigation pane and choose Design View from the pop-up menu that appears.

The macro opens in Design view with the OpenQuery action highlighted.

2. Click the Show All Actions command in the Show/Hide group on the (Macro Tools) Design tab.

Because of security concerns, certain macro actions require the database to have a trusted status in order to run. These macros don't appear in the Action drop-down list unless the Show All Actions command is selected. For more information on security and trusted databases, refer to Chapter 2.

3. Click the Insert Rows command in the Rows group on the (Macro Tools) Design tab.

A blank row appears above the OpenQuery action.

4. Click the arrow in the first row of the Action column (above the OpenQuery action) and select SetWarnings from the drop-down list that appears.

The Action Arguments pane displays the argument for the SetWarnings action. The SetWarnings action prevents modal warnings from stopping the macro and has the same effect as pressing OK or Yes in each dialog box that appears. Error messages and dialog boxes that require user input still appear. A warning symbol (an exclamation point in a triangle) appears in the SetWarnings action's row selector, indicating this macro action requires the database to have a trusted status.

5. Set the Action Argument in the bottom pane to Warnings On: No.

Setting this argument to No turns the warnings off.

6. Click the arrow in the third row of the Action column (below the OpenQuery action) and select SetWarnings from the drop-down list that appears.

The Action Arguments pane displays the argument for the SetWarnings action.

7. Set the Action Argument in the bottom pane to Warnings On: Yes.

Setting this argument to Yes turns the warnings on. You should always turn the warnings back on if you turn them off in a macro; otherwise, you run the risk of running an action without being prompted.

8. Click the arrow in the fourth row of the Action column (below the second SetWarnings action) and select MsgBox from the drop-down list that appears.

   The Action Arguments pane shows the arguments for the MsgBox action. The MsgBox action displays a message box with an OK button along with any message you want to present.

9. Set the Action Arguments in the bottom pane as follows:

   • **Message: tblArtists was successfully backed up to tblArtist_Backup** — This argument specifies the message that appears in the message box window.

   • **Beep: Yes** — This argument specifies whether you want to sound a beep when the message box appears.

   • **Type: Information** — This argument specifies the icon that appears in the message box window. You can choose from None, Critical, Warning?, Warning!, and Information.

   • **Title: Artist Backup Created** — This argument specifies the text that appears in the title bar of the message box window.

10. Click the Save button on the Quick Access Toolbar.

    Access saves the macro.

11. Click the Run command in the Tools group on the (Macro Tools) Design tab.

    A message box appears, displaying the message that you define in Step 9 (shown in Figure 27-5). The other message boxes, asking for your permission to run the make table query, delete the existing table, and append ten rows, don't appear because you turn the warnings off in Step 5 with the SetWarnings action prior to running the OpenQuery action.

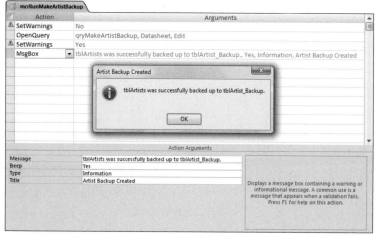

Figure 27-5:
Viewing and running the edited macro.

Chapter 28

Creating a Switchboard

• •

In This Chapter

▶ Making your switchboard

▶ Personalizing your switchboard

▶ Setting your switchboard to open when your database does

• •

*T*he Navigation pane is a great tool for opening the various database objects in your application. However, you might not want some users opening certain objects — or even worse, changing the design of those objects. A *switchboard* is a form that lets you control which objects users can open. You use the Switchboard Manager to maintain your switchboard.

In this chapter, you can create a switchboard that helps you navigate the objects in your database. You can choose which database objects you want to appear in the switchboard. Then, you can learn how to make the switchboard appear automatically when you open the database.

Creating a New Switchboard

Each Access database can have one switchboard form, and you can configure that form by using the Switchboard Manager so the form shows certain sets of commands. If your database doesn't contain a switchboard, Access adds one the first time you open the Switchboard Manager.

Exercise 28-1: Creating a New Switchboard

To create a new switchboard and add switchboard items that open frmArtists and frmAlbums, continue working with the database from Exercise 27-5 or open the `Exercise28-1.accdb` file in the Chapter28 folder, then follow these steps:

1. Click the Switchboard Manager command in the Database Tools group on the Database Tools tab.

A message box appears, stating the Switchboard Manager was unable to find a valid switchboard in the database and asking if you want to create one.

2. Click Yes.

The Switchboard Manager dialog box opens, displaying the Main Switchboard (Default) page in the Switchboard Pages list box (shown in Figure 28-1). The Switchboard Manager also adds a table (Switchboard Items) and a form (Switchboard) to your database.

Switchboard Manager dialog box

Switchboard form   Switchboard Manager command

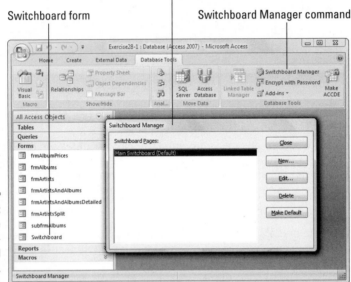

Figure 28-1:
Opening the
Switch-
board
Manager.

3. In the Switchboard Manager dialog box, click the Edit button.

The Edit Switchboard Page dialog box opens, displaying the items on the Main Switchboard (which is currently empty).

4. In the Edit Switchboard Page dialog box, click the New button.

The Edit Switchboard Item dialog box opens (shown in Figure 28-2).

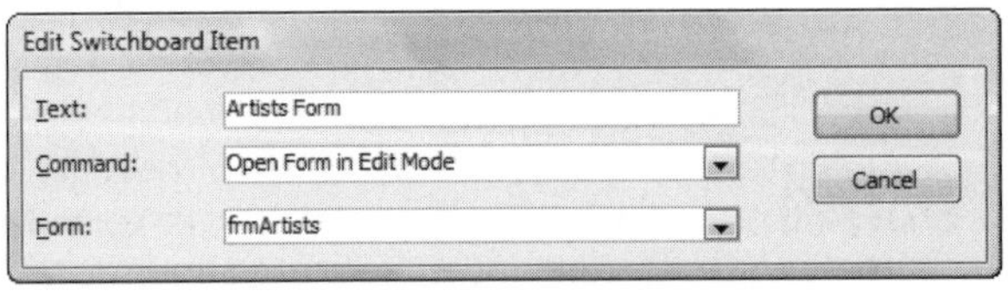

Figure 28-2:
Adding a
switchboard
item.

5. In the Edit Switchboard Item dialog box, fill in the fields as follows:

• Text: Artists Form

• Command: Open Form in Edit Mode

• Form: frmArtists

6. Click OK.

The Edit Switchboard Item dialog box closes, and Artists Form appears in the Items on This Switchboard list box in the Edit Switchboard Page dialog box.

7. In the Edit Switchboard Page dialog box, click the New button.

The Edit Switchboard Item dialog box opens (refer to Figure 28-2).

8. In the Edit Switchboard Item dialog box, fill in the fields as follows:

- Text: Albums Form
- Command: Open Form in Edit Mode
- Form: frmAlbums

9. Click OK.

The Edit Switchboard Item dialog box closes, and Albums Form appears below Artists Form in the Items on This Switchboard list box in the Edit Switchboard Page dialog box.

10. In the Edit Switchboard Page dialog box, click the Close button.

The Edit Switchboard Page dialog box closes, revealing the Switchboard Manager dialog box.

11. In the Switchboard Manager dialog box, click the Close button.

The Switchboard Manager dialog box closes.

12. Double-click the Switchboard form in the Navigation pane.

The Switchboard form opens, displaying buttons that open the Artists Form and the Albums Form, respectively (shown in Figure 28-3).

13. On the Switchboard form, click the Artists Form button.

The Artist Form (frmArtists) opens in Edit mode.

Figure 28-3:
Viewing the
Switchboard
form.

Editing a Switchboard

After you add a switchboard to your database, you can use the Switchboard Manager to add and remove items. You can also add switchboard pages that group commands together, such as creating one screen that opens reports.

Exercise 28-2: Editing a Switchboard

ON THE CD

To edit the switchboard and add a switchboard page to open reports, continue working with the database from Exercise 28-1 or open the `Exercise28-2.accdb` file in the Chapter28 folder, then follow these steps:

1. Click the Switchboard Manager command in the Database Tools group on the Database Tools tab.

The Switchboard Manager dialog box opens, displaying the Main Switchboard (Default) page in the Switchboard Pages list box (refer to Figure 28-1).

2. In the Switchboard Manager dialog box, click the New button.

The Create New dialog box opens.

3. In the Create New dialog box, type **Reports Switchboard** in the Switchboard Page Name text box.

4. Click OK.

The Create New dialog box closes, and Reports Switchboard appears in the Switchboard Pages list box in the Switchboard Manager dialog box.

5. In the Switchboard Manager dialog box, click Reports Switchboard.

Reports Switchboard becomes selected in the Switchboard Pages list box.

6. In the Switchboard Manager dialog box, click the Edit button.

The Edit Switchboard Page dialog box opens, displaying the items on the Reports Switchboard (which is currently empty).

7. In the Edit Switchboard Page dialog box, click the New button.

The Edit Switchboard Item dialog box opens (refer to Figure 28-2).

8. In the Edit Switchboard Item dialog box, fill in the fields as follows:

- Text: Open Artists and Albums Report
- Command: Open Report
- Report: rptArtistsAndAlbums

9. Click OK.

The Edit Switchboard Item dialog box closes, and Open Artists and Albums Report appears in the Items on This Switchboard list box in the Edit Switchboard Page dialog box.

10. In the Edit Switchboard Page dialog box, click the New button.

The Edit Switchboard Item dialog box opens.

11. In the Edit Switchboard Item dialog box, fill in the fields as follows:

- Text: Open Artists Report
- Command: Open Report
- Report: rptArtists

12. Click OK.

The Edit Switchboard Item dialog box closes, and Open Artists Report appears below Open Artists and Albums Report in the Items on This Switchboard list box in the Edit Switchboard Page dialog box.

13. In the Edit Switchboard Page dialog box, click the New button.

The Edit Switchboard Item dialog box opens.

14. In the Edit Switchboard Item dialog box, fill in the fields as follows:

    - Text: Main Switchboard

    - Command: Go to Switchboard

    - Switchboard: Main Switchboard

15. Click OK.

    The Edit Switchboard Item dialog box closes, and Return to Main Switchboard appears below Open Artists Report in the Items on This Switchboard list box in the Edit Switchboard Page dialog box.

16. In the Edit Switchboard Page dialog box, click the Close button.

    The Edit Switchboard Page dialog box closes, revealing the Switchboard Manager dialog box.

17. In the Switchboard Manager dialog box, click Main Switchboard (Default).

    Main Switchboard (Default) becomes selected in the Switchboard Pages list box.

18. In the Switchboard Manager dialog box, click the Edit button.

    The Edit Switchboard Page dialog box opens, displaying the items on the Main Switchboard.

19. In the Edit Switchboard Page dialog box, click the New button.

    The Edit Switchboard Item dialog box opens.

20. In the Edit Switchboard Item dialog box, fill in the fields as follows:

    - Text: Reports Switchboard

    - Command: Go to Switchboard

    - Switchboard: Reports Switchboard

21. Click OK.

    The Edit Switchboard Item dialog box closes, and Reports Switchboard appears below Albums Form in the Items on This Switchboard list box in the Edit Switchboard Page dialog box.

22. In the Edit Switchboard Page dialog box, click the Close button.

    The Edit Switchboard Page dialog box closes, revealing the Switchboard Manager dialog box.

23. In the Switchboard Manager dialog box, click the Close button.

    The Switchboard Manager dialog box closes.

24. Double-click the Switchboard form in the Navigation pane.

    The Switchboard form opens, displaying buttons that open the Artists Form, Albums Form, and the Reports Switchboard, respectively.

25. On the Switchboard form, click the Reports Switchboard button.

    The Reports Switchboard opens.

26. On the Reports Switchboard form, click the Open Artists Report button.

    The Artist Report (rptArtists) opens in Report view.

To change the order of items on your switchboard, highlight a switchboard page in the Edit Switchboard Page dialog box and use the Move Up and Move Down buttons.

Setting the Startup Form

If you're creating a switchboard for your database, you probably want the Switchboard form to open when you open the database. You can get this form to open automatically when you open your database by changing settings in the Access Options window.

Exercise 28-3: Setting the Startup Form

To automatically open the Switchboard form when you open the database, continue working with the database from Exercise 28-2 or open the `Exercise28-3.accdb` file in the Chapter28 folder, then follow these steps:

1. Click the Microsoft Office Button and choose Access Options in the lower-right section of the menu that appears.

The Access Options window appears.

2. In the left pane of the Access Options window, click Current Database.

The Access Options window displays the options that pertain to the currently open database.

3. In the Application Options section in the right pane of the Access Options window, click the arrow to the right of Display Form and select Switchboard from the Display Form drop-down list that appears.

4. In the lower-right of the Access Options window, click OK.

The Access Options window closes, and a message appears, stating that you must close and reopen the current database for the specified option to take effect.

5. Click OK.

The dialog box closes.

6. Click the Microsoft Office Button and choose Close Database from the menu that appears.

The database closes.

7. Click the Microsoft Office Button and select the first database in the Recent Documents list (`Exercise28-3.accdb`).

The database opens and automatically displays the Switchboard form.

To hide the Navigation pane so users can't see the database objects, open the Access Options window, click Current Database, and uncheck the Display Navigation Pane check box in the Navigation section.

Chapter 29

Importing and Exporting Data

• •

In This Chapter

▶ Exporting data to formats other than a database

▶ Importing data from different formats

• •

*A*fter you put data into an Access database, it's not stuck there forever. Not everyone in the world has Access, and sometimes, you need to get information from
your database to those Access-less folks. Luckily, Access supports a number of formats
that should take care of all your exporting needs. And if you happen to receive data in
some other format, you can import that data into Access, as well.

In this chapter, you can export data from Access to an Excel spreadsheet and learn how
to export data to other formats. Then, you can import data from another Access database
and an Excel spreadsheet.

Exporting Data

If you have to get data from your database into some other format, such as an Excel
spreadsheet, a text file, or another database format, you can export the data from Access
into that format.

Exercise 29-1: Exporting Data to an Excel Spreadsheet

To export data from tblArtists to an Excel spreadsheet, continue working with the database from Exercise 28-3 or open the `Exercise29-1.accdb` file in the Chapter29 folder,
then follow these steps:

1. In the Navigation pane, click tblArtists.

   tblArtists becomes highlighted in the Navigation pane. When you export data,
   always select the table or query that you're exporting in the Navigation pane.

2. Click the Excel command in the Export group on the External Data tab.

   The Export — Excel Spreadsheet dialog box opens (shown in Figure 29-1).

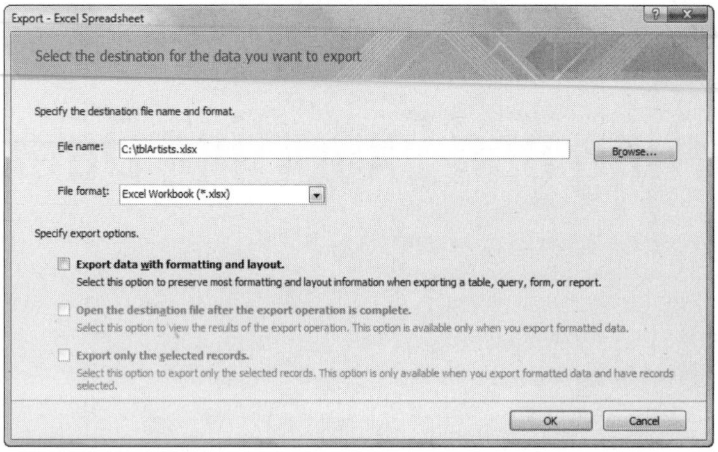

Figure 29-1:
Exporting
data to an
Excel
spread-
sheet.

3. Click the File Name text box and type **C:\tblArtists.xlsx**.

4. Click the arrow to the right of File Format and select Excel Workbook (*.xlsx) from the drop-down list that appears.

   You can export data to Excel so different versions of Excel can open the file. Choose from the following options:

   - **Excel Binary Workbook (*.xlsb):** Excel 2007 format designed to optimize large spreadsheets

   - **Excel Workbook (*.xlsx):** Excel 2007 format

   - **Microsoft Excel 5.0/95 Workbook (*.xls):** Format compatible with Excel versions 5.0 and 95 format

   - **Excel 97 — Excel 2003 Workbook (*.xls):** Format compatible with Excel versions 97 through 2003

5. Select the Export Data with Formatting and Layout check box.

   When you export to Excel, you can preserve most of the formatting within the table, query, form, or report.

6. Select the Open the Destination File After the Export Operation Is Complete check box.

   If you don't have Microsoft Excel on your computer, don't check this option.

7. Click OK.

   Access creates the spreadsheet and opens Microsoft Excel, displaying the new spreadsheet (shown in Figure 29-2).

8. Click the Close button in the top-right corner of the Excel window.

   Excel closes, and Access displays the Export dialog box that states the table was exported successfully and asks if you want to save the export steps. Leave the Save Export Steps checkbox unchecked.

9. Click the Close button in the bottom-right corner of the Export — Excel Spreadsheet dialog box.

   The Export — Excel Spreadsheet dialog box closes.

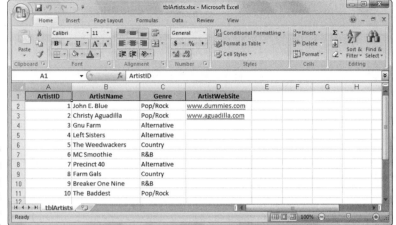

Exercise 29-2: Exporting Data to Other Formats

To export data from tblArtists to other formats, continue working with the database from Exercise 29-1 or open the `Exercise29-2.accdb` file in the Chapter29 folder, then follow these steps:

1. In the Navigation pane, click tblArtists.

tblArtists becomes highlighted in the Navigation pane.

2. In the Export group on the External Data tab, choose from one of the following commands to export data to different formats:

- **SharePoint List:** Exports data to a SharePoint site

- **Word:** Exports data to an RTF file

- **Text File:** Exports data to a delimited text file or a fixed-width text file

- **Access Database:** Exports data to a different Access database

- **XML File:** Exports data to an XML file

- **HTML Document:** Exports data to an HTML file

The appropriate Export dialog box opens, prompting you for the required information to export data.

3. Follow the instructions on the screen to export the data to the format you chose in Step 2.

Some exports require additional steps, and Access asks different questions about file formats, server locations, and other miscellaneous information.

Importing Data

If you have data in some format (including Access), and you want to add that data to your database, don't print that data out and type it all in. Instead, import the data into a table and use that table in your database. Save the typing for another day.

Exercise 29-3: Importing Data from an Excel Spreadsheet

To import data from an Excel spreadsheet, continue working with the database from Exercise 29-2 or open the `Exercise29-3.accdb` file in the Chapter29 folder, then follow these steps:

1. Click the Excel command in the Import group on the External Data tab.

The Get External Data — Excel Spreadsheet dialog box opens.

2. Click the File Name text box and type **C:\tblArtists.xlsx**.

You create the Excel spreadsheet `tblArtists.xlsx` in Exercise 29-1. You can also use the Browse button to navigate to the Excel spreadsheet on your computer.

3. Select the Import the Source Data into a New Table in the Current Database option button.

This option creates a new table in the database with the data from the Excel spreadsheet. The other two option buttons are

- **Append a Copy of the Record to the Table** *tablename:* This option appends the records to an existing table in the database. When you choose this option, make sure the structure of the data you're importing matches the structure of the table.

- **Link to the Data Source by Creating a Linked Table:** This option doesn't import the data to the Access database. Instead, it creates a link to the spreadsheet, so changes made in the spreadsheet are reflected in the linked table and vice-versa.

4. Click OK.

The Import Spreadsheet Wizard appears, asking if the first row of data contains column headings. A preview of the data appears in the lower half of the wizard.

5. Select the First Row Contains Column Headings check box.

The spreadsheet you export in Exercise 29-1 contains the names of the columns in the first row (refer to Figure 29-2).

6. Click Next.

The wizard displays the next page, asking you to specify information about each field. You can specify field names, data types, and indexes, or you can choose not to import a particular field. For this exercise, accept the default choices.

7. Click Next.

The wizard displays the next page, asking you to define a primary key.

8. Select the Choose My Own Primary Key option button.

ArtistID (the first field) appears in the drop down of fields available for the primary key to the right of the Choose My Own Primary Key option button. ArtistID is the field you want for the primary key.

9. Click Next.

The wizard displays the next page, asking you to name the table.

10. Click the Import to Table text box and type **tblArtistsXL**.

11. Click Finish.

The Get External Data — Excel Spreadsheet dialog box appears, asking if you want to save the import steps. Leave the Save Import Steps checkbox unchecked.

12. In the Get External Data — Excel Spreadsheet dialog box, click Close.

The table tblArtistsXL appears in the Navigation pane.

Exercise 29-4: Importing Data from Other Formats

To import data from other formats (try using the ones you export in Exercise 29-2), continue working with the database from Exercise 29-3 or open the `Exercise29-4.accdb` file in the Chapter29 folder, then follow these steps:

1. In the Import group on the External Data tab, choose from one of the following commands to import data from different formats:

- **Access:** Imports data from a different Access database
- **SharePoint List:** Imports data from a SharePoint site
- **Text File:** Imports data from a delimited text file or a fixed-width text file
- **XML File:** Imports data from an XML file
- **ODBC Database:** Imports data from an ODBC compliant database, such as SQL Server
- **HTML Document:** Imports data from an HTML file
- **Outlook Folder:** Imports data from an Outlook folder
- **dBase File:** Imports data from a dBase file
- **Paradox File:** Imports data from a Paradox file
- **Lotus 1-2-3 File:** Imports data from a Lotus 1-2-3 file

The appropriate Get External Data dialog box opens, prompting you for the required information to import data.

2. Follow the instructions on the screen to import the data from the format you choose in Step 1.

Some imports require additional steps, and Access asks different questions about file formats, server locations, and other miscellaneous information.

Part IX
The Part of Tens

The 5th Wave   By Rich Tennant

"Ms. Lamont, how long have you been sending out bills listing charges for 'Freight,' 'Handling,' and 'Sales Tax,' as 'This,' 'That,' and 'The Other Thing'?"

In this part . . .

Alas you've reached the Part of Tens — the section of the book that has lists of ten tips to help you use Access to its full potential. Sure, the entire book is full of exercises that teach how to perform different tasks in Access, but this section points out some key areas to focus on as well as lists of shortcut keys in you're tired of using the mouse. The chapters in this section list ten ways to use Access like a pro and more than ten (I lost count) shortcut keys for using access and entering data.

Chapter 30

Ten Tips for Using Access Like a Pro

*P*erforming exercises in this workbook gives you an opportunity to work with many important features of Access, especially those related to building and maintaining databases. To help you make the most of your hands-on experience, this chapter brings together ten key guidelines to work efficiently and design the best possible databases.

Back Up Your Database

If you take away one thing from this book (and I hope you take away a lot more than one!), remember that you *must* regularly back up your database — Chapter 2 shows you how.

Back up your database once a day if you use it on a daily basis. You can adjust how often you back up your database, based on how often you use it and how important the data is.

In addition to backing up regularly, you should also back up your database before you make any major changes, such as

- ✔ Deleting data
- ✔ Deleting database objects (such as tables, queries, forms, reports, and macros)
- ✔ Changing tables structures
- ✔ Altering relationships
- ✔ Changing a form's design
- ✔ Modifying a report
- ✔ Running action queries

If you make a mistake and delete something you weren't supposed to or change everyone's last name when you meant to change the city, you can simply open the backup copy and resume working with good data or with the accidentally deleted object back in place.

Plan Your Database's Design

In order to create a database that does what you expect, you have to know what those expectations are. When you're going on a trip and you don't know the destination, you have to plan your route, print maps, or program the GPS. Unfortunately, no one has invented a magical electronic device that shows you how to create a database. But this section should put you on the right path.

First, determine what type of information you plan to put in the database. Are you tracking a CD collection, monitoring employees and sales for your company, or scheduling appointments? Also, determine what you want to get out of your application. Do you want to print schedules, labels, or lists upon lists of addresses?

After you know what type of information your database tracks, you can gather some sample information and begin planning the tables and forms. Think about what screens you want in your application for users to enter and edit data, and what fields you need on those screens — then design the tables to support those fields. Also, think about the data you plan on printing and make sure you have the fields in your table structured to print, group, and summarize data.

If you jump right into building your database without proper planning, you can work yourself into a corner and have to change table structures and the design of forms and reports. If you forget one field in a table, then create five forms and five reports based on that table, when you add the field to the table, you also have to add it to those forms and reports. Proper planning can help you avoid extra work down the road.

Define Primary Keys and Relationships

Every table in your database should have a primary key! Many professional developers simply use an AutoNumber field as the primary key for each table. Using an AutoNumber field ensures that you won't have any duplicate values in your primary key field.

You can also use other types of fields as primary keys. You might use a person's Social Security Number, a company's tax ID number, a book's ISBN, or some other unique identifier for the row of data.

Creating primary keys lets you build relationships between tables. For example, you can create a list of customers that uses a CustomerID field as the primary key, then create a table of orders that also contains the CustomerID field as the foreign key. By creating relationships and enforcing referential integrity, you ensure that you can't create an order for a customer that doesn't exist.

Part II covers creating primary keys and building relationships.

Use a Naming Convention

If you want to use Access like a professional, you should really use a naming convention. When you use a naming convention, you can identify the type of object simply by looking at the object's name. A naming convention also helps you keep objects organized, especially if you create a database with many tables, forms, and reports.

To use a naming convention, you simply add a prefix to the object's name. Instead of naming a table Employees, call the table tblEmployees. If you happen to create a query, form, or report based on tblEmployees, you can give those objects unique names by using these prefixes:

✔ **tbl:** Table

✔ **qry:** Query

✔ **frm:** Form

✔ **rpt:** Report

✔ **mcr:** Macro

✔ **bas:** Module (bas is short for Basic, the language used in a module)

You can also use a naming convention for controls on your forms and reports. By default, the names of controls that display data from an underlying table are the field names in the underlying table. That naming system works okay, unless you add additional controls to forms and reports, in which case, use a prefix before the control name. Some common prefixes for controls are

✔ **cbo:** Combo box

✔ **lst:** List box

✔ **txt:** Text box

✔ **lbl:** Label

✔ **chk:** Check box

✔ **cmd:** Command button

Don't put spaces in your object names. Having spaces in object names complicates things, especially when you want to access another form's control's value. For example, you may want to include spaces in the name of a form or report (for example, rpt employee address book), but you can just as easily read the name if you capitalize the first letter of each word without including spaces (for example, rptEmployeeAddressBook).

Change Captions

Although you, as the database developer, need a naming convention to identify the different types of objects, other users of your application don't need to see those names.

Start at the database object level after you create new forms and reports. Change the Caption properties of the forms and reports to a meaningful name that another user finds useful. Changing the Caption property takes just a few seconds, and doing so makes your application appear more professional. Your document tabs and title bars can display user-friendly text such as Contact Entry Form or Quarterly Sales Report, rather than frmThis and rptThat.

After you add data controls to forms and reports, the labels associated with those controls typically have the same name as the field in the underlying table. Add spaces or expand abbreviations that you might have used to shorten the field name. For example, if you named a field ContactAddr1, change the label for that field to Address 1 on a Contacts form.

Here's a good general rule: Change the caption if you see the naming convention on a form or report's document tab when you're not in Design view, labels without spaces between words, or any caption that includes obscure abbreviations.

Use the Clipboard

Cut and copy and paste — oh, my! These elements of the Windows Clipboard can make developing a database a breeze. Not only can you cut, copy, and paste text and data, you can copy and paste objects within Access.

Here are some useful scenarios for using the Windows Clipboard:

- ✔ **Using the Paste Table As dialog box:** Copy a table in the Navigation pane and paste the table back into the Navigation pane to bring up the Paste Table As dialog box. In this dialog box, you can create a new table with or without the data — or append the data to an existing table.

- ✔ **Copying an object:** Copy a query, form, report, or macro in the Navigation pane and paste the object back into the Navigation pane to either make a backup copy of that object or create a new object with a similar look and feel.

- ✔ **Transferring buttons from one form to another:** Copy a button (or group of buttons) from a form and paste it onto another form. As long as the button doesn't contain any form-specific macro actions, the button should operate on the new form.

- ✔ **Using Paste Append:** Copy one or more records from a table and append them to a table with a similar structure by using Paste Append (accessible by clicking the down arrow under the Paste Command in the Clipboard group of the Home tab).

- ✔ **Moving records from Access to Excel:** Copy records from a table and paste them into an Excel spreadsheet.

- ✔ **Moving cells from Excel to Access:** Copy cells from an Excel spreadsheet and paste them as a new table in the Navigation pane.

If you find yourself trying to recreate an object or retype data, try copying from an existing object and pasting into Access (or another application) just to see what happens.

Back up your database before you start tinkering around.

Right-Click Everything

When you're in doubt about what you can do with an object, right-click that object to bring up the context-sensitive pop-up menu that shows you some common tasks you can perform. You can learn just as much (if not more) from right-clicking the different objects within Access and examining the pop-up menu as you can from reading any book on Access — especially if the book is called *Right-Clicking Access Objects For Dummies*.

This list gives you a few examples of what you can accomplish by right-clicking different kinds of Access objects:

- **Database object:** Right-click a database object in the Navigation pane to open it in a specific view, export the object, rename or delete the object, or view the object's properties.

- **Document tab:** Right-click a document tab to save the object, close the object (or all the open objects), or switch views.

- **Control:** Right-click a control in a form or report's Design view to build a macro; change it to another object; change the tab order; or cut, copy, paste, align, size, position, layout, or delete the object. You can also change the back color, font color, special effects, or conditional formatting, and you can view the control's properties.

- **Field:** Right-click a field in Datasheet view, Form view, or Report view to sort and filter the data on that field.

- **Report:** Right-click a report in Print Preview to switch views, change the zoom level, change the number of pages, open the Page Setup dialog box, print the report, export the report, or send it to an e-mail recipient.

Try right-clicking objects rather than using the Ribbon commands to perform operations in your database. You can navigate and change the design of your database much more quickly when you master the right mouse button.

Automate Your Database

If you perform repetitive tasks while working with your database, try automating those tasks by using macros. Macros let you choose actions that you want to run in a specific order, and they can do simple tasks, such as opening and closing forms, as well as run a set of action queries to manipulate your data.

Here are some examples of how you can automate your database:

- Add buttons to forms that perform common operations, such as closing the form, navigating between records, and finding data.

- Create action queries that manipulate data, then build a macro that runs the action queries in the order you want.

✔ Create a switchboard that allows you to navigate to the most common database objects without using the Navigation pane.

✔ Build macros that export your data to other databases or other formats (such as Excel) so users without Access or who can't open your database (for example, if they work in another city) can use your data.

✔ When you can no longer accomplish what you want with macros, consider using Access VBA (Visual Basic for Applications) to automate your database.

Whatever tasks you decide to automate in your database, you can simplify the repetitive nature of certain operations and make navigating and finding information in your database much easier. Part VIII covers automating your database.

Explore and Customize Access Options

The Access Options window contains a slew of options that customizes how Access works and how your database operates. You can customize many areas of Access, such as color schemes, file formats, the Ribbon, how the spell checker works, and security.

To learn the various options, simply open the Access Options window and browse through the different screens. Chapter 2 explores the different options available in Access, and knowing what options are available helps you when you're building a database. Some of the following options appear in the Access Options window:

✔ **Popular:** Customize screen tips, change the color scheme, the default folder and file type for new databases, and your name and initials.

✔ **Current Database:** Change the title bar and icon, specify whether to compact the database when you close it, show the Navigation pane, and customize the Ribbon.

✔ **Datasheet:** Specify the color schemes, how gridlines appear between rows and columns, and the default font for the data.

✔ **Object Designers:** Customize how you create and modify tables, queries, forms, and reports.

✔ **Proofing:** Change how Access automatically corrects and formats the contents of your databases and how it indicates the errors that it finds.

✔ **Advanced:** Change how the keyboard operates moving around datasheets and forms, specify whether to confirm record changes and object deletions, show/hide the status bar, adjust the default print margins, define the date formatting.

✔ **Customize:** Change the commands that appear on the Quick Access Toolbar.

✔ **Add-ins:** View and manage Microsoft Office add-ins.

✔ **Trust Center:** Keep your documents safe and your computer secure and healthy. Also, set up trusted publishers and locations.

✔ **Resources:** Find out how to contact Microsoft, find online resources, and maintain the health and reliability of your Microsoft Office programs.

Search til You Drop

Sure, Access Help is invaluable when you're creating a database. Simply click the area you need help with and press F1, and more than likely, you get the specific information you're looking for (sometimes, you have to search Access Help for the information you need).

However, you can find an entire world outside of Microsoft's headquarters in Redmond, Washington, that's equally as valuable. Just type a question into your favorite search engine and click the Search button, and you're rewarded with a slew of results. Include the words `Access` or `Microsoft Access` to narrow down your results to Access-related topics, specifically.

Here are some search topics to get you started:

- Access user groups
- Access naming convention
- Access wildcard character
- Access combo box
- Access 2007 changes
- Access VBA
- Access SQL

Chapter 31

Ten (More or Less) Shortcut Keys for Using Access

*Y*ou can use the keyboard for much more than typing. Okay, you're still typing if you're pressing keys, but I mean using the keyboard for more than entering data. You can use the keyboard to navigate Access, show and hide screen elements, and save database objects. Table 31-1 shows you some common — and not-so-common — keyboard shortcuts that you can use throughout Access. Instead of searching for commands and buttons in the Access interface, try using these shortcut keys.

Table 31-1	Miscellaneous Shortcut Keys
Key	*Shortcut*
F1	Open Access Help window
F2	Toggle selection
F4	Show/hide Property Sheet in Design and Layout views
F6	Move between panes, database objects, and the Ribbon
F10	Display keyboard shortcuts for the Ribbon
F11	Show/hide Navigation pane
F12	Opens Save As dialog box
Ctrl+F1	Show/hide the Ribbon
Ctrl+F4	Close current document window
Ctrl+S	Save object
Ctrl+O	Open database

(continued)

Table 31-1 *(continued)*

Key	Shortcut
Ctrl+X	Cut selection to Windows Clipboard
Ctrl+C	Copy selection to Windows Clipboard
Ctrl+V	Paste last selection from Windows Clipboard
Ctrl+F6	Move to next document tab
Shift+F2	Open Zoom window

Chapter 32

Ten (More or Less) Shortcut Keys for Entering Data

*Y*ou inevitably have to enter data into a datasheet or form when you use Access. Without data in your database, that database is just a big empty repository, like an abandoned building. Table 32-1 can make your data-entry life easier by giving you some alternatives to reaching for the mouse and searching for commands on the Ribbon. Try using these shortcut keys to navigate your datasheets and forms, and keep both hands on the keyboard.

Table 32-1	Entering Data Shortcut Keys
Key(s)	*Shortcut*
Tab	Move to next field
Enter	Move to next field
Shift+Tab	Move to previous field
Shift+Enter	Save record
Ctrl++	New record
Delete	Delete selection, next character, or selected record
Esc	Undo changes to current field
Esc Esc (press twice)	Undo changes to current record
Ctrl+Z	Undo changes to current field
Ctrl+X	Cut selection to Windows Clipboard
Ctrl+C	Copy selection to Windows Clipboard

(continued)

Table 32-1 *(continued)*

Key(s)	Shortcut
Ctrl+V	Paste last selection from Windows Clipboard
F2	Toggle field selection
F7	Open Spelling dialog box
F8	Extended Selection (press repeatedly to select word, field, record, and all)
Shift+F2	Open Zoom window for current field
Ctrl+P	Open Print dialog box
Ctrl+F	Open Find and Replace dialog box's Find tab
Ctrl+H	Open Find and Replace dialog box's Replace tab
Ctrl+;	Insert current date
Ctrl+:	Insert current time
Ctrl+'	Insert data from current field in previous record
Home	Move to first field in current record
End	Move to last field in current record
Ctrl+Home	Move to first field in first record
Ctrl+End	Move to last field in last record
→	Move to next field
←	Move to previous field
↑	Move to current field in previous record
↓	Move to current field in next record
Ctrl+↑	Move to current field in first record
Ctrl+↓	Move to current field in last record
Page Dn	Scroll down one page of data
Page Up	Scroll up one page of data
Ctrl+Page Dn	Scroll right one page of data
Ctrl+Page Up	Scroll left one page of data

Appendix A

About the CD

System Requirements

Make sure that your computer meets the minimum system requirements shown in the following list. If your computer doesn't match up to most of these requirements, you may have problems using the software and files on the CD. For the latest and greatest information, please refer to the ReadMe file located at the root of the CD-ROM.

- ✔ A PC running Microsoft Windows XP with Service Pack (SP) 2, Windows Server 2003 with SP1, or Windows Vista.

- ✔ An Internet connection (for some exercises)

- ✔ A CD-ROM drive

If you need more information on the basics, check out these books published by Wiley Publishing, Inc.: *PCs For Dummies,* by Dan Gookin; *Windows XP For Dummies,* 2nd Edition, by Andy Rathbone, *Windows Server 2003 For Dummies,* by Ed Tittel and James Michael Stewart, *Windows Vista For Dummies,* by Andy Rathbone.

Using the CD

To install the items from the CD to your hard drive, follow these steps.

1. **Insert the CD into your computer's CD-ROM drive.**

The license agreement appears.

The interface won't launch if you have autorun disabled. In that case, click Start⇨ Run (For Windows Vista, Start⇨All Programs⇨Accessories⇨Run). In the dialog box that appears, type D:\Start.exe. (Replace D with the proper letter if your CD drive uses a different letter. If you don't know the letter, see how your CD drive is listed under My Computer.) Click OK.

2. **Read through the license agreement, and then click the Accept button if you want to use the CD.**

   The CD interface appears. The interface allows you to run the demos with just a click of a button (or two).

What You'll Find on the CD

The following sections are arranged by category and provide a summary of the software and other goodies you'll find on the CD. If you need help with installing the items provided on the CD, refer back to the installation instructions in the preceding section.

Trial, demo, or *evaluation* versions of software are usually limited either by time or functionality (such as not letting you save a project after you create it).

Author-created material

The CD-ROM that comes with this workbook is an integral part of the workbook experience. It contains the practice material that you need to complete most of the exercises as well as videos that walk through select exercises

All the practice material for this book is located in a single My Practice Databases folder on the CD-ROM. This My Practice Databases folder contains 29 chapter folders for the exercises in chapters 1 through 29. Each folder contains databases that correspond to the exercises in the book.

The Access 2007 Workbook Videos folder contains the sample videos for select exercises in this book.

Before you start working through the exercises in this workbook, I suggest that you copy the My Practice Databases folder and the Access 2007 Workbook Videos folders to the My Documents folder on your computer's hard disk as follows:

1. Insert the CD-ROM into your computer's CD/DVD drive.

2. Click the Start button on the Windows taskbar and then click Computer (Windows Vista) or My Computer (Windows XP) to open explorer to your computer.

3. Double-click the icon for the CD/DVD to open its contents in the Windows Explorer window.

4. Click the My Practice Databases folder to select it.

5. Hold Ctrl and click the Access 2007 Workbook Videos folder to select it.

6. Right-click the selected files and select Copy from the pop-up menu.

7. In the left pane of the Windows Explorer window, click Documents (Windows Vista) or My Documents (Windows XP) to open the documents folder on your computer.

8. In the right pane of the Windows Explorer window, right-click a blank area of the window and select Paste from the pop-up menu.

You are now ready to tackle any of the exercises in the workbook using the practice files saved in the My Practice Databases folder inside the Documents (Windows Vista) or My Documents (Windows XP) folder on your hard disk. You can also open any of the videos in the Access 2007 Workbook Videos folder.

Troubleshooting

I tried my best to compile programs that work on most computers with the minimum system requirements. Alas, your computer may differ, and some programs may not work properly for some reason.

The two likeliest problems are that you don't have enough memory (RAM) for the programs you want to use, or you have other programs running that are affecting installation or running of a program. If you get an error message such as Not enough memory or Setup cannot continue, try one or more of the following suggestions and then try using the software again:

- **Turn off any antivirus software running on your computer.** Installation programs sometimes mimic virus activity and may make your computer incorrectly believe that it's being infected by a virus.

- **Close all running programs.** The more programs you have running, the less memory is available to other programs. Installation programs typically update files and programs; so if you keep other programs running, installation may not work properly.

- **Have your local computer store add more RAM to your computer.** This is, admittedly, a drastic and somewhat expensive step. However, adding more memory can really help the speed of your computer and allow more programs to run at the same time.

Customer Care

If you have trouble with the CD-ROM, please call the Wiley Product Technical Support phone number at (800) 762-2974. Outside the United States, call 1(317) 572-3994. You can also contact Wiley Product Technical Support at **http://support.wiley.com**. John Wiley & Sons will provide technical support only for installation and other general quality control items. For technical support on the applications themselves, consult the program's vendor or author.

To place additional orders or to request information about other Wiley products, please call (877) 762-2974.

Appendix B
Exercises

Chapter 1: Getting Started with Access

Exercise 1-1: Launching Access

Exercise 1-2: Creating Additional Icons to Launch Access

Exercise 1-3: Creating a New Blank Database from Access

Exercise 1-4: Creating a New Blank Database from Explorer

Exercise 1-5: Creating a Database from a Local Template

Exercise 1-6: Creating a Database from an Online Template

Exercise 1-7: Opening an Existing Database

Exercise 1-8: Using the Ribbon

Exercise 1-9: Manipulating the Navigation Pane

Exercise 1-10: Getting Help

Chapter 2: Managing Databases

Exercise 2-1: Backing up a Database from Access

Exercise 2-2: Backing up a Database from Windows Explorer

Exercise 2-3: Compacting and Repairing an Open Database

Exercise 2-4: Compacting and Repairing Any Database

Exercise 2-5: Saving an Access Database to an Earlier Version

Exercise 2-6: Exploring Access Options

Exercise 2-7: Using the Tabbed Documents Interface

Exercise 2-8: Using the Overlapping Windows Interface

Chapter 5: Viewing Data in Tables

Exercise 5-1: Sorting Data by One Column

Exercise 5-2: Clearing the Sort

Exercise 5-3: Sorting Data by Multiple Columns

Exercise 5-4: Filtering Data by Selection (One Value)

Exercise 5-5: Turning the Filter On and Off

Exercise 5-6: Removing the Filter

Exercise 5-7: Filtering Data by Multiple Values

Exercise 5-8: Filtering Data on Multiple Columns

Exercise 5-9: Filtering Data by Form

Exercise 5-10: Changing the Datasheet's Font

Exercise 5-11: Changing the Row Colors

Exercise 5-12: Formatting Gridlines

Exercise 5-13: Adding a 3-D Look to Your Datasheet

Exercise 5-14: Aligning Text in a Datasheet Column

Chapter 6: Building Relationships

Exercise 6-1: Adding Tables to the Relationships Window

Exercise 6-2: Rearranging the Relationships Layout

Exercise 6-3: Creating a Relationship

Exercise 6-4: Editing an Existing Relationship

Exercise 6-5: Deleting a Relationship

Exercise 6-6: Creating the Genre Table

Exercise 6-7: Creating Relationships with Referential Integrity

Exercise 6-8: Testing Referential Integrity

Chapter 10: Changing Data with Update Queries

Chapter 11: Adding Data with Append Queries

Chapter 12: Removing Data with Delete Queries

Chapter 13: Creating Tables with Make Table Queries

Chapter 14: Creating and Using Forms

Chapter 15: Basic Form Design

Chapter 16: Changing Control Properties

Chapter 17: Changing Form Properties

Exercise 17-1: Selecting the Form

Exercise 17-2: Changing the Form's Caption Property

Exercise 17-3: Showing and Hiding Form Elements

Exercise 17-4: Changing Data Entry Properties

Exercise 17-5: Allowing Different Views

Exercise 17-6: Changing the Default View

Exercise 17-7: Creating a Modal Pop-Up Form

Chapter 18: Creating Calculated Controls

Exercise 18-1: Adding a Text Box to Display a Mathematical Calculation

Exercise 18-2: Concatenating Text Fields into One Text Box

Exercise 18-3: Showing the Date on a Form

Exercise 18-4: Creating a Multiple Items Form with Totals

Chapter 19: Formatting a Form

Exercise 19-1: Using AutoFormat

Exercise 19-2: Adjusting Control Padding and Margins

Exercise 19-3: Using Conditional Formatting

Exercise 19-4: Adding a Picture

Exercise 19-5: Changing an Existing Graphic

Chapter 20: Arranging and Sizing Controls on a Form

Exercise 20-1: Grouping and Ungrouping Controls

Exercise 20-2: Sizing Controls

Chapter 29: Importing and Exporting Data

Exercise 29-1: Exporting Data to an Excel Spreadsheet

Exercise 29-2: Exporting Data to Other Formats

Exercise 29-3: Importing Data from an Excel Spreadsheet

Exercise 29-4: Importing Data from Other Formats

Index

• Symbols and Numerics •

& (ampersand), for concatenation, 108
* (asterisk)
  as field name in query, 99
  in queries, 93–94
  as wildcard character, 67
[ ] (brackets), for query prompts, 95
∞ (infinity symbol), 99, 100
(pound sign), for Date/Time field, 92, 118
" (quotation marks)
  for concatenating fields, 109
  for text field criteria, 92
3-D look for datasheet, 69–70

• A •

.accdb extension, converting to .mdb, 23–24
Access
  basic database parts, 10–11
  launching, 11–12
  shortcut keys for, 295–296
  user interface (UI), 17–20
Access 2007 Workbook Videos folder, 300
Access objects, opening using Tabbed
    Documents interface, 26
Access Options window
  basics, 25, 27–28
  choices in, 292
  for setting startup form, 278
  Trust Center, 30
Action Arguments pane in macro design
    window, 264–265, 270, 271
action queries
  append queries
    creating, 126–129
    defined, 125
    design, 128
    for single record, 129–130
    source table creation, 125–126

  basics, 115
  delete queries
    creating, 131–133
    criteria for, 133–135
    defined, 131
  macro to run, 269–270
  make table query
    creating, 137–139
    defined, 137
Actions pane in macro design window,
    264–265
Add-ins
  basics, 26
  options for, 292
Advanced options, 26
aligning
  controls, 200–202
  text in columns, 71
Alignment commands, in Layout view, 160
All tab, on Property Sheet, 165
Allow Design View property, 177
Allow Layout View property, 177
Allow Value List Edits property, for combo
    boxes and list boxes, 212
Alternate Fill Color, in Layout view, 160
ampersand (&), for concatenation, 108
AND operator, 67
antivirus software, and software setup, 301
Append dialog box, 127, 129
append queries
  creating, 126–129
  defined, 125
  design, 128
  for single record, 129–130
  source table creation, 125–126
ArtistID Footer for report, 244
asterisk (*)
  as field name in query, 99
  in queries, 93–94
  as wildcard character, 67
Attachment data type, 40

● *G* ●

● *H* ●

Yes/No data type
  basics, 40
  filtering choices, 63
  sort choices, 61
"You cannot save this database
    in an earlier version format"
    message, 24

• Z •

zipping file, 23
Zoom Slider, in Print Preview, 231
Zoom window
  shortcut key for, 296, 298

Notes

Notes

Notes

Wiley Publishing, Inc.
End-User License Agreement

4. **Restrictions on Use of Individual Programs.** You must follow the individual requirements and restrictions detailed for each individual program in the "About the CD" appendix of this Book or on the Software Media. These limitations are also contained in the individual license agreements recorded on the Software Media. These limitations may include a requirement that after using the program for a specified period of time, the user must pay a registration fee or discontinue use. By opening the Software packet(s), you agree to abide by the licenses and restrictions for these individual programs that are detailed in the "About the CD" appendix and/or on the Software Media. None of the material on this Software Media or listed in this Book may ever be redistributed, in original or modified form, for commercial purposes.

5. **Limited Warranty.**

   (a) WPI warrants that the Software and Software Media are free from defects in materials and workmanship under normal use for a period of sixty (60) days from the date of purchase of this Book. If WPI receives notification within the warranty period of defects in materials or workmanship, WPI will replace the defective Software Media.

   (b) WPI AND THE AUTHOR(S) OF THE BOOK DISCLAIM ALL OTHER WAR-RANTIES, EXPRESS OR IMPLIED, INCLUDING WITHOUT LIMITATION IMPLIED WARRANTIES OF MERCHANTABILITY AND FITNESS FOR A PARTICULAR PUR-POSE, WITH RESPECT TO THE SOFTWARE, THE PROGRAMS, THE SOURCE CODE CONTAINED THEREIN, AND/OR THE TECHNIQUES DESCRIBED IN THIS BOOK. WPI DOES NOT WARRANT THAT THE FUNCTIONS CONTAINED IN THE SOFTWARE WILL MEET YOUR REQUIREMENTS OR THAT THE OPERATION OF THE SOFTWARE WILL BE ERROR FREE.

   (c) This limited warranty gives you specific legal rights, and you may have other rights that vary from jurisdiction to jurisdiction.

6. **Remedies.**

   (a) WPI's entire liability and your exclusive remedy for defects in materials and workmanship shall be limited to replacement of the Software Media, which may be returned to WPI with a copy of your receipt at the following address: Software Media Fulfillment Department, Attn.: *Microsoft Office Access 2007 Workbook For Dummies*, Wiley Publishing, Inc., 10475 Crosspoint Blvd., Indianapolis, IN 46256, or call 1-800-762-2974. Please allow four to six weeks for delivery. This Limited Warranty is void if failure of the Software Media has resulted from accident, abuse, or misapplication. Any replacement Software Media will be warranted for the remainder of the original warranty period or thirty (30) days, whichever is longer.

   (b) In no event shall WPI or the author be liable for any damages whatsoever (including without limitation damages for loss of business profits, business interruption, loss of business information, or any other pecuniary loss) aris-ing from the use of or inability to use the Book or the Software, even if WPI has been advised of the possibility of such damages.

   (c) Because some jurisdictions do not allow the exclusion or limitation of liabil-ity for consequential or incidental damages, the above limitation or exclusion may not apply to you.

7. **U.S. Government Restricted Rights.** Use, duplication, or disclosure of the Software for or on behalf of the United States of America, its agencies and/or instrumentalities "U.S. Government" is subject to restrictions as stated in paragraph (c)(1)(ii) of the Rights in Technical Data and Computer Software clause of DFARS 252.227-7013, or subparagraphs (c) (1) and (2) of the Commercial Computer Software - Restricted Rights clause at FAR 52.227-19, and in similar clauses in the NASA FAR supplement, as applicable.

8. **General.** This Agreement constitutes the entire understanding of the parties and revokes and supersedes all prior agreements, oral or written, between them and may not be modified or amended except in a writing signed by both parties hereto that specifically refers to this Agreement. This Agreement shall take precedence over any other documents that may be in conflict herewith. If any one or more provisions contained in this Agreement are held by any court or tribunal to be invalid, illegal, or otherwise unenforceable, each and every other provision shall remain in full force and effect.

BUSINESS, CAREERS & PERSONAL FINANCE

0-7645-9847-3

0-7645-2431-3

Also available:
- Business Plans Kit For Dummies
  0-7645-9794-9
- Economics For Dummies
  0-7645-5726-2
- Grant Writing For Dummies
  0-7645-8416-2
- Home Buying For Dummies
  0-7645-5331-3
- Managing For Dummies
  0-7645-1771-6
- Marketing For Dummies
  0-7645-5600-2

- Personal Finance For Dummies
  0-7645-2590-5*
- Resumes For Dummies
  0-7645-5471-9
- Selling For Dummies
  0-7645-5363-1
- Six Sigma For Dummies
  0-7645-6798-5
- Small Business Kit For Dummies
  0-7645-5984-2
- Starting an eBay Business For Dummies
  0-7645-6924-4
- Your Dream Career For Dummies
  0-7645-9795-7

HOME & BUSINESS COMPUTER BASICS

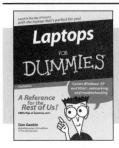

0-470-05432-8

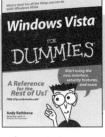

0-471-75421-8

Also available:
- Cleaning Windows Vista For Dummies
  0-471-78293-9
- Excel 2007 For Dummies
  0-470-03737-7
- Mac OS X Tiger For Dummies
  0-7645-7675-5
- MacBook For Dummies
  0-470-04859-X
- Macs For Dummies
  0-470-04849-2
- Office 2007 For Dummies
  0-470-00923-3

- Outlook 2007 For Dummies
  0-470-03830-6
- PCs For Dummies
  0-7645-8958-X
- Salesforce.com For Dummies
  0-470-04893-X
- Upgrading & Fixing Laptops For Dummies
  0-7645-8959-8
- Word 2007 For Dummies
  0-470-03658-3
- Quicken 2007 For Dummies
  0-470-04600-7

FOOD, HOME, GARDEN, HOBBIES, MUSIC & PETS

0-7645-8404-9

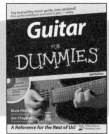

0-7645-9904-6

Also available:
- Candy Making For Dummies
  0-7645-9734-5
- Card Games For Dummies
  0-7645-9910-0
- Crocheting For Dummies
  0-7645-4151-X
- Dog Training For Dummies
  0-7645-8418-9
- Healthy Carb Cookbook For Dummies
  0-7645-8476-6
- Home Maintenance For Dummies
  0-7645-5215-5

- Horses For Dummies
  0-7645-9797-3
- Jewelry Making & Beading For Dummies
  0-7645-2571-9
- Orchids For Dummies
  0-7645-6759-4
- Puppies For Dummies
  0-7645-5255-4
- Rock Guitar For Dummies
  0-7645-5356-9
- Sewing For Dummies
  0-7645-6847-7
- Singing For Dummies
  0-7645-2475-5

INTERNET & DIGITAL MEDIA

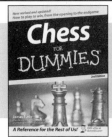

0-470-04529-9

0-470-04894-8

Also available:
- Blogging For Dummies
  0-471-77084-1
- Digital Photography For Dummies
  0-7645-9802-3
- Digital Photography All-in-One Desk Reference For Dummies
  0-470-03743-1
- Digital SLR Cameras and Photography For Dummies
  0-7645-9803-1
- eBay Business All-in-One Desk Reference For Dummies
  0-7645-8438-3
- HDTV For Dummies
  0-470-09673-X

- Home Entertainment PCs For Dummies
  0-470-05523-5
- MySpace For Dummies
  0-470-09529-6
- Search Engine Optimization For Dummies
  0-471-97998-8
- Skype For Dummies
  0-470-04891-3
- The Internet For Dummies
  0-7645-8996-2
- Wiring Your Digital Home For Dummies
  0-471-91830-X

* Separate Canadian edition also available
† Separate U.K. edition also available

Available wherever books are sold. For more information or to order direct: U.S. customers visit www.dummies.com or call 1-877-762-2974.
U.K. customers visit www.wileyeurope.com or call 0800 243407. Canadian customers visit www.wiley.ca or call 1-800-567-4797.

SPORTS, FITNESS, PARENTING, RELIGION & SPIRITUALITY

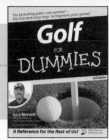

0-471-76871-5

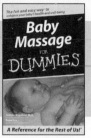

0-7645-7841-3

Also available:
- Catholicism For Dummies
  0-7645-5391-7
- Exercise Balls For Dummies
  0-7645-5623-1
- Fitness For Dummies
  0-7645-7851-0
- Football For Dummies
  0-7645-3936-1
- Judaism For Dummies
  0-7645-5299-6
- Potty Training For Dummies
  0-7645-5417-4
- Buddhism For Dummies
  0-7645-5359-3

- Pregnancy For Dummies
  0-7645-4483-7 †
- Ten Minute Tone-Ups For Dummies
  0-7645-7207-5
- NASCAR For Dummies
  0-7645-7681-X
- Religion For Dummies
  0-7645-5264-3
- Soccer For Dummies
  0-7645-5229-5
- Women in the Bible For Dummies
  0-7645-8475-8

TRAVEL

0-7645-7749-2

0-7645-6945-7

Also available:
- Alaska For Dummies
  0-7645-7746-8
- Cruise Vacations For Dummies
  0-7645-6941-4
- England For Dummies
  0-7645-4276-1
- Europe For Dummies
  0-7645-7529-5
- Germany For Dummies
  0-7645-7823-5
- Hawaii For Dummies
  0-7645-7402-7

- Italy For Dummies
  0-7645-7386-1
- Las Vegas For Dummies
  0-7645-7382-9
- London For Dummies
  0-7645-4277-X
- Paris For Dummies
  0-7645-7630-5
- RV Vacations For Dummies
  0-7645-4442-X
- Walt Disney World & Orlando
  For Dummies
  0-7645-9660-8

GRAPHICS, DESIGN & WEB DEVELOPMENT

0-7645-8815-X

0-7645-9571-7

Also available:
- 3D Game Animation For Dummies
  0-7645-8789-7
- AutoCAD 2006 For Dummies
  0-7645-8925-3
- Building a Web Site For Dummies
  0-7645-7144-3
- Creating Web Pages For Dummies
  0-470-08030-2
- Creating Web Pages All-in-One Desk
  Reference For Dummies
  0-7645-4345-8
- Dreamweaver 8 For Dummies
  0-7645-9649-7

- InDesign CS2 For Dummies
  0-7645-9572-5
- Macromedia Flash 8 For Dummies
  0-7645-9691-8
- Photoshop CS2 and Digital
  Photography For Dummies
  0-7645-9580-6
- Photoshop Elements 4 For Dummies
  0-471-77483-9
- Syndicating Web Sites with RSS Feeds
  For Dummies
  0-7645-8848-6
- Yahoo! SiteBuilder For Dummies
  0-7645-9800-7

NETWORKING, SECURITY, PROGRAMMING & DATABASES

0-7645-7728-X

0-471-74940-0

Also available:
- Access 2007 For Dummies
  0-470-04612-0
- ASP.NET 2 For Dummies
  0-7645-7907-X
- C# 2005 For Dummies
  0-7645-9704-3
- Hacking For Dummies
  0-470-05235-X
- Hacking Wireless Networks
  For Dummies
  0-7645-9730-2
- Java For Dummies
  0-470-08716-1

- Microsoft SQL Server 2005 For Dummies
  0-7645-7755-7
- Networking All-in-One Desk Reference
  For Dummies
  0-7645-9939-9
- Preventing Identity Theft For Dummies
  0-7645-7336-5
- Telecom For Dummies
  0-471-77085-X
- Visual Studio 2005 All-in-One Desk
  Reference For Dummies
  0-7645-9775-2
- XML For Dummies
  0-7645-8845-1

HEALTH & SELF-HELP

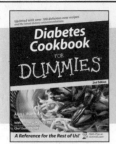

0-7645-8450-2

0-7645-4149-8

Also available:

- Bipolar Disorder For Dummies
  0-7645-8451-0
- Chemotherapy and Radiation
  For Dummies
  0-7645-7832-4
- Controlling Cholesterol For Dummies
  0-7645-5440-9
- Diabetes For Dummies
  0-7645-6820-5* †
- Divorce For Dummies
  0-7645-8417-0 †

- Fibromyalgia For Dummies
  0-7645-5441-7
- Low-Calorie Dieting For Dummies
  0-7645-9905-4
- Meditation For Dummies
  0-471-77774-9
- Osteoporosis For Dummies
  0-7645-7621-6
- Overcoming Anxiety For Dummies
  0-7645-5447-6
- Reiki For Dummies
  0-7645-9907-0
- Stress Management For Dummies
  0-7645-5144-2

EDUCATION, HISTORY, REFERENCE & TEST PREPARATION

0-7645-8381-6

0-7645-9554-7

Also available:

- The ACT For Dummies
  0-7645-9652-7
- Algebra For Dummies
  0-7645-5325-9
- Algebra Workbook For Dummies
  0-7645-8467-7
- Astronomy For Dummies
  0-7645-8465-0
- Calculus For Dummies
  0-7645-2498-4
- Chemistry For Dummies
  0-7645-5430-1
- Forensics For Dummies
  0-7645-5580-4

- Freemasons For Dummies
  0-7645-9796-5
- French For Dummies
  0-7645-5193-0
- Geometry For Dummies
  0-7645-5324-0
- Organic Chemistry I For Dummies
  0-7645-6902-3
- The SAT I For Dummies
  0-7645-7193-1
- Spanish For Dummies
  0-7645-5194-9
- Statistics For Dummies
  0-7645-5423-9

Get smart @ dummies.com®

- **Find a full list of Dummies titles**
- **Look into loads of FREE on-site articles**
- **Sign up for FREE eTips e-mailed to you weekly**
- **See what other products carry the Dummies name**
- **Shop directly from the Dummies bookstore**
- **Enter to win new prizes every month!**

* Separate Canadian edition also available

† Separate U.K. edition also available

Available wherever books are sold. For more information or to order direct: U.S. customers visit www.dummies.com or call 1-877-762-2974.
U.K. customers visit www.wileyeurope.com or call 0800 243407. Canadian customers visit www.wiley.ca or call 1-800-567-4797.